Media and the
American Mind

DANIEL J. CZITROM

M☆E☆D☆I☆A

AND THE AMERICAN MIND

From Morse to McLuhan

University of North Carolina Press ☆ Chapel Hill

Manufactured in the United States of America

10 09 08 07 06   13 12 11 10 9

Library of Congress Cataloging in Publication Data

Czitrom, Daniel J., 1951–
Media and the American Mind.

Bibliography: p.
Includes index.
1. Mass media—Social aspects—United States.
2. United States—Popular culture.   I. Title.
HN90.M3C96   302.2'3   81-14810

ISBN-13: 978-0-8078-1500-7 AACR2
ISBN-10: 0-8078-1500-4 AACR2
ISBN-13: 978-0-8078-4107-5 (pbk.)
ISBN-10: 0-8078-4107-2 (pbk.)

Frontispiece
Early Radio Demonstrated at a Farmhouse, ca. 1925.
Courtesy of Smithsonian Institution, Washington, D.C.

For my mother and father, with love

Contents

Tables

Preface

Most works of history contain the kernel of autobiography. My own fascination with the history of modern media can be traced to their ubiquitous and highly charged presence in my personal experience, particularly while growing up in New York City. What must life have been like, I wondered, before radio and television, motion pictures, phonographs, and our incredibly diverse periodical press? My original concern, in the broadest sense, was to explore how media of communication have altered the American environment over the past century and a half. How did the new media affect traditional notions of space and time, the nature of leisure and consumption, the socialization process, and the intellectual climate? How, in fact, did they become so prominent in American everyday life?

The omnipresence of the mass media in both space and time, coupled with their insistent emphasis on the new, present us with perhaps the most formidable barriers to historical understanding. Among other impulses, this book is the end product of the desire to somehow get behind what the media are today, to recapture the past that they subtly deny, to peel back their public faces, and to place in historical context the ways we have come to measure and interpret their cultural import.

The breadth of my concerns, along with the surprising dearth of historical precedents, pushed me toward the strategy of attempting an American intellectual history of modern communication—but one that would be firmly rooted in social context. My conception of intellectual history leans toward the broadest possible definition: an understanding of the field not merely as the formal history of ideas but ultimately as the history of symbolic action and meaning, and their relation to human behavior. The phrase "American mind" in the title is thus not meant to suggest some overarching, mystical unity. It simply signifies, perhaps a bit ironically, my attempt to consider the widest possible universe of historical thought and feeling about new means of communication.

I formulated my central questions this way: How have the attempts of Americans to comprehend the impact of modern communication evolved since the mid-nineteenth century? How have these efforts fit into the larger realm of American social thought?

What has been the relationship between these ideas and changing communications technologies and institutions? What role did early popular responses play in the development of new media forms?

I divided my inquiry into two parts in order to obtain two different angles of vision on these questions. Part one analyzes the contemporary responses, including popular reactions, to three new media. For each one of these chapters I have explored the ideas and their intimate connections with the technological and institutional growth of the media themselves. I began with the telegraph because it marked the first separation of communication from transportation and also opened the age of electronic media. The motion picture heralded the arrival of a startling new form of popular culture and challenged the received notions of culture itself. A study of radio provided a chance to examine the rise of broadcasting, the most powerful and ubiquitous form of modern communication.

In part two I consider the three major traditions, or persuasions, in American thought concerning the impact of modern media in toto. The Progressive trio of Charles Horton Cooley, John Dewey, and Robert Park made pioneering probes into the holistic nature of modern communications media. The behavioral approach in empirical research, the study of "effects," was for decades the dominant model for American communications studies. Finally, the radical media theories of Harold Innis and Marshall McLuhan emphasized, in different ways, changes in communications technology as the central force in the historical process.

I am aware of an inevitable overlap in treating the categories of culture and communication. Modern media have become integral to both the conception and reality of culture, especially popular culture. I argue that the term *popular culture*, in its current sense, dates back to the rise of the movies. An important subtext throughout part two is the steady erosion of any clear boundary between notions of culture and communication in the twentieth century. The interplay between these categories in the book reflects, I think, their (often unconscious) blending by the thinkers considered herein.

The genuine confusion surrounding the term *media* is more fully examined in the epilogue. Historical research and writing may not have proved as successful as I had imagined in helping to clear up this state of affairs. Hopefully, it can at least allow us to see more clearly how the various media are, and always have been, simultaneously different things. We may accurately speak of "television," for example, as a powerful economic institution; as an aesthetic form; as the major purveyor of advertising and arbiter of *life-style*; as the chief determinant of the parameters of contemporary politics; as a deceptively complex system of signs; or as a highly individuated, democratically distributed ritual object at the center of many people's everyday lives. The full range of media history, including the range of popular responses within it, needs to be brought to bear in our attempts at meaningful discourse about both the present situation and future possibilities.

My sense of frustration at having barely scratched the surface remains, although I admit to having marked out a very wide surface. The profusion of new research over the past few years, particularly in film and broadcasting, has lessened the eerie sense of intellectual isolation that accompanied the fitful beginnings of this project. Still, our historical knowledge remains sketchy at best, with large gaps to be filled. Metahistorical and epistemological questions concerning how new media reshape our perceptions of the past and the contours of knowledge itself remain almost totally unexplored. Throughout this book I have interpolated what seem to me some fruitful possibilities for further historical inquiry. I am hopeful that my effort might encourage new diachronic analyses of modern media, perhaps helping to balance the proliferation over the past two decades of synchronic approaches to communications studies.

A diverse group of friends and comrades gave me important support toward the completion of this book, especially in the form of ongoing speculative dialogues. Simultaneously serious and playful, these speculations were rooted in common concerns: understanding how the media intervene directly in our intellectual and emotional lives, in our politics, in our work, in our aesthetic stance, and in our collective memory. My small effort has been aimed at advancing the historical side of that understanding. My involvement with the magazine *Cultural Correspondence* as an editor and contributor centered on the task of recovering and reclaiming lost or forgotten nodes of popular culture, especially as these might relate to the potential for political change. The collaborative work around *CC* allowed me to profit greatly from the insights and sympathetic support offered by Paul Buhle, George Lipsitz, and Dave Wagner. I am grateful as well for the steady encouragement I have received from David Marc, Michael Starr, Jim Hoberman, Bob Schneider, Margaret Haller, Ziva Kwitney, Richard Kilberg, and Jim Murray. Thanks, too, to my conscientious editor, Pamela Morrison, for helping to make this a better book.

James W. Carey made a strong impression on me when I first heard him speak in Madison in 1974. In subsequent conversations and correspondence, Jim offered much-needed advice and encouragement during the amorphous early stages of defining my subject. He provided me with important bibliographic leads and some of his own unpublished work. His published essays have also been a key source of intellectual inspiration.

Russell Merritt read and commented on early drafts of each chapter. He graciously shared with me the results of his research into early nickelodeon theaters. His thoughtful criticisms and bibliographical help were a great aid.

Paul K. Conkin also read and commented on early drafts of all the chapters. My study first took solid shape in his intellectual history seminar, which I took part in for two years at the University of Wisconsin. His careful critical readings significantly sharpened my thinking and writing.

My largest intellectual debt is to my friend Daniel T. Rodgers. Dan's astute criticism and unflagging faith over the last few years played a crucial part in the conceptualization and development of this book. He gave each chapter draft a close reading and supplied me with substantial constructive comments. But his greatest contribution has been to urge me consistently and patiently toward finding my own voice.

Finally, my thanks to the New York Public Library, one of the last truly democratic institutions of higher learning in this country. I trust it will continue to treat all scholars equally, regardless of whether they are distinguished professors or taxi drivers.

D. J. C.
New York City
July 1981

PART ONE

Contemporary Reactions to Three New Media

CHAPTER 1

"Lightning Lines" and the Birth of Modern Communication, 1838–1900

The success of the first electric telegraph line in 1844 opened the era of modern communication in America. Before the telegraph there existed no separation between transportation and communication. Information traveled only as fast as the messenger who carried it. The telegraph dissolved that unity and quickly spread across the land to form the first of the great communication networks. Contemporaries of the early telegraph had no way of foreseeing the intricate wonders of our current communications media, many of them institutional and technological descendants of the "lightning lines." The awesome fact of instantaneous communication provided cause enough for intense speculation; no future possibilities seemed as dazzling as present reality.

But in puzzling over the implications of the telegraph, "this most remarkable invention of this most remarkable age," as many styled it, mid-nineteenth century Americans opened an important cultural debate that has steadily intensified and expanded through the present. The intellectual and popular responses to the telegraph included the first attempts at comprehending the impact of modern communication on American culture and society. Then as today, reckoning with new forms of communication provided a forum to consider rather ancient issues charged with new meaning and urgency by technological advance. What might the telegraph, "annihilator of space and time," augur for thought, politics, commerce, the press, and the moral life?

Consideration of these questions paralleled and often interlocked with the issues raised by the economic development of the telegraph system: those of corporate power, monopoly, and government regulation. The institutional history of the telegraph forms only a necessary background for exploring the cultural reception given the first breakthrough into modern communication. But the tension between what the communications revolution implied and what the telegraph became, between fervent visions and prosaic reality, make up a key portion of that story.

In 1858, speaking during a mammoth New York jubilee celebrating completion of the Atlantic cable, the American scientist Joseph Henry hailed the telegraph as the ultimate demonstration of the nation's genius. "The distinctive feature of the history of the Nineteenth Century," he declared, "is the application of abstract science to the useful arts, and the subjection of the innate powers of the material world to the control of the intellect as the obedient slave of civilized man." Henry's statement also serves to accurately define contemporary understanding of that curious new word, *technology*. He was certainly not alone in holding up the telegraph as perhaps the most remarkable technological triumph of the age, the clearest demonstration yet of the harvest to be reaped from the application of science to the arts.[1]

Only after numerous fundamental discoveries in chemistry, magnetism, and electricity could a practical electromagnetic (as opposed to semaphoric) telegraph take shape. Nineteenth-century accounts of telegraph history invariably begin with the discovery of electricity by Thales of Miletus and other ancients. Watson of England and Franklin of America pioneered in the sending of electricity through wires in the eighteenth century. In the 1790s the Italians Galvani and Volta revealed the nature of galvanism, or the generation of electricity by the chemical action of acids upon metals. Oersted of Denmark and Ampere of France discovered electromagnetism about 1820. By 1831 Joseph Henry, then at Princeton University, solved the critical problem of creating a strong electromagnet capable of producing mechanical effects at a distance; he did this by substituting a battery of many small cells for the customary battery of one large cell. In the 1820s and 1830s scientists from all over the world worked to create a viable electric telegraph: Ampere in France; Schilling in Russia; Steinheil in Germany; Davy, Cooke, and Wheatstone in England.[2]

Samuel Finley Breese Morse, artist, daguerrotypist, "the American Leonardo," gave the world its first practical electromagnetic telegraph in 1838. Morse's career exemplified that union of science and art so lauded by nineteenth-century boosters of technology. As a youth he had studied painting and sculpture in Europe and he achieved some prominence in America with his portraiture and landscapes. He became a professor of painting and design at the University of the City of New York in 1832; later he served as first president of the National Academy of Design. Morse had also exhibited an avid interest in scientific and mechanical experiments, particularly those involving electricity. In 1832 he conceived a plan for applying sequential electrical impulses through wires for the transmission of intelligence. His original motivation lay in the hope of obtaining an income from his invention that might free him to pursue painting full time.

But over the next twelve years, a period marked by personal poverty and public indifference, Morse gradually turned his attentions entirely to the telegraph. Morse remained ignorant of most of the work that preceded him. The conception of the telegraph, its early mechanical form, and the signaling code were his achievements. After 1837 he received important scientific, mechanical, and financial assistance from several associates: Leonard Gale, Joseph Henry, Alfred Vail, and later Ezra Cornell. Morse's sending apparatus was a crude version of the familiar telegraph key; the receiver consisted of an electromagnet that attracted an iron armature mounting a pen or stylus. A clockwork motor drew a paper tape under the pen or stylus, which marked the tape in accordance with the pulse of current in the circuit. Alfred Vail later worked out a simplified receiving device, allowing the operator to read messages by listening to the clicks emitted by a sounder.

After a series of public demonstrations of his device in early 1838, Morse petitioned Congress for an appropriation to build an experimental line. These exhibitions, at the Vail family iron works in Morristown, New Jersey, at the Franklin Institute of Philadelphia, and in Washington before the House Committee on Commerce, provoked keen local curiosity wherever they took place. Morse himself reported that the Morristown showing of 13 January 1838, at which he sent a long letter through two miles of wire, was "the talk of all the people round, and the principal inhabitants of Newark made a special excursion on Friday to see it." President Van Buren and his cabinet requested and received a private viewing on 21 February 1838. Yet the doubts, disbelief, and ridicule surrounding Morse's efforts were not easily overcome. Five lonely and frustrating years passed before he obtained a thirty-thousand-dollar grant to construct a line between Baltimore and Washington, D.C. Even then, the appropriation passed the House only after a jocular discussion of a satirical amendment that would have required half the sum to be spent "for trying mesmeric experiments." Morse finally opened the nation's first telegraph line on 24 May 1844 with the famous query, "What hath God wrought?"

Morse and his partners had hoped to sell their invention to the federal government, but though Congress subsidized the initial line, it refused offers to buy the patent rights. A period of wildcat speculation and building followed, marked by byzantine legal tangles involving Morse, his partners, and the various individuals who were leased construction rights under the patents. Still, only eight years later, the nation boasted over twenty-three thousand miles of telegraph lines. During these early years, a host of astonished Americans pondered the answer to Morse's first telegraphic message.[3]

The public greeted the first "lightning lines" with a combination of pride, excitement, and sheer wonder. But there were plenty of expressions of doubt, incredulity, and superstitious fear. Not infrequently, observers recorded an uneasy mixture of these feelings. In dozens of cities and towns, as telegraph construction proceeded quickly in all directions, skeptics, believers, and the merely curious flocked to get a firsthand look.

While readying the experimental line in early May, Morse reported from Washington that "there is great excitement about the Telegraph and my room is thronged." He understood the need for publicity to counter widespread incredulity. "A good way of exciting wonder," he advised Alfred Vail on the Baltimore end, "will be to tell the passengers to give you some short sentence to send me; let them note time and call at the Capitol to verify the time I received it." In the days immediately following the 24 May message, the telegraph played a sensational role in the Democratic National Convention being held in Baltimore. Morse and Vail astounded crowds in Washington with the news of James Polk's nomination. Silas Wright, nominated for vice president, declined by telegraph. A dubious convention verified the report by sending a committee by train to interview Wright in Washington. A committee tried to change Wright's mind by telegraph the next day, but failed.

The attendant press coverage and eyewitness accounts from government officials helped legitimize Morse's breakthrough. On 31 May the exultant inventor described the scene: "The enthusiasm of the crowd before the window of the Telegraph Room in the Capitol was excited to the highest pitch at the announcement of the nomination of the Presidential candidate, and the whole of it afterward seemed turned upon the Telegraph." Alfred Vail reported from Baltimore that crowds besieged the office daily, pressing for a glimpse of the machine. They promised "they would not say a word or stir and didn't care whether they understood or not, only they wanted to say they had seen it."[4]

A palpable scepticism no doubt fueled the desire to observe the telegraph in person. As a Rochester newspaper put it, anxiously awaiting the extension of the telegraph to that city in May 1846: "The actual realization of the astonishing fact, that instantaneous personal conversation can be held between persons hundreds of miles apart, can only be fully attained by witnessing the wonderful fact itself." The press referred variously to "that strange invention," "that almost superhuman agency," or "this extraordinary discovery." Noting the large numbers of people visiting the first Philadelphia telegraph office in early 1846, a local paper concluded, "It is difficult to realize, at first, the importance of a result so wholly unlike anything with which we have been familiar; and the revolution to be effected by the annihilation of time . . . will not be appreciated until it is felt and seen."[5]

Western and southern communities, reached later, were no less enthusiastic. Telegraph entrepreneurs and stock promoters toured frontier districts, offering exhibitions to audiences in public halls. Telegraph offices set aside ample space for spectators, usually allowing visitors to have their name sent and returned for a small fee. "One of the greatest events ever," exulted a Cincinnati daily upon the telegraph's arrival: "We shall be in instantaneous communication with all the great Eastern cities." As the "lightning" reached Zanesville, Ohio, in the summer of 1847, the press described local response: "The Wires and other apparatus of the Telegraph are exciting considerable discussion among our fellow citizens. With those by far the larger part, who view it understandingly, there are some gentlemen who are perfectly incredulous of all its boasted capacity for the transmission of news."[6]

The incredulous were not limited to Zanesville, and neither were the nervous. Ezra Cornell, Morse's assistant who had supervised the actual building of the first telegraph line, ran up against the gnawing anxiety which accompanied public acclaim. Traveling to New York City to put up demonstration lines in the autumn of 1844, Cornell found city authorities fearful of unspecified dangers to the populace. They forced Cornell to pay a fee for an eminent professor, Benjamin Silliman, to certify that the telegraph wires posed no threat to public safety.[7]

Reminiscing in 1902 about his days as a messenger boy for an early Pennsylvania line of the 1840s, the writer William Bender Wilson noted that "few can credit the curiosity and credulity which characterized the people in connection with the telegraph, and how few had even an idea of the principles governing it." The wires swaying in the wind

> gave the wintry blasts the opportunity of producing some-what musical, weird, and fantastic sounds that could be heard for some distance, to the great discomfort of the rustics. The public mind having something of a superstitious bend, many people in the neighborhood of the line, alarmed by the sounds proceeding from the wire as the winds swept over it, would walk a very considerable distance out of their way, often placing themselves at great inconvenience, particularly after sundown, to avoid passing under or near it.[8]

The more cosmopolitan contemporaries of Wilson's rustics took a bemused view of such popular fears. And newspapers were filled with glib anecdotes such as the one concerning a local who offered to bet his entire farm that his best team of horses could outrace the telegraph in delivery of a message. Yet even the most scientifically minded meditations on the significance of the telegraph revealed uneasiness about a new technology whose essence, electricity, no one really understood. And although the intellectual paeans to the telegraph's possibilities were virtually unanimous, the cause for celebration was by no means agreed upon. At the root of this tension lay the changing meaning of communication itself.

★

Serious considerations of the telegraph usually touched upon the other technological marvels of the age, the railroad and the steamboat. Yet the inscrutable nature of the telegraph's driving force made it seem somehow more extraordinary. Nineteenth-century science, although beginning to harness the power of electricity in several areas, could still not explain precisely what it was. Daniel Davis, a Boston electrician and mechanic who manufactured telegraph equipment for Morse, noted that electricity was a very familiar agent visible in lightning, the hair of animals, and other everyday contexts. But electricity was also unseen, "a central power

. . . endowing matter with a large proportion of its chemical and mechanical properties."

Although tamed by the telegraph, the electric spark, wrote a chronicler of electricity's progress, remained "shadowy, mysterious, and impalpable. It still lives in the skies, and seems to connect the spiritual and the material." Contemporary historians of telegraphy recurringly commented on the paradox. "The mighty power of electricity, sleeping latent in all forms of matter, in the earth, the air, the water, permeating every part and particle of the universe, carrying creation in its arms, is yet invisible and too subtle to be analyzed." Its potential appeared boundless; "its mighty triumphs are but half revealed, and the vast extent of its extraordinary power but half understood."[9]

Electricity, Reverend Ezra S. Gannett told his Boston congregation, was both "the swift winged messenger of destruction" and "the vital energy of material creation." "The invisible, imponderable substance, force, whatever it be—we do not even certainly know what it is which we are dealing with . . . is brought under our control, to do our errands, like any menial, nay, like a very slave."

Insofar as it markedly increased man's control over the environment, electricity resembled that other grand force, the steam engine. But steam was gross and material in comparison; "there is little poetical or great in the rattle of the train or the roar of a monstrous engine." As one typical historian argued: "Electricity is the poetry of science; no romance—no tale of fiction—excel in wonder its history and achievement." The new science of electromagnetism promised further development and application; "the gigantic power of the steam engine may dwindle into insignificance before the powers of nature which are yet to be revealed."[10]

"Canst thou send lightnings, that they may go, and say unto thee, Here we are?" (Job 38:35). This Biblical quotation, one of the impossibilities enumerated to convince Job of his ignorance and weakness, frequently prefaced nineteenth-century writings on the telegraph. It expressed well the sense of miracle that these works invariably sought to convey. As the most astounding product of electrical science, the telegraph promised miraculous consequences. T. P. Shaffner, historian and early telegraph booster, concluded a history of all the past forms of communication: "But what is all this to subjugating the lightnings, the mythological voice of Jehovah, the fearful omnipotence of the clouds, causing them in the fine agony of chained submission to do the offices of a common messenger—to whisper to the four corners of the earth the lordly behests of lordly man!"[11]

While Shaffner and others seized upon the telegraph as a means of recasting all history in the terms of the growth of communication, some became intoxicated with what the telegraph would bring to the future. Always they spoke of a twin miracle: the grand moral effects of instantaneous communication and the wonderful mystery of the lightning lines themselves. "Universal communication" became the key phrase in these exhortations. The electric telegraph promised a unity of interest, men linked by a single mind, and the worldwide victory of Christianity. "It gives the preponderance of power to the nations representing the highest elements in humanity . . . It is the civilized and Christian nations, who, though weak comparatively in numbers, are by these means of communication made more than a match for the hordes of barbarism." Universal peace and harmony seem at this time more possible than ever before, as the telegraph "binds together by a vital cord all the nations of the earth. It is impossible that old prejudices and hostilities should longer exist, while such an instrument has been created for an exchange of thought between all the nations of the earth."[12]

Just as the telegraph promised "a revolution in moral grandeur," the instrument itself seemed "a perpetual miracle, which no familiarity can render commonplace. This character it deserves from the nature employed and the end subserved. For what is the end to be accomplished but the most spiritual ever possible? Not the modification or transportation of matter, but the transmission of thought."

"The Telegraph," asserted the *New York Times* in 1858, "undoubtedly ranks foremost among that series of mighty discoveries that have gone to subjugate matter under the domain of mind." Not only did the new electrical technology further man's ability to conquer nature, it actually allowed him to penetrate it. By successfully liberating the subtle spark latent in all forms of matter, man became more godlike. "Piercing so the secret of Nature, man makes himself symmetrical with nature. Penetrating to the working of creative energies, he becomes himself a creator."[13]

Underpinning the grand moral claims made on behalf of the telegraph lay a special understanding of an elusive term, *communication*. The word has had a complex history. Praisers of "universal communication" no doubt had in mind the most archaic sense of the word: a noun of action meaning to make common to many (or the object thus made common). The notion of common participation suggested communion, and the two words shared the same Latin root, *communis*. Sometime in the late seventeenth century the meaning was extended to include the imparting, conveying, or exchanging of information and materials. In this sense the means of communication also included roads, canals, and railroads. The telegraph thus split communication (of information, thought) from transportation (of people, materials). But the ambiguity between the two poles of meaning, between communication as a mutual process or sharing and communication as a one-way or private transmission, remained unresolved.[14]

Those who celebrated the promise of universal communication stressed religious imagery and the sense of miracle in describing the telegraph. They subtly united the technological advance in communication with the ancient meaning of that word as common participation or communion. They presumed the triumph of certain messages; but they suggested too that the creation of a new communications technology itself, "the wonderful vehicle," was perhaps the most important message of all.

Henry Thoreau's sceptical view of the telegraph, one of very few pessimistic expressions on the subject, sought to deflate just such moral claims made on behalf of the new technology. In *Walden* (1854) he argued that the telegraph represented simply another illusory modern improvement rather than a positive advance, "an improved means to an unimproved end. . . . We are in great haste to construct a magnetic telegraph from Maine to Texas; but Maine and Texas, it may be, have nothing important to communicate. . . . We are eager to tunnel under the Atlantic and bring the old world some weeks nearer to the new; but perchance the first news that will leak through into the broad, flapping American ear will be that Princess Adelaide has the whooping cough."[15] Thoreau was perhaps a bit churlish here, for Maine and Texas did indeed have a great deal to communicate. But the essence of that communication would not be the celestial commerce savored by both Thoreau and those who deemed the telegraph a sublime moral force.

For the telegraph promised to transform the earthly realms of politics and trade as well. The presumed annihilation of time and space held a special meaning for a country of seemingly limitless size. And here for the first time, one finds the repeated use of organic metaphor and symbol to describe how modern communication would change American life. As early as 1838, in trying to convince Congress to subsidize his work, Morse anticipated twentieth-century notions of the "global village." It would not be long, he wrote, "ere the whole surface of this country would be channelled for those

from working men's clubs to immigrant societies and temperance groups, marched from the Crystal Palace to Battery Park. Along with the nods to international cooperation, banners and speakers continually reminded the crowds of the distinctively American genius at work. Cyrus W. Field, hero of the day, joined the American pantheon of popular heroes; for, as one ditty put it, " 'Twas Franklin's hand/That caught the horse/'Twas harnessed by/Professor Morse."

The *New York Times* referred to the "divine boon" of the telegraph in describing the tumult: "From some such source must the deep joy that seizes all minds at the thought of this unapproachable triumph spring. It is the thought that it has metaphysical roots and relations that makes it sublime."[20] This "wondrous event of a wondrous age," creation of "the international spinal connection," spectacularly confirmed the telegraph's dual potential as both a sublime moral force and a technology that would make a significant intervention in everyday life.

★

Yet the conception of the telegraph as an autonomous influence in American culture was flawed from the start. In 1852 Alexander Jones prefaced his *Historical Sketch of the Electric Telegraph* with a dedication to the merchants of New York, "to whose patronage, with that of the public press, the electric telegraphs are largely indebted for their support and success." Jones accurately summarized the economic reality faced by the early telegraph companies. Their survival as solvent businesses depended more on the patronage of newspapers and traders than on messages between individuals. But Jones's assessment gave only half of an historical equation. Although the press and commercial interests made the telegraph economically viable, the telegraph itself dramatically transformed the press. Telegraphy gave rise to both the modern conception of news and our present methods of news gathering. The telegraph ultimately touched the public consciousness primarily through the mediation of the press. The cultural debate over the telegraph's import thus shifted to encompass larger questions raised by the new journalism.

Newspapers of the colonial and early national period, usually weeklies or semiweeklies, printed the news as it arrived through the mails or by word of mouth. Very seldom did they seek out news. Reporters and correspondents of the modern type were unknown; national and foreign news was obtained mostly through press "exchanges." The bulk of news in colonial papers consisted of reports on

English affairs and on European events that affected England. But news from European capitals took from two to six weeks to reach London, and from four to eight weeks to get to America. Thus the original idea of news, that is, something that is "new," became transformed in colonial papers. Emphasis on timeliness gave way to a concern merely with keeping a historical record of events long after they occurred.[21]

From the Revolution through the Civil War mercantile dailies and various political papers dominated journalism in America. But in the 1830s a new kind of newspaper arose to challenge the partisan and commercial press; this new variety eventually prevailed both economically and conceptually. The "penny papers" of this period, led by Benjamin Day's *New York Sun*, James G. Bennett's *New York Herald*, and William Swain's *Philadelphia Public Ledger*, revolutionized the idea of news. They brought back the element of timeliness and gave new life to the old notion that the most important news is what the public looks for. Because these penny papers appealed to a mass public, news no longer needed to be respectable or even significant. These journals shifted to a greater stress on local and sensational news (especially crime and sex) and invented the so-called human-interest story. With their big circulations and large advertising revenues, the penny papers could spend huge sums for procuring news from all over the country in speedy fashion. Inevitably, the news function won out over editorial and political comment as the key component of the American newspaper.[22]

All of the latest forms of transportation and communication were utilized by the penny press, at great expense: chartered steamboats and railroads, horse and stage expresses, harbor patrols, and carrier pigeons. But the telegraph, more than all of these combined, made possible the rapid transmission of news and large-scale cooperative news gathering on a regular basis. The dramatic impact of the telegraph on national politics during the first days of Morse's experimental line demonstrated the extraordinary potential of the telegraph for news dissemination.[23]

Two of the leading proprietors of penny papers played prominent roles in early telegraph growth. William Swain, owner of the *Philadelphia Public Ledger*, invested heavily in the Magnetic Telegraph Company, the first commercial telegraph corporation. He served as one of its first directors and later became its president in 1850. James G. Bennett of the *New York Herald* became the heaviest patron of the telegraph, spending tens of thousands of dollars on dispatches. In the first week of 1848 he boasted of his *Herald* containing seventy-nine thousand words of telegraphic content, at a cost of $12,381.[24] The Mexican War provided a public demand for news; at its outbreak a mere 130 miles of wire existed, reaching only as far south as Richmond, Virginia. Bennett and others set up a combination of pony express routes to complement the infant telegraph system, and they beat the government mails between New Orleans and New York. The biggest scoop of the war, the fall of Vera Cruz, was credited to the *Baltimore Sun*, which received the news ahead of the War Department and telegraphed the victory message to President Polk.[25]

Bennett pioneered in the reporting of political speeches as well. In November 1847, Henry Clay delivered an important address on war policy in Lexington. The *Herald* arranged to run an express of over eighty miles between Lexington and Cincinnati where the speech was telegraphed to New York via Pittsburgh, and published in the next day's edition. Obtaining the speech cost five hundred dollars. Bennett himself wrote extensively on the subject of telegraphy. He predicted that all newspapers must eventually publish and rely on telegraphic news or go out of existence. Journalism was destined to become more influential than ever: "The public mind will be stimulated to greater activity by the rapid circulation of news. The swift communication of tidings of great events will evoke in the masses of the community still keener interest in public affairs. . . . The whole nation is impressed with the same ideas at the moment. One feeling and one impulse are thus created and maintained from the center of the land to its uttermost extremities."[26]

Telegraphy made possible, indeed demanded, systematic cooperative news gathering by the nation's press. The original Associated Press consisted of six New York dailies. Until the early 1840s joint news-gathering efforts had been temporary alliances with usually local scope; these were not organized and regular attempts to report daily events. A frantic competition among New York papers was interrupted only occasionally by these truces. The AP formally originated in 1849 as the Harbor News Association, created for the purpose of collecting "marine intelligence." Here we find the regulations that caused so much controversy in years to come: "'No new member will be admitted to the association unless by unanimous and written consent of all existing partners but news may be sold to newspapers outside of New York City upon a majority vote of all existing partners.'" Two years later the seven members of Harbor News consolidated that service with the Telegraph and General News Association, formed "for the purpose of collecting and receiving telegraphic and other intelligence." By 1852 the AP consisted of seven papers operating two complex systems of news gathering. Foreign news came in through a harbor patrol in New York; the patrol also received and forwarded dispatches with packets at Boston and Halifax. A domestic news service operated out of New York under a general agent and staff.[27]

Although an expanding telegraph network encouraged and in turn was nourished by news gathering agencies, a good deal of friction arose between the two groups. In 1846, before it had even completed its first line, the Magnetic Telegraph Company knew the press would be potentially its best customer. The directors decided that for messages exceeding a hundred words, the price on all words over that number should be reduced to one-third of the regular rate. But a provision allowing papers to maintain charge accounts led to trouble, with several journals refusing to pay. For their part, newspapers charged that long delays and many errors frequently marred the telegraph service.

Disconnected and uncoordinated lines, the great expense of early telegraphy, inadequate facilities, inexperienced operators, and fierce competition for the use of the few existing wires made the period between 1846 and 1849 a chaotic one for both press and telegraph companies. Furthermore, the newspapers feared the incursion of the telegraph companies themselves into the news gathering process. At open issue was who ought to gather telegraph news. Operators sometimes supplied news messages free to the press in an effort to popularize the telegraph; eastern operators would also send items from a New York or Philadelphia morning paper to the West.[28] The formation and consolidation of the AP in this period was essentially a response to the unsettled conditions in the young telegraph industry.

Between the two sides there emerged an independent third party: telegraph reporters. As early as 1847, a handful of these men sent and received commercial reports between cities, selling them to newspapers. Alexander Jones, one of the pioneers, wrote: "It became apparent that the employees in the telegraphic offices could not be expected to collect news at important points, and forward it. Their occupation confined them to the immediate duties of their offices. Hence, the business of telegraphing brought into requisition the Telegraph Reporters." Jones devised the first systems of commercial and political ciphers for abbreviating news transmissions. For about a year these reporters operated independently until they joined the AP, with Jones as its first general agent.

Until he retired in 1851, Jones helped put the fledgling AP on a sound financial and organizational footing. "We received and distributed the news, paid all tolls and other expenses necessary to conduct the business. We employed reporters in all the principal cities in the United States and Canada and on receiving it in New York, would make about eight or nine copies of it, on manifold—six for the New York press, and the remaining copies for reforwarding to the press in other cities and towns. To this had daily to be added the New York local and commercial news, etc."[29] Under Jones the AP began its climb, eventually becoming the most ubiquitous and powerful news-gathering agency of the nineteenth century.

In 1800 there had been approximately 235 newspapers of all kinds published in the United States, or about one for every 22,500 people; by 1899 the figures were 16,000 newspapers, or one for every 4,750 people. "At the end of the century," wrote one historian of the press in 1899, "journalism is the history of the world written day by day, the chief medium of enlightenment for the masses, the universal forum of scholar, sage, and scientist."[30] Insofar as the invention and spread of the telegraph provided the crucial catalyst and means for regular, cooperative news gathering, it supplied the technological underpinning of the modern press; that is, it transformed the newspaper from a personal journal and party organ into primarily a disseminator of news.

Other technological developments helped reshape the nineteenth-century press too. Steam presses in the 1830s and later rotary presses of the 1890s allowed faster and larger press runs; linotypes developed in the 1880s introduced automatic typesetting; photo-engraving, beginning with halftones in 1877, played an important part in the pictorial journalism and sensationalism of the 1880s and 1890s. But the telegraph led the way not only to large-scale news gathering and modern news concepts, but also to standardization, perhaps the most remarkable characteristic of modern journalism. Simon N. D. North, in his 1884 census report on the history and current state of the American press, concluded: "The influence of the telegraph upon the journalism of the United States has been one of equalization. It has placed the provincial newspaper on a par with the metropolitan journal, so far as the prompt transmission of news —the first and always to be chiefest function of journalism—is concerned.[31]

Although a broad consensus existed regarding the ways in which the press had changed since the advent of the telegraph, there was no agreement about their effect on the nation's cultural life. The post–Civil War years brought the first rush of literature on the pathology of mass communication, with which we are so familiar today. Here one finds a clear prefiguring of the twentieth century ethical and behavioral critiques of the mass media. Reproofs of "newspaperism" and the assorted evils of modern journalism singled out the telegraph as the main culprit responsible for the debilitating changes wrought in the press.

The London *Spectator* looked dubiously on the net effect of electricity as an intellectual force. The crucial result had been the pervasive diffusion of news, "the recording of every event, and especially every crime, everywhere without perceptible interval of time—The world is for purposes of intelligence reduced to a village." But was this desirable? "All men are compelled to think of all things, at the same time, on imperfect information, and with too little interval for reflection. . . . The constant diffusion of statements in snippets, the constant excitements of feeling unjustified by fact, the constant formation of hasty or erroneous opinions, must in the end, one would think, deteriorate the intelligence of all to whom the telegraph appeals. . . . This unnatural excitement, this perpetual dissipation of the mind" was the legacy of the electric telegraph.[32]

Across the Atlantic, American press critic W. J. Stillman charged the telegraph with having "put out of the field the chief fruit of culture in journalism. . . . America has in fact transformed journalism from what it once was, the periodical expression of the thought of the time, the opportune record of the questions and answers of contemporary life, into an agency for collecting, condensing, and assimilating the trivialities of the entire human existence. In this chaos for the days' accidents we still keep the lead, as in the consequent neglect and oversight of what is permanent and therefore vital in its importance to the intellectual character."[33]

A sentimental nostalgia for the standards of pre–Civil War journalism reverberated in these complaints. The old style of personal journalism, in which a single man's personality had thoroughly defined what a paper stood for, had disappeared. The triumph of the reporter over the editor meant the ascendancy of news over opinion. At the same time the press's role in popular education had drastically increased. "In politics, in literature, in religion the newspaper is accepted as an infallible guide"; the result could only be "a debauch of the intellect." "Newspaperism" created a new and poisonous atmosphere that was "daily breathed into the lungs of society." The modern newspaper, based on a huge system of procuring telegraphic news, produced decadence.

companies to build lines. The government would also build a telegraph network of its own, independent of private lines. Although Congress subsidized the first experimental line, it refused to buy Morse out, despite the recommendations of the House Ways and Means Committee (1845) and the postmaster general (1845, 1846). As a congressman in 1844 Cave Johnson had ridiculed Morse's request for an appropriation, but as postmaster general two years later he changed this view. In 1846 he warned that "the evils which the community may suffer or the benefits which individuals may derive from the possession of such an instrument, under the control of private associations or unincorporated companies, not controlled by law, cannot be overestimated." Johnson and others worried that the Post Office, given the exclusive power for the transmission of intelligence by the Constitution, would inevitably be superseded if the telegraph remained in private hands. Just as the Post Office had adopted other progressive means of communication and transportation, it ought to establish its own telegraph line, if not take' it over totally. Thus the federal government, after initially encouraging the telegraph, lost its chance to own it and supervise its subsequent development.[36]

By the early 1850s the young telegraph industry found itself in an institutional chaos. Over fifty telegraph companies existed, some for no other reason than to sell stock. Duplicate lines went up all over, hurting the few firms that managed to turn a profit. The West in particular suffered from cheap and hastily built lines, unequal tariffs, and poor coordination of lines. Out of this confusion emerged Western Union, which grew into America's first great industrial monopoly and its largest corporation in the space of ten years.

Western Union resulted from the consolidation in 1856 of two companies, the New York and Mississippi Valley Printing Telegraph Company and the Erie and Michigan Telegraph Company. The latter was controlled by Ezra Cornell, one of Morse's earliest backers; he had obtained valuable grants under the Morse patent to build lines over a large stretch of the West. This patent right proved the key item in the deal, for it gave to Western Union the basis of its immense power. Ironically, the New York and Mississippi Company had originally been set up under the patent rights of the House printing telegraph; this was a rival to Morse's system, which printed its messages in letters rather than in dots and dashes. But Morse's machine was by far the simpler and more adaptable to use on railroad lines and Western Union's exclusive contracts with western railroad companies helped give it a great advantage over its rivals in early years.

Through an aggressive policy of acquiring various telegraph properties and patents, rebuilding and consolidation, and signing exclusive railroad contracts, Western Union achieved supremacy in a decade. After 1866 the company consistently swallowed up virtually all competition (while simultaneously issuing new stock) until 1909, when Western Union itself came under control of a new corporate giant, American Telephone and Telegraph.[37] Table 1 illustrates this growth.

Table 1
Western Union Development, 1856–1883

Year	Miles of Line	Miles of Wire	Offices	Messages	Profits
1856		550			
1867	46,270	85,291	2,565	5,879,282	$2,624,930
1874	71,585	175,735	6,188	16,329,256	2,506,920
1880	85,645	233,534	9,077	29,215,509	5,833,938
1883	143,452	428,546	12,917	40,581,177	7,660,349

By 1880 the U.S. Census deemed it appropriate and desirable to compare the statistics of the nation's telegraph system as a whole with those of Western Union, on account of "the transcendent importance" of that company (see Table 2).[38]

Table 2
Total U.S. Telegraph System Compared to Western Union, 1880

	Total	Western Union	WU%
Miles of Line	110,727	85,645	77
Miles of Wire	291,213	233,534	80
Messages	31,703,181	29,215,509	92
Press Messages	3,154,398	3,000,000	91
Receipts from Messages	$13,512,116	$12,000,000	89

While Western Union built a monopoly in the telegraph industry, it also aided the establishment of a news monopoly through mutual benefit contracts with the AP. Before the ascendancy of Western

Union, relations between AP and telegraph companies wavered between cozy encouragement and fierce rivalry. Prior to 1866 the AP held the upper hand in the relationship by favoring one telegraph company over another and by threatening to finance new lines. In 1853, for example, the failing Commercial Telegraph Company offered its lines between New York and Boston to the AP for forty thousand dollars. The association declined to buy the lines outright, but agreed to send all reports over the line as an incentive for other investors to purchase and manage it. In order to maintain regular, unbroken service between major news centers, the AP frequently encouraged additional construction, repairs, and changes in ownership.

Some thirty years later, Daniel H. Craig, general agent of AP between 1851 and 1866, lamented the refusal of New York's seven AP members to buy up telegraph lines. "Had they assented to my wishes," he argued, "the Western Union Telegraph Company would have been buried in its infancy, or if permitted to live, it would have been as the tail to the Associated Press kite, instead of the association's being in that relation to the Western Union Company, as it is, and has been for the last sixteen years."[39]

Associated Press had to beat down at least one organized and well-financed attempt to make a telegraph company collector and distributor of the news rather than the mere agent of transmission. In 1859 the American Telegraph Company, then one of the most powerful systems in the country, with key lines between Nova Scotia and New York, threatened AP with rate hikes and cancellation of its policy of priority for all AP messages. The ploy failed only after a bitter public relations war and the reorganization of American Telegraph. In the aftermath, the Newfoundland to Boston line, which carried the latest foreign news, was leased to the AP.[40]

As the first telegraphic news agency, the New York Associated Press gained the advantage over any opposition that might arise. When new cities were linked up to the telegraph system, the AP made their daily papers customers for the news dispatches. By 1860, the seven New York dailies comprising the AP spent over two hundred thousand dollars annually on news gathering, more than half of which they got back from customers outside the city. They were in total control of America's domestic and foreign news gathering, obtaining the news they wanted and settling all questions of policy.

In 1866 the New York AP faced its first major challenge from another news agency, but out of this conflict emerged a stronger AP in alliance with Western Union and a concept of news as a commercial franchise. The Western Associated Press had been founded in 1865 as a result of dissatisfaction with New York domination over news gathering. Western customers of New York AP wanted more news concerned with events in the West and Washington, D.C.; the New York papers emphasized news suited to the commercial interests of the city. The Western group also complained about the high cost of cable news from Europe. (The first permanently successful Atlantic cable began transmitting in 1866; New York AP members paid one-third of the cable costs, its customers the remaining two-thirds.)

An agreement reached in early 1867 outlined a division of territory with exchanges of news between the New York AP and the Western AP, plus certain payments to the New York group for foreign news and special services. In effect, this meant a federation of news gathering associations with mutual respect for each other's territorial monopoly. The New York AP still held the upper hand because it controlled European news, market reports, and Washington, D.C. dispatches. This truce paved the way for other auxiliary associations modeled on the Western AP, such as the New England AP, the Southern AP, and the New York State AP. These groups became something less than junior partners in the AP; membership in them was akin to holding a franchise, a privilege to be guarded and defended from outsiders.

Western Union played a critical role in forging peace and rationalizing the news gathering process. In 1866 Western Union also swallowed up its last two big rivals, the United States Telegraph Company and the American Telegraph Company, thus creating a corporation with a combined capital of over forty million dollars and virtual control of the nation's telegraph wires. Western Union feared that its system could not bear the strain of transmitting reports for two press associations, especially in areas where facilities were thin. Each of the three parties, New York AP, Western AP, and Western Union, signed contracts with the other two, thus formalizing and perpetuating the existence of three monopolies. Western AP's contract was regional, whereas the New York AP's and Western Union's were national. Both news associations pledged not to use the wires of companies other than Western Union and promised to oppose any new telegraph companies. Western Union agreed not to enter the news gathering field (except to sell market reports) and offered special discount rates to the two press associations.[41]

Throughout the final decades of the century, attacks on the AP news monopoly and the Western Union telegraph monopoly reverberated in Congress, in angry pamphlets, and in the press. Critics consistently tied the two organizations together as threats to freedom. Collusion between them was especially dangerous in a democracy, where "the perpetuation of the Government must have its ultimate guarantee in the intelligence of the people." In 1872 the House Committee on Appropriations, reporting favorably on a bill to establish a postal telegraph, emphasized the dangers inherent in the alliance. For the telegraph companies in the United States had

> so hedged themselves in by alliance with the press associations that no new or projected journal can have the use of the telegraph at rates not absolutely ruinous, and many journals, long established and receiving reports, are in the absolute power of the telegraph companies. The press associations, on their part, formally bind themselves to employ no opposition telegraph line for the transmission of their regular or special reports; and the telegraph companies, on their part, refuse to transmit the reports and messages of rival press associations except at exorbitant rates.[42]

A Senate investigation of 1874 documented instances in which Western Union cut off transmission of news reports to papers that criticized the telegraph company and the content of AP dispatches.

> Western Union has bound the Associated Press, as part of the price paid for the transmission of its news, to oppose any other telegraph company, and then points to the columns of the papers as evidence that neither the journals themselves nor the public desire a change. . . . The power of the telegraph, continually and rapidly increasing, can scarcely be estimated. It is the means of influencing public opinion through the press, of acting upon the markets of the country, and of seriously affecting the interests of the people.[43]

One of the central issues revolved around the AP claim that news was a franchise, a commercial commodity like any other. Many told of attempts to start newspapers, only to be shut out from news dispatches by the local AP group. Henry George, in a famous example, tried to found a Democratic paper in San Francisco in 1879, but the AP members in that city refused to sell him the news; that is, they refused to grant him a franchise. George traveled to Philadelphia to start a rival news agency to supply his paper with reports. After complaints from the San Francisco AP, Western Union cut George off from the only telegraph line to the West; his paper failed and he lost his investment. Other rival news agencies argued that since the large number of AP clients divided the cost of telegraphing and received special rates from Western Union, any real competition was doomed.[44]

Associated Press officials defended their organization as "a great mutual benefit or cooperative association of business men. . . . We are dealing in news," asserted AP general agent James W. Simonton in 1879. "I claim that there is a property in news, and that property is created by the fact of our collecting it and concentrating it." Answering charges made in 1884 that the AP unfairly controlled American news, William H. Smith, AP general manager, expanded on this idea: "Complaint is made because members of the Associated Press choose their partners, and do not throw open the doors to every newcomer. What private business is conducted on that principle? Does the dry-goods merchant divide the orders of his commercial agent with his neighbors? Does the broker supply competing brokers with his dispatches? And yet it has been suggested here that this principle be applied to the Associated Press, a business as distinctly as the others." The AP, of course, did not distinguish, as one angry senator put it, "between that kind of business which affects public affairs and the general interest of the people, and that which merely affects the private affairs of the citizens."[45]

Similarly, Western Union President William Orton defended the privatization of America's telegraph system when, in 1870, he told a special house committee investigating the telegraph industry: "The mere fact of monopoly proves nothing. The only question to be considered is, whether those who control its affairs administer them properly and in the interest, first, of the owners of the property, and second, of the public."[46]

Between 1866 and 1900 Congress considered over seventy bills designed to reform the telegraph system; some twenty committees from the House and Senate investigated, held hearings, and reported on the question. They compiled a staggering amount of testimony and statistics in the process. In 1866 Congress passed a law giving all telegraph companies the right to build lines along post and military roads on the condition that, at any time five years hence, the United States could buy all lines and property of these companies if it chose to. A board of five persons (two government representatives, two company representatives, and a neutral fifth party agreeable to all) would make an appraisal of any property the government wished to buy. This law became the legal basis for most reform bills of the period.

Virtually all of these can be classed in two categories. One set of schemes, known as the "postal telegraph," provided for the government to charter and subsidize a private telegraph corporation that would contract with telegraph companies as the government contracted with railroads to move the mail. The aim here was to set up a competitor to Western Union. Existing telegraph companies would be permitted to sell their plants to the new corporation under the act of 1866; the postmaster general would decide where to establish offices. A variation of this plan called for the government to build and operate its own independent telegraph system. A second, more radical plan, known as the "governmental system," urged the Congress to obtain absolute ownership and control of all telegraph lines, under the act of 1866.[47]

Telegraph reformers hoped to democratize America's communications network through either government ownership or government competition with Western Union. "This glorious invention," claimed Charles A. Sumner, Henry George's business partner, "was vouchsafed to mankind, that we might salute and converse with one another respectively stationed at remote and isolated points for a nominal sum. A wicked monopoly has seized hold of this beneficient capacity and design, and made it tributary, by exorbitant tariffs, to a most miserly and despicable greed." Cheaper and more uniform rates would bring the telegraph within the reach of all classes, not just business men and the press. Reformers made a Constitutional argument as well, claiming the telegraph as an extension of the Post Office; the government must have control over the transmission of intelligence.[48]

Telegraph reform of some sort received support from a wide strata of the American public in the late nineteenth century. The National Grange, the American Federation of Labor, the Populist party, and the Knights of Labor all lobbied for a government telegraph. Petitions with more than two million signatures reached Congress by 1890, demanding a postal telegraph system. Business groups such as the National Board of Trade, the New York Board of Trade and Transportation, and scores of chambers of commerce also joined the campaign. "Certain limited classes are against this consolidation, but the masses of people are strongly for it," asserted Postmaster General John Wanamaker in 1890. "That man must be willfully blind who does not see the vast and rising tide of public sentiment against monopoly."[49]

But the movement for telegraph reform dissipated around 1900, partly owing to the decline of the Populist movement and the inability to offset Western Union's strong lobbying presence in Congress. The latter included liberal franking privileges for government officials. Like the Populists, who included planks for the government takeover of the telegraph in all their platforms, the telegraph reformers expressed a profound sense of betrayal. A golden opportunity had presented itself in 1844, when Congress could easily have purchased the rights to Morse's invention. Instead, the nation suffered under the heel of Western Union, "the most exacting, the most extortionate, the most corrupt monopoly" in the land.[50] Such descriptions of the telegraph's situation were common, but they had more to do with the antimonopoly fervor of the day than with early moral concerns about the telegraph's ultimate meaning. Discussions about the telegraph's place in American society had passed into the purely political realm. Telegraphy had become merely another feature of modern industrial life requiring government regulation.

By 1900 the auspicious promise of the telegraph seemed quite distant, as antique as the original Morse instrument that gathered dust in the Smithsonian. It had developed as a private monopoly rather than a shared resource; though a common carrier, it was not a truly public means of communication. These institutional precedents would prove crucial to the future of American communication, particularly that of broadcasting. Although its presence was not directly felt in everyday life, the telegraph eventually touched most people indirectly through the mass press it helped create. It could not be an independent moral force, sublime or otherwise. Never again would new communications technology evince such a universal quality of hope. But newer media, on the horizon by the 1890s, would both amplify and extend all the cultural questions raised when the telegraph revolutionized the meaning of communication. Indeed, the motion pictures, a medium with a far more direct effect upon the everyday lives of people, would challenge the established definitions of culture itself.

CHAPTER 2

American Motion Pictures and the New Popular Culture, 1893–1918

The telegraph truly amazed contemporaries as the first agency of instantaneous communication. It seemed capable of annihilating space and time, those stubborn barriers to more perfect social cohesion. The telegraph impressed early commentators as a pure medium that would surely act as a moral force in everyday life. The mere fact of this new means of communication, which was separated from transportation, portended a great advance for American society. Extravagant predictions made on behalf of telegraphy, as well as the idea of universal communication, rested on affirming powers thought to be inherent in the medium itself. But as a medium that transmitted and received coded messages from point to point, the telegraph had its most palpable effect on the modernization of America's press and commercial system.

The motion picture did not enjoy the near unanimous praise afforded the lightning lines. Unlike the telegraph, movies never held forth the promise of a pure medium of communication. Whereas the telegraph had inspired mystery and wonder by transforming the nature of communication, the motion picture confronted the accepted standards of culture itself. Movies introduced more than a new communication technology; they quickly became the principal new (and most popular) art form of the twentieth century. Films communicated not with coded messages but with familiar idioms of photography and narrative. They brought people together in public exhibitions, and the most successful entrepreneurs of these exhibitions soon won control of the entire industry. With origins deep in the gritty cauldron of urban amusements, motion pictures found their first audiences and showmen mainly in the immigrant and working class districts of the large cities.

Insofar as contemporary popular culture has become inextricably linked to modern media of communication, the birth of the movies marked a crucial cultural turning point. The motion picture's curious amalgam of technology, commercial entertainment, art, and spectacle set it off as something quite unfamiliar and threatening to the old cultural elite. But this strange blend of elements also produced a peculiarly American alloy, one that ironically recalled and perhaps even fulfilled one of the oldest dreams of America's cultural nationalists.

To argue that the motion pictures created a new popular culture requires first a consideration of the varied meanings of the term *culture* in Anglo-American thought between the Civil War and World War I. Edward B. Tylor established the modern anthropological definition in English at the beginning of his 1871 classic, *Primitive Culture*: "that complex whole which includes knowledge, belief, custom, art, law, morals, and any other capabilities and habits acquired by man as a member of society." However, Tylor's definition did not enter any British or American dictionary until over fifty years later; it failed to gain recognition in standard encyclopedias, reference works, or popular periodicals until well into the twentieth century. Although this notion of culture has since become familiar to the public and important to disciplines other than anthropology, it was essentially ignored in the time frame considered here.[1]

The main usage of the word in these years referred to the "doctrine of culture," a somewhat ethereal yet vivid concept for those who held it. Popular and learned discourse on the subject described variations on a process of cultivation aimed at an ethical and spiritual ideal of human perfection. The English critical tradition, most notably the work of Matthew Arnold, provided the key referents. Culture, according to Arnold in his influential essay *Culture and Anarchy* (1869), sought "to make the best that has been thought and known in the world current everywhere; to make all men live in an atmosphere of sweetness and light where they may use ideas as it uses them itself, freely—nourished, and not bound to them." John Addington Symonds, the English literary scholar, also stressed the organic metaphor in characterizing culture as "self-tillage, the ploughing and the harrowing of self by use of what the ages have transmitted to us from the work of gifted minds."[2]

Arnold tied culture closely to religion: "Religion says the kingdom of God is within you; and culture, in like manner, places human perfection in an internal condition, in the growth and predominance of our humanity proper, as distinguished from our animality." True culture set itself apart by "becoming something rather than in having something, in a universal condition of the mind and spirit, not in an outward set of circumstances." Culture represented something more than mere education; it was a further goal pursued by the individual. "Education," wrote Symonds, "educes or draws forth faculties. Culture improves, refines, and enlarges them, when they have been brought out." Culture raised "previously educated intellectual faculties to their highest potency by the conscious effort of their possessors."[3]

What is striking about most American writings on the subject of culture is their defensive tone regarding the Arnoldian tenet. This was a response in part to works such as Arnold's *Civilization in the United States*, which attacked the Philistine deficiencies of American middle-class life. America was not an "interesting" civilization, by which Arnold meant it lacked distinction and beauty. Americans generally did not even recognize that a problem existed; "in what concerns the higher civilization they live in a fool's paradise."[4]

Middle-class American thought, as represented in popular magazines, largely accepted the English doctrine of culture. Writers concentrated on proving to European critics that Americans were at least becoming aware of their nation's inadequacies. Thomas Wentworth Higginson, for example, defined culture this way in 1867: "Culture is the training and finishing of the whole man, until he sees physical demands to be merely secondary, and pursues science and art as objects of intrinsic worth. It places fine art above useful art and is willingly impoverished in material comforts, if it can thereby obtain nobler living." In his appeal for culture, Higginson argued that America lacked a first-class university and that its culture was still sadly provincial. He echoed the old complaint that the "true great want is of an atmosphere of sympathy in intellectual aims."[5]

Other writers bemoaned the fact that America appeared somehow cut off from that precious heritage of art and literature deemed so crucial by the doctrine of culture. Middle-class life in America, "peculiarly unassuaged as it is by picturesque or mitigating features," yielded a people with little appreciation for aesthetics. In the continual struggle against vulgar materialism, everything that "teaches or stimulates man to set a value on any kind of life other than the material or the sensational or the hysterically emotional may be called an instrument of culture." Writing on American culture in 1868, the Philadelphia physician Henry Hartshorne thought the nation's greatest deficiency to be "a class of men of leisure— independent of the daily necessity of self support." Such a class was a prerequisite for America's cultural progress. "True culture," wrote another critic, "involves a maturing of taste, intellect, and nature which comes only with time, tranquility, and reposeful association of the best sort."[6]

Advocates of the doctrine of culture perpetually worried about its degradation at the hands of their audience, the educated middle and upper classes. The idea of culture as a process too easily slipped into a view of culture as a product, something that one could simply appropriate or buy. But the more one really cared for culture, warned its defenders, the less one professed it; the more one came into possession of it, the less conscious did his pursuit of it become. The transformation of an ideal process into a mere commodity deeply troubled the upholders of culture; they spent as much energy castigating such abasement as they did celebrating the ideal. For, as John Addington Symonds lamented, "all the good things that culture implies in common parlance are understood to be alloyed with pedantry, affectation, and aesthetical priggishness."[7]

The doctrine of culture contained an implicit tension between the belief that culture was the province of an elite and the desire to see culture spread to the great masses of people. In both England and America the specter of class warfare hovered over the appeals for culture. Certainly for Arnold, anarchy, the hopelessly fragmented society, seemed the bleak alternative to culture. The endeavor to diffuse the best that had been thought and known was itself a mark of the greatest men of culture. These were the people, Arnold wrote, "who have labored to divest knowledge of all that was brash, uncouth, difficult, abstract, professional, exclusive"; those who tried to "humanize it, to make it efficient outside the clique of the cultivated and learned, yet still remaining the best knowledge and thought of the time, and a true source, therefore of sweetness and light."

Culture in this sense was the true cement of society, generated at the top and spread downward. Arnold himself, in his work as inspector of schools and as an active educational reformer, tried to apply the principles set forth in his theoretical writings. He believed that true culture could produce a sense of community transcending personal, sectarian, and class interests. But Arnold, in his fierce opposition to the suffrage and working class movements of his day, also confused the present ordering of political and economic interests with human society. The populace, "our playful giant," was beginning to assert "his right to march where he likes, meet where he likes, enter where he likes, hoot as he likes, threaten as he likes, smash as he likes. All this, I say, tends to anarchy." Arnold thus looked to culture to protect "that profound sense of settled order and security, without which a society like ours cannot live and grow at all."[8]

American writers were no less conscious of the connections between culture and class conflict. In 1872 Charles Dudley Warner, newspaper editor, essayist, and coauthor with Mark Twain of *The Gilded Age*, addressed the relationship between culture and the common day laborer. Speaking at the commencement ceremonies of his alma mater, Warner identified the great problem of the times as "the reconciliation of the interests of classes. . . . Unless the culture of the age finds means to diffuse itself, working downward and reconciling antagonisms by a commonness of thought and feeling and aim in life, society must more and more separate itself into jarring classes, with mutual misunderstanding and hatred and war." The educated man, the scholar, the man of culture, had a responsibility to the masses: "His culture is out of sympathy with the great mass that needs it, and must have it, or it will remain a blind force in the world, the lever of demagogues who preach social anarchy and misname it progress." Warner concluded that men of culture were needed "to shape and control the strong growth of material development here, to guide the blind instincts of the mass of men who are struggling for a freer place and a breath of fresh air." The working man asked derisively, "What is your culture to me?"; and Warner regarded as a menace the "question which the man with the spade asks about the use of your culture to him."

Similarly, in 1892, F. W. Gunsaulus, a prominent Ohio Methodist minister who wrote fiction and poetry, argued that the ideal of culture must help stem the present trend toward social revolt. True culture must teach laboring men that there is nothing so sacred as law; and "to bandage the eyes of ignorant men against the fact that there is and will be a righteous accumulation of wealth in the name of civilization, is to commit an outrage against truth." Men of culture must fill the worker's brain with "noble ideas and impulses" in order to curb his tendencies toward revolting against capital.[9]

Yet the problem remained of how to bring about the wider diffusion of culture without cheapening it. One made a great error in supposing one could simplify culture or make it easy; this resulted in "culturine," or imitation culture. Neither British nor American writers used the phrase "popular culture" in this period. Clearly,

they viewed what we today refer to as popular culture as a distract-
ing and baneful influence. Arnold warned that "plenty of people will
try to give the masses, as they call them, an intellectual food prepared and adapted in the way they think proper for the actual condition of the masses. The ordinary popular literature is an example
of this way of working on the masses." The American Alfred Berlyn,
writing an article entitled "Culture for the Million," thought it "a
matter of common observation that the reading of the great bulk of
the people is still limited almost exclusively to daily and weekly
newspapers, penny novelettes, journals of the 'bits' and 'arts' order,
and the cheapest kind of illustrated magazines." The pace of industrial society itself, of which cheap periodical literature was an omnipresent expression, formed a serious obstacle to culture: "The restless rush of present day life, its constant distractions, its perpetual
movement, its ubiquitous newspapers, with their ever shifting ka-
leidoscope of events and interests—these things are inimical to the
contemplative mood in which alone the companionship of good books
can be sought with profit."[10]

Although the doctrine of culture enjoyed a broad consensus among
educated classes, at least as a desirable ideal, important American
dissenters had always been heard. The young Emerson, for one, had
rejected the idea of culture as a process of refinement. All of Nature
was on the side of spiritual rebirth; man could "go nowhere without
meeting objects which solicit his senses, and yield him new meanings. . . . Culture comes not alone from the good and beautiful but
also from the trivial and sordid." Culture must present all the attrac-
tions of nature, "that the slumbering attributes of man may burst
their sleep and rush into day."

Emerson extended the organic metaphor of culture to include
much more than self-tillage. Culture encompassed not merely the
study and understanding of ancient classics, but a willingness to
explore and experience unknown and even threatening terrain:
"The effect of Culture on the man will not be like the trimming and
turfing of gardens, but the educating the eye to the true harmony of
the unshorn landscape, with horrid thickets, wide morasses, bald
mountains, and the balance of the land and sea." For Emerson, no
extreme veneration of past great works could ever substitute for
trusting one's own experience.[11]

A new generation of twentieth-century intellectuals shared the
spirit of Emerson's attitude as they discussed the barriers to the
creation of distinctly American art and thought. Van Wyck Brooks
wondered why his peers felt "the chill of the grave" when they

thought of the "Arnoldian doctrine about knowing the best that has been thought and said in the world." The doctrine of culture had allowed nineteenth-century Americans to attend to material tasks. "It upholstered their lives with everything that is best in history, with all mankind's most sumptuous effects quite sanitarily purged of their ugly and awkward organic relationships. It set side by side in the Elysian calm of their bookshelves all the warring works of the mighty ones of the past. It made creative life synonymous in their minds with finished things, things that repeat their message over and over, and 'stay put.'"

The reverence for European and classical texts had perverted the ideal of culture. Randolph Bourne argued that "culture is not an acquired familiarity with things outside, but an inner and continually operating taste, a fresh and responsive power of discrimination and the insistent judging of everything that comes to our minds and senses." Arnold and his followers had reversed the normal psychological process by maintaining that one must know the classics to successfully discriminate in the present. "Our cultural humility before the civilization of Europe, then, is the chief obstacle which prevents us from producing any true indigenous culture of our own."[12]

Fifty years earlier Walt Whitman had made perhaps the most radical and prescient appeal for a new American culture. Like Emerson, Whitman emphasized the value of confronting the unknown; like Brooks and Bourne, he preferred to speculate on the possibilities for the future instead of pursuing an ideal based on the past. In his 1867 essay "Democracy," Whitman replied to an attack on universal suffrage made by Thomas Carlyle. He used the pretense of a political debate to hold forth in a strikingly grandiloquent fashion on the cultural prospects of democracy.

Whitman described his deep disappointment with the present aesthetic products of America. He felt a "singular awe" when he mixed with the

> interminable swarm of alert, turbulent, good natured independent citizens, mechanics, clerks, young persons. . . . I feel, with dejection and amazement, that among our geniuses and talented writers or speakers, few or none have yet really spoken to this people, or absorbed the central spirit and idiosyncracies which are theirs, and which, thus, in the highest ranges, so far remain entirely uncelebrated, unexpressed. . . . I say I have not seen one single writer, artist, lecturer, or what not, that has confronted the voiceless but ever erect and active,

pervading, underlying will and typic Aspiration of the land,
in a spirit kindred to itself. Do you call these genteel little
creatures American poets? Do you term that perpetual, pista-
reen, pasteboard work, American art, American opera, drama,
taste, verse? I think I hear, echoed as from some mountain
top afar in the the West, the scornful laugh of the Genius
of These States.[13]

Whitman outlined a vision of culture as the authentic expression
of the "grand, common stock," a culture that tapped the "measure-
less wealth of latent power and capacity" of the people. "The literature of These States, a new projection, when it comes, must be the
born outcrop, through all rich and luxuriant forms, but stern and
exclusive, of the sole Idea of The States, belonging here alone."

His new projection arrived about a generation later, made possible
by a new means of communication: motion pictures. The movies produced a new sort of culture, both a product and process with explic-
itly popular appeal. It recalled, in fact, the cultural program set
forth in *Democratic Vistas*: "drawn out not for a single class alone,
or for the parlors or lecture rooms, but with an eye to practical life,
the west, the working man, the facts of farm and jackplane and engineers, and of the broad range of the women also of the middle and
working strata."[14] But for believers in the traditional doctrine of
culture, the arrival of the movies meant a serious confrontation with
a strange phenomenon that did not fit neatly into any of the old
categories.

★

Projected motion picture photography became a reality in the 1890s,
but the dream of throwing moving pictures on a screen stretched
back at least three centuries. Various European inventors described
and created "magic lanterns" (primitive slide projectors) as early as
the mid-seventeenth century. But not until the early nineteenth
century did Peter Mark Roget and others seriously consider the principle of persistence of vision, a concept fundamental to all moving
pictures, drawn or photographed.

In the 1870s and 1880s several scientists engaged in the investigation of animal and human movement turned to photography as
a research tool. The most important of these, Etienne Jules Marey of
France and Eadweard Muybridge, an Englishman living in America,
created varieties of protocinema that greatly advanced visual time-
and-motion study. They also inspired inventors around the world to

try their hand at constructing devices capable of producing the illusion of motion photography. Most of these inventors, including Thomas Edison, took up motion picture work for quite a different reason than Marey and Muybridge: the lure of a profit-making commercial amusement.[15]

Early film historians and journalists chose to perpetuate and embellish the legend of Edison's preeminence in the development of motion pictures. In fact, as the painstaking and voluminous research of Gordon Hendricks has shown, the true credit for the creation of the first motion picture camera (*kinetograph*) and viewing machine (*kinetoscope*) belongs to Edison's employee, W. K. L. Dickson. Between 1888 and 1896, Dickson was "the center of all Edison's motion picture work during the crucial period of its technical perfection, and when others were led to the commercial use of the new medium, he was the instrument by which the others brought it into function." Edison himself admitted in 1895 that his reason for toying with motion pictures was "to devise an instrument which should do for the eye what the phonograph does for the ear"; however, his interest in motion pictures always remained subordinate to his passion for the phonograph.[16]

With the perfection of a moving picture camera in 1892, and the subsequent invention of the peep hole kinetoscope in 1893, the stage was set for the modern film industry. Previewed at the Columbian Exposition in Chicago during the summer of 1893, the kinetoscope could handle only one customer at a time. For a penny or a nickel in the slot, one could watch brief, unenlarged 35-mm black-and-white motion pictures. The kinetoscope provided a source of inspiration to other inventors; and, more importantly, its successful commercial exploitation convinced investors that motion pictures had a solid financial future. Kinetoscope parlors had opened in New York, Chicago, San Francisco, and scores of other cities all over the country by the end of 1894. The kinetoscope spread quickly to Europe as well, where Edison, revealing his minimal commitment to motion pictures, never even bothered to take out patents.[17]

At this time the Dickson-Edison kinetograph was the sole source of film subjects for the kinetoscopes. These early films were only fifty feet long, lasting only fifteen seconds or so. Beginning in 1893 dozens of dancers, acrobats, animal acts, lasso throwers, prize fighters, and assorted vaudevillians traveled to the Edison compound in West Orange, New Jersey. There they posed for the kinetograph, an immobile camera housed in a tarpaper shack dubbed the "Black Maria," the world's first studio built specifically for making movies.[18]

Although it virtually disappeared by 1900, the kinetoscope provided a critical catalyst to further invention and investment. With its diffusion all over America and Europe, the competitive pressure to create a viable motion picture projector, as well as other cameras, intensified. During the middle 1890s various people worked furiously at the task. By 1895, in Washington, D.C., C. Francis Jenkins and Thomas Armat had discovered the basic principle of the projector: intermittent motion for the film with a period of rest and illumination in excess of the period of movement from frame to frame. In New York, Major Woodville Latham and his two sons, along with Enoch Rector and Eugene Lauste, contributed the famous *Latham loop*, which allowed the use of longer lengths of film. William Paul successfully demonstrated his *animatograph* projector in London in early 1896. The Frenchmen Auguste and Louis Lumiere opened a commercial showing of their *cinematograph* in Paris in late 1895—a remarkable combination of camera, projector, and developer all in one. W. K. L. Dickson and Herman Casler perfected their *biograph* in 1896, clearly the superior projector of its day and the foundation for the American Mutoscope and Biograph Company.[19]

Once again, the name of Edison is most closely associated in the popular mind with the invention of the first projection machine. Actually, the basis of the *Edison Vitascope*, first publicly displayed in New York on 24 April 1896, was essentially the projector created by Thomas Armat. The Edison interests persuaded Armat "that in order to secure the largest profit in the shortest time it is necessary that we attach Mr. Edison's name in some prominent capacity to this new machine. . . . We should not of course misrepresent the facts to any inquirer, but we think we can use Mr. Edison's name in such a manner as to keep with the actual truth and yet get the benefit of his prestige."[20]

With the technology for the projection of motion pictures a reality, where were they to be shown? Between 1895 and 1905, prior to the nickelodeon boom, films were presented mainly in vaudeville performances, traveling shows, and penny arcades. Movies fit naturally into vaudeville; at first they were merely another novelty act. Audiences literally cheered the first exhibitions of the vitascope, biograph, and cinematograph in the years 1895 to 1897. But the triteness and poor quality of these early films soon dimmed the novelty and by 1900 or so vaudeville shows used films mainly as chasers that were calculated to clear the house for the next performance. Itinerant film exhibitors also became active in these years, as different inventors leased the territorial rights to projectors or sold them outright to enterprising showmen. From rural New England and upstate New York to Louisiana and Alaska, numerous visitors made movies a profitable attraction in theaters and tent shows. Finally, the penny arcades provided the third means of exposure for the infant cinema. Aside from their use of kinetoscopes, arcade owners quickly seized on other possibilities. Arcade patrons included a hard core of devoted movie fans, who wandered from place to place in search of films they had not seen yet. Some arcade owners bought, rented, or built their own projectors; they then partitioned off part of the arcade for screening movies. They acquired films from vaudeville managers who discarded them.[21]

The combination of the new audience and a growing class of profit-minded small entrepreneurs resulted in the explosion of store theaters (nickelodeons) after 1905. A supply of film subjects and equipment was necessary to meet the demand, and the first of several periods of wildcat development ran from 1896 to 1909. The three pioneer companies of Edison, Vitagraph, and Biograph in effect controlled the production of motion picture equipment, but a black market quickly developed. Each company that sprang up in these years became a manufacturer of instruments in addition to producing films. Many firms had long lists of patent claims, each arguing that it had a legal right to do business. Aside from the few real inventors and holders of legitimate patents, a good deal of stealing and copying of equipment took place. Lawsuits ran a close second to movies in production priorities. In 1909 the ten major manufacturers finally achieved a temporary peace with the formation of the Motion Picture Patents Company, a patent pooling and licensing organization. In addition to granting only ten licenses to use equipment and produce films, the Patents Company created the General Film Exchange to distribute films only to licensed exhibitors, who were forced to pay a two dollar weekly fee. The immediate impetus for this agreement, aside from the desire to rationalize profits, offers one clue as to how early motion pictures became a big business. Edison and Biograph had been the main rivals in the patents struggle, and the Empire Trust Company, holder of two hundred thousand dollars in Biograph mortgage bonds, sent J. J. Kennedy (an executive and efficiency expert) to hammer out an agreement and save their investment.[22]

By 1909 motion pictures had clearly become a large industry, with three distinct phases of production, exhibition, and distribution; in addition, directing, acting, photography, writing, and lab work emerged as separate crafts. The agreement of 1909, however, rather than establishing peace, touched off another round of intense speculative development, because numerous independent producers and exhibitors openly and vigorously challenged the licensing of the Patent Company. In 1914, after five years of guerrilla warfare with the independents, the trust lay dormant; the courts declared it legally dead in 1917. Several momentous results accrued from the intense battle won by the innovative and adventurous independents. They produced a higher quality of pictures and pioneered the multireel feature film. Under their leadership Hollywood replaced New York as the center of production, and the star system was born. At the close of the world war, they controlled the movie industry not only in America, but all over the globe.[23]

Of all the facets of motion picture history, none is so stunning as the extraordinarily rapid growth in the audience during the brief period between 1905 and 1918. Two key factors, closely connected, made this boom possible. First, the introduction and refinement of the story film liberated the moving picture from its previous length of a minute or two, allowing exhibitors to present a longer program of films. One-reel westerns, comedies, melodramas, and travelogues, lasting ten to fifteen minutes each, became the staple of film programs until they were replaced by feature pictures around World War I. George Melies, Edwin S. Porter (*The Great Train Robbery*, 1903), and D. W. Griffith, in his early work with Biograph (1908 to 1913), all set the pace for transforming the motion picture from a novelty into an art.

Secondly, the emergence of the nickelodeon as a place devoted to screening motion pictures meant that movies could now stand on their own as an entertainment. These store theaters, presenting a continuous show of moving pictures, may have begun as early as 1896 in New Orleans and Chicago. In 1902 Thomas Tally closed down his penny arcade in Los Angeles and opened the Electric Theater, charging ten cents for "Up to Date High Class Moving Picture Entertainment, Especially for Ladies and Children." But the first to use the term *nickelodeon* were John P. Harris and Harry Davis, who converted a vacant store front in Pittsburgh in late 1905.[24]

News of their success spread quickly and spawned imitators everywhere. All over America adventurous exhibitors converted penny arcades, empty store rooms, tenement lofts, and almost any available space into movie theaters. Because no official statistics remain from those years, we must rely on contemporary estimates. By 1907 between three and five thousand nickelodeons had been established, with over two million admissions a day. In 1911 the Patents Company reported 11,500 theaters across America devoted solely to showing motion pictures, with hundreds more showing them occasionally; daily attendance that year probably reached five million. By 1914 the figures reached about 18,000 theaters, with more than seven million daily admissions totaling about $300 million.[25]

Perhaps more graphic (and accurate) than these national statistics, local surveys revealed the terrific popularity of movies, especially in the larger cities. Table 3 summarizes data from a number of contemporary estimates of movie attendance in eight cities during these years.[26]

Table 3
Urban Movie Attendance, 1911–1918

City	Population (1910)	Year	Weekly Attendance	Number Theaters
New York	4,766,883	1911	1,500,000	400
Cleveland	560,663	1913	890,000	131
Detroit	465,766	1912	400,000	
San Francisco	416,912	1913	327,500	
Milwaukee	373,857	1911	210,630	50
Kansas City	248,381	1912	449,064	81
Indianapolis	233,650	1914	320,000	70
Toledo	187,840 (1915)	1918	316,000	58

Although data for smaller cities and towns is more scarce, what little we have suggests that the "nickel madness" was not limited to large urban centers. For example, in Ipswich, Massachusetts, an industrial town of six thousand in 1914, movie attendance was substantial among school children. Of 127 children in grades five through eight, 69 percent of the boys went once a week or more to the movies, as did 55 percent of the girls. Among 179 high school students, 81 percent attended moving picture shows, on the average of 1.23 times per week for boys and 1.08 for girls. A 1914 study of Springfield, Illinois (1910 population, 51,678) revealed that 813 of the 857 high school students interviewed went to the movies regularly. Forty-one percent of the boys and 30 percent of the girls attended at least seven times a month, whereas 59 percent of the boys and 53 percent of the girls attended at least four times a month. A similar survey in 1914 of four Iowa cities (Iowa City, Dubuque, Burlington, Ottumwa) questioned fourteen hundred high school students. It showed that 30 percent of the boys and 21 percent of the girls in these communities went to the movies at least seven times a month, with 60 percent of the boys and 45 percent of the girls going at least four times each month.[27]

This sudden and staggering boom in movie attendance evoked strenuous reactions from the nation's cultural traditionalists, those whose values and sensibilities had been shaped largely by some version of the doctrine of culture. Although the motion picture held out great promise for many of the traditionalists in the abstract, few of them could accept as positive advance the new popular culture and all it implied. Their consideration of motion pictures centered on three points, all interrelated: the context of exhibition, the nature of the audience, and the content of the films themselves.

★

All of the surveys of motion picture popularity, and indeed a large fraction of all discussions of the new medium, placed movies in a larger context of urban commercial amusements. Movies represented "the most spectacular single feature of the amusement situation in recent years," a situation that included penny arcades, dance academies and dance halls, vaudeville and burlesque theaters, pool rooms, amusement parks, and even saloons. Motion pictures inhabited the physical and psychic space of the urban street life. Standing opposite these commercial amusements, in the minds of the cultural traditionalists, were municipal parks, playgrounds, libraries, museums, school recreation centers, YMCAs, and church-sponsored recreation. The competition between the two sides, noted sociologist Edward A. Ross, was nothing less than a battle between "warring sides of human nature—appetite and will, impulse and reason, inclination and ideal." The mushrooming growth of movies and other commercial amusements thus signaled a weakness and perhaps a fundamental shift in the values of American civilization. "Why has the love of spontaneous play," wondered Reverend Richard H. Edwards, "given way so largely to the love of merely being amused?"

For those who spoke about "the moral significance of play" and preferred the literal meaning of the term *recreation*, the flood of commercial amusements posed a grave cultural threat. Most identified the amusement situation as inseparable from the expansion of the city and factory labor. Referring to the enormous vogue of the movies in Providence, Rhode Island before World War I, Francis R. North noted the "great alluring power in an amusement which for a few cents . . . can make a humdrum mill hand become an absorbed

witness of stirring scenes otherwise unattainable, a quick transference from the real to the unreal."

Commercial amusements tempted rural folk as well, and some
writers argued that "the young people coming from the country
form the mainstay of the amusement resorts." Frederick C. Howe
warned in 1914 that "commercialized leisure is moulding our civilization—not as it should be moulded but as commerce dictates. . . .
And leisure must be controlled by the community, if it is to become
an agency of civilization rather than the reverse."

A scientific assessment of the situation, as attempted by the
myriad of recreation and amusement surveys of the early twentieth
century, seemed a logical first step. Beyond this, the drive for municipal supervision of public recreation and commercial amusements
fit comfortably into the Progressive ethos of philanthropists, social
workers, and urban reformers all over America. "In a word," asserted Michael M. Davis of the Russell Sage Foundation in 1912,
"recreation within the modern city has become a matter of public
concern; laissez faire, in recreation as in industry, can no longer be
the policy of the state."[28]

What actually transpired in and around the early nickelodeons
varied from theater to theater and city to city. On the whole they do
not seem to have been an especially pleasant place to watch a show.
A 1911 report made on moving picture shows by New York City
authorities disclosed that "the conditions found to exist are such as
to attach to cheap and impermanent places of amusement, to wit:
poor sanitation, dangerous overcrowding, and inadequate protection
from fire or panic." Despite the foul smells, poor ventilation, and
frequent breakdowns in projection, investigators found overflow
crowds in a majority of theaters. Managers scurried around their
halls, halfheartedly spraying the fetid air with deodorizers and
vainly trying to calm the quarrels and shoving matches that com-
monly broke out over attempts to better one's view. The overall
atmosphere was perhaps no more rowdy or squalid than the tenement home life endured by much of the audience; but the nickelodeons offered a place of escape for its eager patrons.[29]

The darkness of the nickelodeon theater, argued some doctors and
social workers, caused eye strain and related disorders: "Intense
ocular and cerebral weariness, a sort of dazed 'good-for-nothing'
feeling, lack of energy, or appetite, etc.," as one physician put it. The
health problem melted into a moral one, as critics condemned the
darkness. Declared John Collier at a child welfare conference, "It is
an evil pure and simple, destructive of social interchange, and of

artistic effect." Jane Addams observed that "the very darkness of the theater is an added attraction to many young people, for whom the space is filled with the glamour of love-making." Darkness in the nickelodeon reinforced old fears of theaters as havens for prostitutes and places where innocent girls could be taken advantage of. John Collier asked: "Must moving picture shows be given in a dark auditorium, with all the lack of social spirit and the tendency to careless conduct which a dark auditorium leads to?"[30]

If the inside of the theaters was seamy, the immediate space outside could be severely jolting. Gaudy architecture and lurid, exaggerated posters were literally "a psychological blow in the face," as one writer put it. Sensational handbills, passed out among school children, vividly described movies such as *Temptations of a Great City*: "Wine women and gayety encompass his downfall. Sowing wild oats. See the great cafe scene, trap infested road to youth, and the gilded spider webs that are set in a great city after dark." Phonographs or live barkers would often be placed just outside the theater, exhorting passers-by to come in. Inside, the nickelodeon program varied from theater to theater. An hour-long show might include illustrated song slides accompanying a singer, one or more vaudeville acts, and an illustrated lecture, in addition to several one-reelers. But movies were the prime attraction.[31]

In the summer of 1909, while strolling in a provincial New England town, economist Simon Patten found the library, church, and schools, "the conserving moral agencies of a respectable town," all closed. In contrast to this literally dark side of town, Patten described the brighter side where all the people were. Alongside candy shops, fruit and nut stands, and ice cream parlors, Patten noted the throngs at the nickel theater.

> Opposite the barren school yard was the arcaded entrance
> to the Nickelodeon, finished in white stucco, with the ticket
> seller throned in a chariot drawn by an elephant trimmed with
> red, white and blue lights. A phonograph was going over and
> over its lingo, and a few machines were free to the absorbed
> crowd which circulated through the arcade as through the street.
> Here were groups of working girls—now happy "summer girls"
> —because they had left the grime, ugliness, and dejection of
> their factories behind them, and were freshened and revived by
> doing what they liked to do.[32]

Here the contrast was more than symbolic. Like many others, Patten warned that the traditional cultural institutions needed to adapt quickly in the face of movies and other commercial amusements. They could compete only by transforming themselves into active and "concrete expressions of happiness, security, and pleasure in life."[33]

As for the nickelodeon program itself, everyone concurred that vaudeville was "by far the most pernicious element in the whole motion picture situation." Early projected motion pictures had found their first home in vaudeville houses during the 1890s. But with the rise of theaters devoted to motion pictures, the situation reversed itself. Exhibitors across the nation added vaudeville acts to their film shows as a novelty for attracting patronage in a highly competitive business. Not all movie houses included vaudeville acts on the bill; local demand, availability of talent, and other conditions dictated the exact format of the show. But vaudeville became enough of a commonplace in American nickelodeons for observers to agree that it was the most objectionable feature of them. Particularly in immigrant ghettos, where ethnic vaudeville remained popular until the 1920s, reformers feared the uncontrolled (and uncensorable) quality of the live performance. The singers, dancers, and dialect comics of vaudeville appalled and frustrated those who were struggling to regulate the burgeoning nickelodeon movement.

The mayor's committee in Portland, Oregon complained in 1914, for example, about the numerous shows "where decent and altogether harmless films are combined with the rankest sort of vaudeville. There is a censorship upon the films, but none at all on male and female performers, who in dialog, joke, and song give out as much filth as the audience will stand for." In 1910 an Indianapolis civic committee denounced the vaudeville performances in local movie theaters as unfit for any stage: "Almost without exception the songs were silly and sentimental and often sung suggestively." Robert O. Bartholomew, the Cleveland censor of motion pictures, could not believe some of the things he witnessed in that city's nickelodeons in 1913:

> Many verses of different songs have been gathered which would not bear printing in this report. Dancers were often seen who endeavored to arouse interest and applause by going through vulgar movements of the body. . . . A young woman after dancing in such a manner as to set off all the young men and boys in the audience in a state of pandemonium brought onto the stage a large python snake about ten feet long. The snake was first wrapped about the body, then caressed and finally kissed in its mouth.[34]

Nickelodeon vaudeville was usually cheap, almost impossible to regulate, and socially objectionable—to the authorities, if not to the audience. As a result, police harassment and stricter theater regulations were employed all over the country to exclude vaudeville from movie houses. By 1918 nearly all movie exhibitors had responded to external pressure and internal trade opinion by eliminating vaudeville. They were forced to concede what one exhibitor had written in a trade paper in 1909, that "a properly managed exclusive picture show is in a higher class than a show comprised partly of vaudeville."[35]

In every town and city the place of exhibition proved the most vulnerable point of the industry, a soft underbelly for critics to attack. New York's experience between 1908 and 1913 provides a rough historical model for what transpired all over the country as cultural traditionalists sought to control the sphere of exhibition. By 1908 over five hundred nickelodeons had appeared in New York, a large proportion of them in tenement districts. A city ordinance required only a twenty-five dollar license for theaters with common shows (movies were so designated) that had a capacity below three hundred; the regular theater license of five hundred dollars was well above the means of average exhibitors, so they made certain that their number of seats remained below three hundred. At a stormy public meeting on 23 December 1908, prominent clergymen and laymen urged Mayor George McClellan to close the nickelodeons for a variety of reasons. These included violation of Sunday blue laws (the busiest day for the nickelodeon trade), safety hazards, and degradation of community morals. "Is a man at liberty," demanded Reverend J. M. Foster, "to make money from the morals of people? Is he to profit from the corruption of the minds of children?" The next day Mayor McClellan revoked the licenses of every movie show in the city, some 550 in all.

On Christmas day exhibitors, film producers, and distributors responded by meeting and forming the Moving Picture Exhibitors Association, with William Fox as their leader. The movie men successfully fought the order with injunctions, but the message was clear: some form of regulation was necessary. Marcus Loew began to ask various civic bodies for names of potential inspectors to investigate the theaters. It took several years, however, for New York to enact the first comprehensive law in the United States regulating movie theaters. The 1913 legislation included provisions for fire protection, ventilation, sanitation, exits, and structural requirements. Seating limits increased from three hundred to six hundred to provide exhibitors more funds for making improvements. Significantly, all vaudeville acts were banned from movie houses unless they met the stiffer requirements of regular stage theaters.[36]

★

Although movies contributed to the new web of commercial amusements, they obviously stood apart from them as well. Motion pictures presented a troubling paradox: they clearly departed from traditional forms of recreation, yet they were undoubtedly superior to dance halls and pool rooms. Their potential for uplift was enormous, especially when one considered the makeup of the audience. Contemporary observers never tired of stressing the strong appeal motion pictures held for the working classes and new immigrants. Vigorous movie-phobes thought it impossible to exaggerate "the disintegrating effect of the sensational moving picture." Those more sanguine about its possibilities agreed with publisher Joseph M. Patterson: "The sentient life of the half-civilized beings at the bottom has been enlarged and altered by the introduction of the dramatic motif, to resemble more closely the sentient life of the civilized beings at the top." Both sides agreed that precisely because of the special appeal movies had for these groups, as well as for children, one had an obligation to discover how and why the motion picture captured its enormous audience.[37]

The 1911 Russell Sage study of New York theaters estimated movie audiences in that city to be 72 percent working class. A 1914 study of how one thousand working men spent their leisure time concluded that the popularity of moving pictures was the one outstanding fact of the survey. Sixty percent of those questioned attended movies regularly; those working the longest hours spent the most time at the shows; and those who earned less than ten dollars per week went the most often.[38]

Most writers directly coupled the working-class response to the film with modern industrial conditions. Elizabeth B. Butler, in her classic 1909 study of working-class women in Pittsburgh, thought that grinding and monotonous factory labor radically changed recreation patterns: "Dulled senses demand powerful stimuli; exhaustion of the vital forces leads to a desire for the crude, for violent excitation. . . . In such circumstances, culture of hand or brain seems unattainable, and the sharing of our general heritage a remote dream." Using a prevalent distinction of the day, Butler noted that the working women of Pittsburgh "are spending their leisure, not using it." Thus, of the 22,685 women working in factories and stores, she found less than 2 percent involved with such centers of recreation as the YWCA, Business Women's Club, and sewing circles. The extent to which movies dominated the women's recreational life profoundly impressed Butler, and she vividly described a trip to the nickelodeon:

> I shall not soon forget a Saturday evening when I stood among
> a crowd of pleasure seekers on Fifth Avenue, and watched
> the men and women packed thick at the entrance of every pic-
> ture show. My companion and I bought tickets for one of the five
> cent shows. Our way was barred by a sign, "Performance now
> going on." As we stood near the door, the crowd of people wait-
> ing to enter filled the long vestibule and even part of the side-
> walk. They were determined to be amused, and this was one of
> the things labelled "Amusement." They were hot and tired
> and irritable, but willing to wait until long after our enthusi-
> asm was dampened and we left them standing in line for
> their chance to go in.[39]

Butler did not believe that motion pictures were inherently bad; indeed, the diversion they offered to work-weary women was essential. "Yet there should be possibility for constructive diversion. A diversion is needed which shall be a form of social expression, and with slighter toll from strength and income, be of lasting value to the body and spirit."[40]

Similarly, Margaret F. Byington's 1910 study of ninety households in the mill town of Homestead, Pennsylvania, also acknowledged the great popularity of movies. The nickelodeon was the only theater of any kind available in Homestead. Pittsburgh theaters were out of the reach of working-class families because of travel time and expense. "Many people, therefore, find in the nickelodeons their only relaxation. Men on their way home from work stop for a few minutes to see something of life outside the alternation of mill and home; the shopper rests while she enjoys the music, poor though it be, and the children are always begging for five cents to go to the nickelodeon. In the evening the family often go together for a little treat."[41]

Contemporary observers somewhat overstated both the class and ethnic factors in their analysis of movie audiences. Commercial amusements proved more commercial than they had ever dreamed. Thus, although the working classes made up the bulk of early audiences and provided the basic working capital for the new medium, efforts to woo the middle and upper classes began almost immediately. As Russell Merritt has shown, "The blue collar worker and his family may have supported the nickelodeons. The scandal was that no one connected with the movies much wanted his support—least of all the immigrant film exhibitors who were working their way out of the slums." Merritt's study of the early Boston movie trade shows that after 1908 virtually all new nickelodeons opened in business districts on the outer edges of slums and near white-collar shopping centers, where they hoped to attract middle-class patronage.[42]

Even before the rise of the feature film and the wave of new movie palaces built after 1914, two developments usually cited as correlative with the winning of the middle-class audience, movie men actively sought to leave the slums behind. In Chicago, for example, as early as 1908, the Swann Theater opened in a residential quarter at a cost of sixty-five thousand dollars, and it immediately attracted a large family trade. For five or ten cents, the theater ran an eighty-minute program of three one-reelers and several illustrated songs. "The policy of the house recognizes the eternal feminine as the great factor in determining the nature of any amusement enterprise; and the pictures shown are always carefully selected with the view of pleasing the ladies." Trade papers were filled with advice on how to improve the reputation of movies through higher prices, more attractive and carefully located theaters, and better films.[43]

The presence of large numbers of "undeveloped minds" in the nickelodeons—immigrants and children—evoked endless assertions about movies as a potential agent of Americanization and moral suasion. The notion that movies served to Americanize immigrants had more to do with wish fulfillment than reality. For one thing, perhaps a majority of films screened in early years were produced in Europe. The Americanization argument seems to have been largely another piece of ammunition in the battle to establish a censorship of films.

The image of ignorant immigrants and incorrigible youth uplifted by movies was a potent and reassuring one for social workers and civic leaders sympathetic to films. An anonymous poem entitled "A Newsboy's Point of View," written about 1910, typified this sentimental attitude. It purported to describe how a newsboy witnesses the father of his girlfriend giving up drink after they all see a film about the evils of alcohol. The poem is written in the urban slang appropriate for its narrator, a tough Irish urchin. A stock image of the Progressive imagination, the newsboy quotes his girl's father: "'I never knowed just what a bum I'd gone an' got to be / Until those movin' pitchers went an' showed myself to me.'" But the real revela-

tion comes in the last stanza, as the newsboy reflects on a larger
lesson:

All what I see wit' me own eyes I knows an' unnerstan's
When I see movin pitchers of de far off, furrin' lan's
Where de Hunks an' Ginnes come from—yer can betcher life I
   knows
Dat of all de lan's an' countries, 'taint no matter where yer goes
Dis here country's got 'em beaten—take my oat dat ain't no
   kid—
'Cause we learned it from de movin' pitchers, me an' Maggie
   did.[44]

A far more significant effect of the motion picture, particularly for
children, was in the area of peer socialization. The act of moviegoing
created an important new subculture centered outside of the home.
Jane Addams astutely recognized this development. Although she
actively involved herself in the community supervision of movies
and theaters, Addams always looked upon this work as only a
holding action. To the end of her life she remained ambivalent about
the implications of motion pictures. Her response to the motion picture's growth in Chicago reflected the uneasiness of even the most
sympathetic traditionalists.

In the spring of 1907, responding to pressure from the *Chicago
Tribune*, the city's police department set up a "nickel theater bureau"
charged with investigating movie theaters and penny arcades. One
detective, walking along Milwaukee Avenue, counted eighteen
nickelodeons in a mile-and-a-half stretch. The *Tribune* and various
social agencies were greatly agitated by both the large numbers of
children at the shows and the large proportion of objectionable
films: movies with scenes of robbery, murder, shoplifting, skirt-
lifting, and bedrooms. At Hull House, Addams and her associates
had observed the eagerness of the penniless children to attend the
movies. At first the settlement tried to compete with commercial
exhibitors, establishing its own moving picture show, probably in
early 1907. "Although its success justified its existence," Addams
discovered, "it was so obviously but one in the midst of hundreds
that it seemed much more advisable to turn our attention to the
improvement of all of them or rather to assist, as best we could, the
successful efforts in this direction."[45]

Thus Hull House joined the Juvenile Protection Association, the
Relief and Aid Society, and other civic groups in cooperating with
the police censorship of "5 cent theaters, penny arcades, and other

cheap amusement resorts where juveniles are taught depravity." Addams opposed any ordinances prohibiting children from attending theaters without an adult, arguing that these were unenforceable. "What is needed," she declared, "is a regulation of the theaters. They are useful in providing a place of amusement for those who cannot go to the regular theater and can be made instructive. Police regulation supplemented by the efforts of a citizen's committee will overcome any evil influence."[46]

Young people invariably attended shows in groups, "with something of the 'gang' instinct. . . . What is seen and heard there becomes the sole topic of conversation, forming the ground pattern of their social life. That mutual understanding which in another social circle is provided by books, travel, and all the arts, is here compressed into the topics suggested by the play." But how could this corrupt dramatic art and the crude music that went with it replace the true drama, the real theater, which was "the only place where they can satisfy that craving for a conception of life higher than that which the actual world offers them?"

It could not. Throughout her career Addams championed amateur drama as a vital expression of the "play instinct." Like so many others, she argued for more extensive public recreation as an alternative to the commercial exhibition of films: not only playgrounds, but also patriotic and ethnic festivals, folk dancing, children's theater. She was ahead of her time in her sensitivity to preserving immigrant cultures, and here again she lamented the tendency of movies to erase the ethnic heritage from the minds of so many children. Addams's views on recreation amounted to nothing less than a vision of multicultural communion based on the artistic expression of individuals. One could not achieve communion at the movies. "To insist that young people shall forecast their rose colored future only in a house of dreams, is to deprive the real world of that warmth and reassurance which it so sorely needs and to which it is justly entitled: furthermore we are left outside with a sense of dreariness, in company with that shadow which lurks only around the corner for most of us—a skepticism of life's value."[47]

★

Although both the exhibition milieu and the nature of the audience continued to trouble the cultural traditionalists, they realized that movies were here to stay. Municipal regulation of the theaters, along with the elimination of vaudeville, might improve the moral atmosphere of shows. However, in no way could the size of the audience and the intensity of its devotion be diminished by substituting alternative forms of cheap amusement. Regulation of the films themselves thus remained the focal point for social control.

The 1908 nickelodeon licensing struggle in New York City led directly to the first attempt at a comprehensive censorship of motion pictures, and this attempt was spearheaded by the movie industry itself. In March 1909 the movie exhibitors and producers in New York City requested the People's Institute, a civic and educational foundation, to organize the National Board of Censorship of Motion Pictures. Although administered by the People's Institute, the board was a self-regulating body; it comprised a general committee (electing its own members and an executive board) that formally elected people to the actual censoring committee. Essentially, the NBC was the first of several methods of voluntary trade regulation for the movie industry, with the exhibitors and producers footing the bill. The movie men clearly wanted to counter public criticism of their business, for the standing of each exhibitor and producer depended on every other. The creation of the board may also be viewed as another important method by which the industry could make motion pictures more palatable to the upper and middle classes, "to improve the average quality of the films in order that a larger and larger number of the total population [would] patronize motion pictures."[48]

Here the commercial realities of the movies forced the industry to seek the cooperation of the cultural traditionalists. The board continually defined its mission as the uplifting of both the films and the taste of the audiences; it claimed that its goal was the elimination of any need for censorship. It began with the premise that "the motion picture has become a public power and a moral and cultural influence which must be brought under social control." Hence it made sure that "these censors [were] cultured men and women, trained to look on the activities of life from the broad view of their social significance; . . . persons of culture and more or less prominent in social and other public life in New York—doctors, lawyers, clergymen, and, in fact, men and women of all kinds of activities."

The board presumed a very simple psychology at the core of the moviegoer's experience: "Those who are educated by the movies are educated through their hearts and their sense impressions and that sort of education sticks. Every person in an audience has paid admission and for that reason gives his attention willingly. . . . Therefore he gives it his confidence and opens the window of his mind. And what the movie says sinks in." The board's standards of judgment mostly concerned elimination of excesses in scenes dealing with sex, drugs, and crime, particularly prostitution. While keeping in mind the differences in local standards, it tried "to act on behalf of the general conscience and intelligence of the country in permitting or prohibiting a given scene on film." By 1914 the National Board of Censorship claimed to be reviewing 95 percent of the total film output in the United States; it either passed a film, suggested changes, or condemned a movie entirely. Mayors, police chiefs, some four hundred civic groups, and local censoring committees from all over the country subscribed to the board's weekly bulletin.[49]

Local censorship arrangements remained active despite the work of the national board. Compared to the national board, local censors felt a greater confidence in their absolute right and ability to distinguish between moral and immoral films. Local boards often attacked the national board as too lenient, and they fiercely defended the necessity for community control of the censorship power. They tended to judge films solely as an endless succession of potential morality plays. In Portland, Oregon, for example, the form instituted by the mayor's committee on motion pictures asked investigators of movie theaters to use the following criteria in judging films: "Estimate moral value: Good, bad, or without moral value. Does the wrong doer prosper? Is the way of the transgressor easy? Are the rascals held up for admiration? Are the virtues made sources of mirth?" In Pennsylvania the state censors defined the "standards of the board" in a totally negative fashion. The state board worked out an incredibly detailed list describing scores of scenes that it prohibited from films shown in Pennsylvania.[50]

Compared to the large number of people interested mainly in the social effects of motion pictures, writers who approached movies as an art form were a small circle before World War I. They stand out as a prophetic minority in their efforts to treat the new popular culture from an aesthetic perspective, but they frequently revealed the same assumptions as the traditionalists about the nature of "true culture." At first most critics assessed movies in relation to the art form to which they seemed closest: drama. Indeed, there was a great deal of cross-fertilization between movies and the theater in these early years, both in terms of personnel and in the stylistic fusion of realism and romanticism.[51] But this insistence on judging motion pictures as merely another category of drama blinded many critics to the early achievements of film artists such as Griffith, Chaplin, Sennett, Pickford, Ince, and others. The motion picture, argued Brander Matthews in 1917, can improve on standard theatrical melodrama and farce, but "comedy and tragedy are wholly beyond its reach, and equally unattainable by it are the social drama and the problem play."

Film was not one of the higher or more important forms of drama, Matthews asserted, because it could not combine intellectual cooperation, emotional appeal, and sense gratification, the three elements that made drama the most illustrious art. He grudgingly conceded that motion pictures might be a new art, but because they could not utilize the spoken word, they would never rival the drama. Matthews concluded condescendingly that, as film makers accepted the medium's limitations and began to develop its techniques, "the apparent rivalry between the drama and the moving picture will lessen, and each will be left in possession of its own special field."[52]

Theater critics in general had difficulty with movies as an art form, and their confusion is perhaps best summarized in the work of Walter P. Eaton. As early as 1909, Eaton cited what he perceived as a rise in movie audience taste: "They have come to demand real drama, pictures that tell a coherent, interesting story and tell it well, with genuine settings and competent actors." Several European *films d'art* were already raising people's awareness of acting, story construction, and dramatic unity. For Eaton, however, appreciation of the "canned drama" remained only a means to the true understanding of real drama. He ultimately viewed the improvement of movies merely as a method of rescuing theatrical drama: "When they are well planned and well played, it is quite possible that they can always fill a useful function, in leading the lower strata of society up toward an appreciation of true dramatic art, which is, after all, only brought to flower on the stage of a true theater, where actual men and women speak with the voices God gave them."[53]

Four years later, Eaton still distinguished between movies and "the real thing." The menace of the movies to dramatic art was overstated, he claimed, even if "talking pictures" became a reality. Eaton pointed to the "layers on layers of intelligence and taste in the public," and although movies appealed to the hoi polloi, true drama would always remain a province of the cultural elite. "Talking movies can never give to these people the deep emotional glow, the keen intellectual zest, the warm aesthetic satisfaction which comes from living, vital acting, from distinguished, witty speech, from all the complex and interblended technical problems of the drama brought triumphantly off." In 1914 he saw some hope in the rising popularity of the feature film. Here he found sustained narrative, more clearly allied to dramatic and pictorial art, demanding concentration of two hours or more. Movies such as *Queen Elizabeth* (featuring Sarah Bernhardt) and *The Prisoner of Zenda* (starring James K. Hackett), larger theaters, and higher admission prices brought a more dignified quality to the motion picture. This is precisely what independent film producers such as Adolph Zukor aimed at. Nevertheless, for Eaton feature pictures of famous plays had value only as feeders for live performances.[54]

Finally, by 1915, Eaton even renounced his former optimism that movies might act as a school of appreciation for drama, breeding new audiences for the financially troubled legitimate stage. The drama must take to the offensive and recapture the masses, its gallery, through a program of socialized theater. Only municipal playhouses and branch theaters could compete economically with the movies for the working-class audience. It was time for true drama to fight motion pictures, not accommodate them. "They have a cruel realism which at once dulls the imagination and destroys the illusive romance of the art. They are utterly incapable of intellectual content. . . . All poetry, all music, all flash of wit, all dignity of spoken eloquence, they can never know."[55]

As the movie industry turned away from the simple one- and two-reelers produced by the Patents Company members and moved toward full-length features and spectacles, so too did film slowly achieve an independent critical status. By World War I more and more newspapers, magazines, and trade publications began to employ full-time reviewers to consider the latest in film art. Aside from professional critics, though, increasing numbers of intellectuals and artists began to contemplate seriously the aesthetic possibilities that movies offered. They were excited because film seemed a truly popular art, one that entered to an amazing extent "into the daily thought of the masses." As a new medium of expression, movies had advantages over the drama. It liberated the narrative from constraints of time and space and gave the artist a greater ability to alter his point of view. Robert Coady, writing in the avant-garde little magazine *Soil*, defended the motion picture as "a medium of visual motion." Aesthetic censorship, the attempt to make movies simply imitate drama, would prove just as crippling as the legal kind. "There is a world of visual motion yet to be explored, a world the motion picture is opening up to us."[56]

The two most substantial early treatments of film aesthetics came from antipodal sources. One may be considered the fount of the psychological approach to film analysis. The other sought to somehow adapt the classical notions of beauty to a new democratic art. Hugo Munsterberg's psychological study, *The Photoplay*, wanted to establish the aesthetic independence of motion pictures. But Munsterberg, chairman of the philosophy department at Harvard, wished to combine aesthetic inquiry with an exploration of the psychological factors involved in the movies' appeal. His psychology owed more to Kant and the German idealist tradition than to Freud and the new psychoanalysis.

Munsterberg argued that understanding the psychology of the motion picture must precede consideration of its aesthetic and that this was crucial for appreciating its differences from other arts. Various aspects of the motion picture depended on illusion, for example, depth and movement. "Flatness is an objective part of the technical physical arrangement, but not a feature of that which we really see"; similarly, the motion that a spectator sees "appears to be a true motion, . . . yet is created by his own mind." Both depth and movement "come to us in the moving picture world, not as hard facts, but as a mixture of fact and symbol. They are present yet they are not in the things. We invest the impression with them."

The *close-up* "objectified in our world of perception our mental act of attention," and thereby gave art "a means which far transcend[ed] the power of any theater stage." The *cutback* (flashback) paralleled the close-up by objectifying the mental act of remembering. The technique of *cutting* in movies allowed the objective world to be molded by the interests of the mind: "Events which are far distant from one another so that we could not be physically present at all of them at the same time are fusing in our field of vision, just as they are brought together in our consciousness. . . . This inner division, this awareness of contrasting situations, this interchange of diverging experience in the soul, can never be embodied except in the photoplay." All of these techniques made the power of suggestion great in film; the subtle art of the camera had great potential for deeply touching the emotions and attitudes of the audience.

Once one comprehended the basic psychology of the movies, the aesthetic followed naturally. Art must transcend reality, not imitate it, showing us things and events perfectly complete in themselves. Motion pictures were well suited for this task. They told "the human story by overcoming the forms of the outer world, namely space, time, and causality, and by adjusting the events to the forms of the inner world, namely attention, memory, imagination, and emotion." Human action was thus freed from physical phenomena and transferred to the realm of the mind. This transferral, Munsterberg argued, explained the great popularity of movies and accounted for the aesthetic feeling they gave.

In elaborating his aesthetic, Munsterberg sounded a good deal like those cultural traditionalists who could accept film only as a means to an end; he saw film's greatest mission as aesthetic education. Although Munsterberg hailed the new art of film, his ideas in some ways resembled those of Matthew Arnold: "An enthusiasm for the noble and uplifting, a belief in duty and discipline of the mind, a faith in ideals and eternal values must permeate the world of the screen." Perhaps because he was so involved in discovering why the new medium was so powerful, Munsterberg worried about the average person's ability to handle it: "The people still have to learn the great difference between true enjoyment and fleeting pleasure, between real beauty and the mere tickling of the senses."[57]

In *The Art of the Moving Picture*, the poet Vachel Lindsay tried to outline "a basis for photoplay criticism in America"; it is memorable less for its success in forming a critical theory than for Lindsay's ebullience in extolling the movies on several levels. The book was really a prose poem, still remarkable today in its breadth of vision, urgent commitment, and naiveté. Enormously excited at being present at the creation of a new art, Lindsay predicted that the movies would evolve into a peculiarly American cultural form: "The possibility of showing the entire American population its own face in the Mirror Screen has at last come."

His method was to categorize various types of movies by comparing them with traditional art forms. Thus, "the Action Film is sculpture-in-motion, the Intimate Photoplay is painting-in-motion, [and the] Splendor Pictures [are] architecture-in-motion." These analogies gave Lindsay the opportunity to legitimize the art of film, and he reiterated the theme of its independence: "The photoplays of the future will be written from the foundation of the film. . . . The supreme photoplay will give us things that have been half expressed in all other mediums allied to it."

To a poet who once walked across the nation reciting and selling his work to anyone who might listen, the potential for "a democracy and a photoplay business working in daily rhythm" was dizzying. Movies might succeed where earlier art forms had failed. Lindsay invoked the fervor of his kindred spirit: "Whitman brought the idea of democracy to our sophisticated literati, but did not persuade the democracy itself to read his democratic poems. Sooner or later the kinetoscope will do what he could not, bring the nobler side of the equality idea to the people who are so crassly equal."

Although he discussed a large number of contemporary films, Lindsay thought the future of movies most worthy of attention. We were all in on the ground floor; Edison became the new Gutenberg, and the invention of the motion picture seemed as great an advancement as the beginning of picture writing. Ostensibly an attempt to carve out a theory of film criticism, Lindsay's book went far beyond this, affirming that "the destiny of America from many aspects may be bound up in what the prophet wizards among her photoplaywrights and producers mark out for her, for those things which a whole nation dares to hope for it may in the end attain."[58]

By the end of the Great War, the medium of motion pictures had established a new popular culture: a postprint confluence of entertainment, big business, art, and modern technology that catered to and drew its strength from popular taste. The new popular culture combined product and process, neither of which fit within the matrix of the old doctrine of culture. The achievements of film art could not be measured by traditional critical standards; they demanded their own aesthetic. The act of moviegoing became a powerful social ritual for millions, a new way of experiencing and defining the shared values of peer and family.

Motion pictures thus proved a medium of communication that touched everyday life far more viscerally and immediately than had the more heralded telegraph. Telegraphy rearranged perceptions of time and space with its instantaneous transmission of information. Movies altered patterns of leisure and created a new art form. The new popular culture, however, still found its locus outside of the home. By the 1920s radio broadcasting would combine the impact of these two previous breakthroughs in media development. As a result, the accumulated force of modern communication penetrated the American home itself.

CHAPTER 3

The Ethereal Hearth: American Radio from Wireless through Broadcasting, 1892–1940

The development of the telegraph and the motion picture proceeded in a relatively straight historical line. Pioneers in the creation of those two media struggled to find technological solutions to specific problems: the transmission of intelligence using coded electrical impulses through wires and the perfection of projected motion photography. Early in their history, the implications those media held for prevailing notions of communication and culture seemed startling.

Radio broadcasting added a totally new dimension to modern communication by bringing the outside world into the individual home. The history of radio, however, was far more complex than the histories of previous media breakthroughs. The broadcasting system tied together a bundle of technological and scientific threads that had been dangling for a generation. It thus makes sense to distinguish wireless technology up to and including World War I from the later system of radio broadcasting. Wireless technology presumed a far higher level of scientific knowledge, particularly in mathematics and physics, than that required by previous advances in communication. Although individual experimenters around the world contributed to wireless progress, it ultimately achieved technological sophistication through the research performed and coordinated by science-based industry and the military.

Radio broadcasting began as a marketing tool, a service designed by large electrical equipment manufacturers to sell privately owned receivers. The enormous potential of radio broadcasting for improving the quality of daily life, its ubiquitous power to bring art, entertainment, music, education, and news into the living room, contained severe contradictions. With radio broadcasting, wireless technology went public in the privacy of the home. But if the owner-ship of receivers promised to be democratic, what of the control of transmission? During the 1920s debate over radio's future centered on the questions of structure and finance: Would the electrical inter-ests supply the service indefinitely? If not, who would pay for it and how would it be regulated? By the onset of the Great Depression, ad-vertising had established itself as the basis for American broadcast-ing. Critics wondered about the hidden social costs of free broadcast-ing paid for by commercial sponsors. Meanwhile, with its newfound stability, radio programming regularly featured hybrid combina-tions of traditional entertainment and news forms.

Looking backward, quite a few of the contemporary appraisals of wireless technology and radio broadcasting strike us as rather quix-otic. This is in part because today's broadcasting media continually propound the idea that their current configuration is the only one possible. But the range of opinions on wireless technology's signifi-cance and the variety of proposals for the organization of radio broadcasting remind us that the present incarnation of broadcast media need not be permanent.

Almost as soon as scientists perfected electromagnetic telegraphy, they began searching for ways to eliminate the wires. Both Steinheil in Germany and Morse in America demonstrated telegraphy by con-duction (using the earth or water as a return circuit) early in tele-graph history. Later, various experimenters successfully telegraphed by forms of induction. Using electrostatic induction (whereby an electric charge in one conductor induces one in another nearby), Edi-son in 1885 created a system allowing moving trains to utilize tele graph lines running parallel to the tracks without interfering with the normal message load sent over the wires. Edison's *motograph*, tried briefly on railroad lines in the 1880s, proved a scientific suc-cess but a commercial failure. Using electromagnetic induction (in which an electric current in a wire, while increasing or decreasing, induces another current in its neighborhood), William Preece man-aged to send telegraphic messages over several miles of water. As chief engineer of the British Post Office, Preece conducted numerous experiments in the 1890s using parallel series of wires to maintain communication with islands inaccessible to the wire telegraph.[1]

Despite all of this work, none of the conductive or inductive meth-ods of wireless telegraphy demonstrated clear potential. During the 1880s and 1890s nearly all researchers approached the problem as one of conquering water—communication between ships, between ship and shore, or between islands. Edison's curious motograph was the exception. For use over water, however, neither inductive nor conductive telegraphy could even replace the foghorn. Most observers agreed with the prognosis of the Harvard engineer John Trowbridge, who ended an 1892 review of various plans for wireless telegraphy at sea by declaring: "Telegraphing through the air without wires by means of electricity does not seem at present to have the element of practicality in it." To Trowbridge the question of wireless communication over land did not seem worth deliberating, and it "probably would never be used even if it were practicable."[2]

The ultimate scientific foundation for wireless telegraphy came not from induction or conduction, but from the concept of electromagnetic waves traveling through space. University-trained scientists, largely in England and Germany, pioneered in proving the existence and utility of these waves. In the 1860s James Clerk-Maxwell, one of the great theoretical physicists of the century, mathematically predicted the existence of electromagnetic waves in the ether. Both light and electricity, Maxwell showed, resulted from vibrations in the ether; they differed only in the rate of vibration. He predicted that electric waves could be set up by electric oscillations and, like light or sound waves, could be detected. These electric waves would travel at the speed of light. Although the notion of a mysterious, all-pervasive ether later became discredited among scientists, it served Maxwell as a convenient fiction to help explain the presence and behavior of electromagnetic waves. Over twenty years later, Heinrich Hertz built machines to generate and detect electric waves, confirming Maxwell's electromagnetic wave theory. Between 1888 and 1892 Hertz performed a series of classic experiments showing that electric waves (like sound, heat, or light) could be reflected, refracted, concentrated, and focused.[3]

Throughout the 1890s scores of researchers all over the world took up the intellectual challenge of exploring the wonders of *Hertzian waves*. Edouard Branly in France and Oliver Lodge in England made great strides in perfecting the *coherer*. Branly discovered that loose metal filings in a glass tube (which normally have a high electrical resistance) would lose their resistance in the presence of electric oscillations, cohering and thereby becoming a conductor. Lodge added a tapper arrangement like that of a doorbell to Branly's coherer; each successive impulse produced coherence and de-coherence. The filings took the place of a telegraph key, allowing a recording instrument to receive messages. In Russia, Alexander Popov used a coherer attached to a vertical wire that was designed to record atmospheric disturbances and detect thunderstorms in advance. But none of these scientists had a clear conception of using Hertzian waves for regular wireless communication.[4]

Others in the scientific community, however, did see a great potential for "aetheric telegraphy." In 1892, noting the investigations of Hertz and Lodge into "ethereal vibrations or electric rays," British physicist William Crookes wrote:

> Here is unfolded to us a new and astonishing world —one which it is hard to conceive should contain no possibilities of transmitting and receiving intelligence. . . . What therefore, remains to be discovered is—firstly, simpler and more certain means of generating electrical rays of any desired wavelength . . . secondly, more delicate receivers which will respond to wavelengths between certain defined limits and be silent to all others; thirdly, means of darting the sheaf of rays in any desired direction. . . . This is no mere dream of a visionary philosopher. All the requisites needed to bring it within the grasp of daily life are well within the possibilities of discovery.[5]

Crookes's article inspired the young Anglo-Italian Guglielmo Marconi to develop a truly practical wireless telegraphy based on Hertzian waves. In the popular imagination Marconi's name is the one most closely associated with the invention of the wireless telegraph, but this is a gross simplification. Marconi should be viewed as the crucial innovator in wireless, not as its inventor. By modifying, improving, and perfecting the devices introduced by Hertz, Lodge, Branly, Popov, and others, Marconi achieved the best practical results in wireless communication, beginning in 1895. Unlike the university scientists, he had a clear idea for the commercial development of wireless; from the start he surrounded himself with the best engineers for assistants, as well as top managerial talent. Although his own technical contributions were not radically new, Marconi applied for patents on all of his projects, thus making certain that his company acquired a dominant position. Taking advantage of his family's wealth and contacts in England, Marconi performed extensive experiments under the auspices of the British Post Office, and in 1897, with the backing of English capitalists, he formed the Marconi Wireless Telegraph Company. The organization planned to install wireless equipment on lightships and lighthouses along the English coast.[6]

Marconi's achievements in wireless communication over progressively greater distances attracted enormous attention from the scientific world and the popular press on both sides of the Atlantic. Fifty years earlier wire telegraphy inspired diverse theories about the nature of its driving force, electricity. All the work done with Hertzian waves fueled a similar, if more sophisticated, type of speculation on the nature of the ether. In particular, many scientists agreed with J. Ambrose Fleming, prominent physicist, engineer, and a later close associate of Marconi, who thought the theoretical import of wireless far more intriguing than its capacity to send messages. "Its practical uses are indubitable," he wrote in 1899, "but it has a wider interest from a scientific standpoint, in that it opens up a vista of fascinating speculation into the possible revelations in store for us concerning the powers and potencies of the mysterious ether."

For centuries scientists had postulated various ethers to explain phenomena as diverse as gravity, light, and the motion of the planets. The theoretical work of Maxwell, corroborated by Hertz's experiments, seemed to prove that all electromagnetic and optical phenomena could be explained by a system of mechanical stresses in a single ether. This all-encompassing ether, of fixed position and finite density, sufficed to transmit all the known forces (such as gravity, light, heat, and electromagnetism) that one material object exerted on another through distance. The ether hypothesis enjoyed a wide acceptance by scientists in the late nineteenth century; development of the first wireless devices in the 1890s no doubt added to the prestige of the single ether theory. But when various experiments showed that the ether and its properties were unobservable, the notion of a material ether became untenable. By 1905 Einstein's special theory of relativity had shown, among other things, that there could be no single ether providing an absolute standard of rest and that the velocity of light in empty space is always the same relative to any moving coordinate system.[7]

Oliver Lodge, the British physicist and wireless pioneer, offered this typical description of the ether: "a perfectly continuous, subtle, incomprehensible substance pervading all space and penetrating between the molecules of all ordinary matter, which are embedded in it and connected with one another by its means. And we must regard it as the one universal medium by which all actions between bodies are carried on." Throughout the greater part of space one found simple, unmodified ether, "elastic and massive, squirming and quivering with energy, but stationary as a whole." Here and there, however, were "specks of electrified ether" that were connected by fields of force and in a state of violent motion; these specks were known as matter. For physicists, the ether theory provided a simple unifying principle; ether was a basic category for understanding the physical universe. The "vagueness of the notion," argued Lodge, "will be nothing more than is proper in the present state of our knowledge."[8]

But ether had important metaphysical implications as well, and these might eventually be grasped with the help of the new wireless devices. The feeling that the wireless had somehow put men on the threshold of the innermost secrets of nature paralleled that elicited by wire telegraphy. The relation between the wireless and ether stirred anew the old dream of "universal communication," a dream expressed in religious terms by the early commentators on the telegraph. But with the wireless, the discussion drew its metaphors and vocabulary primarily from physics and biology.

Conceptualizing and explaining just how "ethereal telegraphy" worked proved no easy task for scientists. "We have been so trained to regard currents of electricity as something flowing in one unbroken circuit," wrote William Preece, "that their temporary condition as waves of energy in space is hard to realize; especially in the absence of an *electrical sense.*" But perhaps in the coming "Ether Age" man might evolve a new electrical sense through his knowledge of electromagnetic waves. Oliver Lodge argued that "we are growing a new sense; not indeed an actual sense organ, but not so very unlike a new sense organ. . . . Electroscopes, galvanometers, telephones—delicate instruments these; not yet eclipsing our sense organs of flesh, but in a few cases coming within measurable distance of their surprising sensitiveness. And with these what can we do? Can we smell the ether, or touch it, or what is the closest analogy? Perhaps there is no useful analogy; but nonetheless we deal with it, and that closely."

Telepathy, perhaps the ultimate form of universal communication, might follow from a better understanding of the ether, the universal medium. Among others, the American physicist Amos E. Dolbear postulated that since different kinds of motion in the ether generated heat, light, electricity, and magnetism, scientists might soon be able to manipulate the ether to produce thought transference with brain waves. The English scientist William Ayrton told Marconi that his new method of communication seemed "almost like dreamland and ghostland, not the ghostland of the heated imagination cultivated by the Psychical Society, but a real communication from a distance based on true physical laws."[9]

If the ether theory straddled the physical and the metaphysical, most scientists found this fact more ironic than preposterous. After all, the ether theory had gained greater credence precisely because of the latest discoveries of scientists in the field of the wireless. Oliver Lodge noted that natural philosophy must sometimes be forced into a conviction about something intangible and occult:

> And when next century, or the century after, lets us deeper
> into their secrets (electricity and ether) and into the secrets
> of some other phenomena now for the first time being rationally
> investigated, I feel as if it would be no merely material pros-
> pect that will be opening on our view, but that we shall get
> a glimpse into a region of the universe, as yet unexplored by
> Science, which has been sought from far, and perhaps blindly
> apprehended, by painters and poets, by philosophers and
> scientists.[10]

In 1902 Marconi succeeded in signaling across the Atlantic by wireless telegraphy, fueling further excitement about its possibilities. Two areas of service opened up in these years: the purely commercial sending of messages and the selling or leasing of equipment for the marine wireless. By 1905 the Marconi organization alone had outfitted hundreds of naval and commercial vessels and had set up fifty land stations around the world. At first the Marconi companies sold equipment, but they soon adopted a policy of selling communication like the telephone company. They leased wireless sets and provided a Marconi-trained operator who communicated only with other Marconi-equipped ships or shore stations.[11]

In the United States, the British Marconi interests launched an American subsidiary that soon dominated the wireless field. Other companies began in America at this time, spurred on by government patronage. The U.S. Weather Bureau hired Reginald Fessenden, a Pittsburgh electrical engineer, to conduct experiments in wireless as an aid to forecasting. In 1902 Fessenden formed the National Electric Signalling Company, and he later became a leader in the development of wireless telephony. Lee De Forest, the other important American wireless inventor, formed the first of several wireless companies in 1901. The next year the government commissioned him to build experimental wireless sets and stations, providing desperately needed funds. Later, De Forest became perhaps the preeminent American inventor of the prewar era, and his audion vacuum tube proved crucial for both radio transmission and reception.[12]

The major technical problem in these years was the perfection of "syntony," namely, the tuning of wireless devices so that a transmitter could communicate with one receiver to the exclusion of others and vice versa. The point-to-point model of the wireless stemmed from the military implications that many saw in it. As early as 1897 Marconi himself had pointed out the military potential of wireless telegraphy for exploding gunpowder and the magazines of ships from a distance; he clearly had military uses in mind when discussing the urgency of improved tuning. Others noted the prospects for steering torpedoes, firing mines, and blowing up forts with "radio waves."[13]

The point-to-point model for the wireless did not, however, preclude nonmilitary uses; the perfection of tuning would insure the secrecy of different kinds of messages. Ray Stannard Baker, who reported on Marconi's achievements in 1902, thus projected a not-distant future where organizations and even families could secure their own private frequencies: "Great telegraph companies will each have its own tuned instruments, to receive only its own messages, and there may be special tunes for each of the important governments of the world. Or perhaps (for the system can be operated very cheaply), the time will even come when the great banking houses and business houses, or even families and friends, will each have its own wireless system, with its own secret tune. Having variations of millions of different vibrations, there will be no lack of tunes." The English engineer William Ayrton offered an even more personal vision. Eventually everyone might possess his own wireless transmitter and receiver:

> If a person wanted to call a friend he knew not where, he would call in a loud, electro-magnetic voice, heard by him who had the electro-magnetic ear, silent to him who had it not. "Where are you?" he would say. A small reply would come, "I am at the bottom of a coal mine, or crossing the Andes, or in the middle of the Pacific." Let them think of what that meant, of the calling which went on every day from room to room of a house, and then think of that calling extending from pole to pole; not a noisy babble, but a call audible to him who wanted to hear and absolutely silent to him who did not.[14]

Indeed, a critical new factor entered the wireless scene in the early 1900s, very much in the spirit of Ayrton's fantasy: the amateur wireless operator. All over the nation thousands of amateurs, many of them schoolboys, constructed wireless receivers and transmitters, mastered telegraphic codes, and claimed the ether for themselves. The discovery that several types of crystals would serve as cheap, easy-to-make detectors of radio waves launched the amateur boom around 1907. By 1917 over 8,500 amateurs operated transmitting stations, and between two and three hundred thousand had receiving sets. A burgeoning cottage industry of electrical suppliers and wireless publications sprang up to cater to the amateurs' needs. The rapid spread of the wireless art among amateurs vitally affected the evolution of radio. In the short run, the amateurs contributed to the ethereal chaos by interfering with naval and commercial service, thus making the need for government regulation more imperative. In the long run, amateur wireless sets provided an invaluable training ground for future researchers and broadcasters, and these "hams" formed the first audience for the earliest radio broadcasts.[15]

Government regulation of the wireless began in this period with the report of the Roosevelt board in 1904, which recommended a three-way division of authority over the American wireless. The Department of Labor and Commerce would supervise commercial stations, the War Department would have charge of military stations, and, most importantly, the navy would control coastal stations. This report, though not law, established the dominance of the United States Navy in the wireless field, enabling it to build its own system and pour millions of dollars into research. Congress later passed laws requiring ships to carry wireless equipment and operators, but not until the Radio Act of 1912 did the government produce a comprehensive plan to regulate the wireless. The act divided the wireless spectrum between ship, coastal, amateur, and government frequencies; it also gave the secretary of commerce broad but contradictory powers. He could assign wavelengths and time limits on stations, but he could not refuse to grant a license. This act remained the fundamental radio law until 1927. It did not mention broadcasting, yet it would serve at precisely the time that broadcasting began, thus contributing to the confusion that characterized American radio in the 1920s.[16]

Just as wireless telegraphy appeared to achieve a semblance of stability, two interrelated developments, one scientific and one political, intervened: wireless telephony and World War I. Scientists had worked on the transmission of speech without wires since the turn of the century, trying to overcome several obstacles: the generation of uniform high-frequency electric waves that were sufficiently continuous to transmit the upper harmonics of speech; a means of modulating the electric waves in accordance with sound waves; a continuously responsive receiver sensitive to speech; and the linking of wireless and wire telephones by means of suitable relays. Early experimenters in wireless telephony often found themselves so far ahead of contemporary practice that they needed to wait for years until engineering realities caught up with them. By 1910 both Fessenden and De Forest successfully transmitted speech and music by wireless, startling wireless operators who happened to be listening in. Fessenden pioneered in the use of a high-frequency alternator for the production of the continuous "undamped" waves required to transmit the human voice. De Forest patented the three-element vacuum tube, or *audion*, which could be used both to modulate received radio waves and to create high power waves in transmission.[17]

The perfection of wireless telephony became largely a function of research and development by several large corporations and the federal government; private enterprise and government even joined forces on this project. American Telephone and Telegraph, wary of possible competitive threat from wireless telephony, directed a massive research effort. As Frank Jewett, chief of the Bell system's laboratory research, recalled in later years, "it was clear to the A T & T Company . . . that a full, thorough, and complete understanding of radio must be had at all times if the art of telephony . . . was to be advanced and the money invested in that service safeguarded." In 1913 and 1914 A T & T bought all patent rights to De Forest's audion and related inventions, and it soon possessed all patents and patent rights covering the use of vacuum tubes in wire and wireless telephony.[18]

The U.S. Navy and A T & T cooperated in the first successful tests of transcontinental wire telephony and transoceanic radio telephony in 1915. General Electric entered the field at this time too, focusing on the construction of high-frequency transmitters for the long-distance wireless and the perfection of vacuum tubes. American Marconi also held valuable patents on the vacuum tube and other wireless components. World War I brought even greater attention to the wireless; European and American armed forces demanded radio units for airplanes, ships, and infantry. As soon as America entered the war, the government took over all wireless stations, and, more importantly for future events, guaranteed manufacturers protection against legal action over patent infringements. Thus, pressure for the mass production of radio equipment during the war broke the patent stalemate and stimulated a boom in radio research. The war led to a vast coordinated effort in the manufacture of radio parts, particularly the vacuum tube.[19]

The main uses of postwar radio, the consensus of corporate and military researchers held, would be in transoceanic and marine communication and as a subordinate technology serving long-distance telephony. General Electric and Westinghouse, manufacturers of vacuum tubes, transmitters, and other radio equipment during the war, looked for ways to keep this lucrative business in peace time. A T & T continued experiments utilizing the new radio technology to improve telephone service. And American Marconi, expecting to have all its radio stations returned by the federal government, hoped to resume its position as the leading force in American wireless.

The federal government also took a strong interest in radio's postwar future. The Wilson administration hoped to challenge British domination of international communication and to thereby advance American commercial interests. After failing to get Congress to pass legislation for making the wartime government control of wireless stations permanent, the administration pursued a different strategy. In 1919 the British Marconi interests negotiated with General Electric to buy exclusive rights to the Alexanderson Alternator, a high-powered radio transmitter used for transoceanic work during the war. The British company appeared to be the only potential customer for GE, which was strapped for funds as government war patronage dried up. Through a series of long and delicate negotiations, the government stepped in and served as the midwife to the birth of the Radio Corporation of America. RCA, with GE as the major stockholder, bought out American Marconi (which had been controlled by the British), thus assuring America a powerful position in world communication. The government's control of all wireless land stations was the trump card that forced the British to sell.

GE and RCA formed an alliance with A T & T (which bought a large share of RCA stock) and its subsidiary Western Electric, pooling thousands of radio patents in the process. A complex group of cross-licensing agreements divided the business up as follows: GE would manufacture receivers and parts and market these through RCA; A T & T would sell transmitters and have control of telephony as a service, wired or wireless; RCA would have as its chief function international communication. Government and amateur orders were exempted from these agreements. Thus, the close wartime relationship between the government and large corporations involved in radio research carried over into peace.[20]

But the new and generally unforeseen element of broadcasting almost immediately shattered the peace brought to the radio world. Virtually no one in the scientific, amateur, military, or corporate communities had expected broadcasting to become the main use of wireless technology. The sending of uncoded messages to an undifferentiated audience transformed wireless into a popular medium of communication.

★

The "radio mania" of the early 1920s began in response to the first regular broadcasting, done by station KDKA of the Westinghouse Corporation. Westinghouse executive Harry P. Davis noticed that amateur broadcasts from the garage of an employee, Frank Conrad, attracted attention in the local Pittsburgh press; a department store advertised wireless sets capable of picking up Conrad's "wireless concerts." The ad, Davis later wrote, "caused the thought to come to me that the efforts that were then being made to develop radiotelephony as a confidential means of communication were wrong, and that instead its field was really one of wide publicity; in fact, the only means of instantaneous collective communication ever devised." In the fall of 1920, the company converted Conrad's amateur station into a stronger one at its main plant. Starting with the Harding-Cox election returns, it began regular nightly broadcasts that were probably heard by only a few hundred people. After its wartime conversion to the production of radio equipment, Westinghouse found itself in the economic doldrums when peace came. Shut out of the RCA-GE-A T & T axis, it aggressively promoted broadcasting as a service that could sell cheap receiving sets and give the company publicity. Seizing the initiative in broadcasting enabled Westinghouse to enter the corporate alliance of the radio group in the spring of 1921. It bought 20 percent of RCA and would share the manufacturing of receivers and parts with GE.[21]

Immediately after KDKA started its service, scores and then hundreds of broadcasters entered the field. By May 1922 the Commerce Department had granted over 300 licenses for broadcasting; at the end of that year the number stood at 570. Tens of thousands of people began purchasing receiving sets and accessories. Swamped by this unanticipated demand, the radio group manufacturers struggled to produce radio equipment for the new audience and the legion of broadcasters; new and often shady companies sprang up to help meet the demand. Newspapers and periodicals around the country printed special radio supplements, eagerly accepting their share of the new industry's advertising. The public bought about a hundred thousand receiving sets in 1922 and over half a million in 1923. Total sales revenue from radio receivers and parts reached $136 million in 1923.

Early broadcasting did not proceed as an independent commercial enterprise, but, following the lead of KDKA, instead became basically a merchandising offshoot. The first broadcasters divided into three classes: those selling radio sets; those seeking goodwill and free advertising, such as newspapers, hotels, and department stores; and religious and educational institutions. For example, of the 570 stations licensed in 1922, radio and electrical manufacturers owned 231; newspapers owned 70; educational institutions owned 65; and department stores owned 30. The turnover rate was high, with ninety-four stations having shut down already by the end of 1922. Although some of these stations purchased their transmitters from the patent allies, many more bypassed the radio group and had theirs built by zealous amateurs, thousands of whom had received radio training during the war.

At first all of these stations operated on the same wavelength, 360 meters, wreaking havoc in the air, particularly in urban centers. Secretary of Commerce Herbert Hoover, saddled with the now obsolete Radio Act of 1912, called a series of four annual radio conferences. These began in 1922 and aimed at attaining some semblance of regulation. Broadcasters, manufacturers, amateurs, and researchers gradually worked out ways to allocate the broadcast spectrum. In 1923 the conference divided the stations into three classes: high power (later called "clear channels," designed to serve large areas and be free of interference), medium power (often sharing time), and low power (local stations, all on the 360 meter wavelength).[22]

The programming in these first years included a broad variety of material. Regular shows were rare in the early 1920s, and most stations depended on phonograph records, popular and light classical music performed live by local talent, and talks (such as storytelling for children). For example, the early program logs of WHA, pioneer station of the University of Wisconsin, reveal radio programs on nearly every imaginable topic. Faculty members, mostly on a one-time basis, gave dramatic readings and talks on music appreciation, gardening, electronics, and history. Such talks became a staple in radio, particularly on the stations run by universities. On station KDKA musical concerts, singers, and phonograph records predominated, along with rudimentary news reports and remote broadcasts of church services. KDKA, like other stations owned by radio manufacturers and dealers, also featured lectures on the technical aspects of radio; these were aimed at the nucleus of early broadcast listeners, the wireless amateurs. Itinerant vaudevillians began to perform on radio stations during these years. Singer Wendell Hall, one of the first of this group, performed in stations all over the country (often without fee) as a means of boosting the sales of his records and sheet music. Hall attracted thousands of fan letters wherever he went, a testament to the publicizing power of radio for entertainers.[23]

Today we think of radio as synonymous with broadcasting, but in the first few years after KDKA's start this was by no means obvious to the thousands of radio amateurs and longtime observers of the wireless. By 1922 about fifteen thousand amateur transmitting stations held licenses in the United States, and these "hams" constituted an organized and active lobby in radio circles. Along with perhaps another quarter of a million prebroadcasting wireless amateurs (capable of receiving), these people had provided the original seed capital and audience for the radio industry. They bought radio equipment and kept up with the latest technical advances before and after the first broadcasting stations. For amateurs, broadcasting remained merely one of several applications of radio; the notion of organizing radio around a few big broadcasting stations rather than individuals appalled them. They looked condescendingly on those new radio fans interested only in the content of broadcasts and not in the other aspects of radio. Advertisements for the American Radio Relay League, the amateur's national organization, urged readers of radio periodicals: After You Grow Tired of the Broadcast Stuff—Come In with Us and Enjoy Real Radio. Their vision of radio's future centered on a legion of amateurs performing several functions: "To conceive of thousands of boys, young men, and grownups through out the United States using the same medium to talk with one another . . . to listen at given intervals to concerts where all manner of instrumental and vocal performances are faithfully reproduced; to intercept the news of the nation as broadcasted by various central stations in the larger cities; to receive timely and valuable agricultural reports of importance to farmers." But broadcasting, originally conceived by manufacturers as an inducement for buying radio equipment, eventually shoved aside the very people who had nurtured it.[24]

Still, listening to the early broadcasts proved an active rather than a passive entertainment, requiring that at least one member of the family acquire some technical knowledge. One had to constantly adjust and rearrange batteries, crystal detectors, and vacuum tubes for the best reception. In 1924, Robert and Helen Lynd found Middletown residents of all classes taking to radio: "Here skill and ingenuity can in part offset money as an open sesame to swift sharing of the enjoyment of the wealthy.... Far from being simply one more means of passive enjoyment, the radio has given rise to much ingenious manipulative activity." For numerous radio fans the excitement lay precisely in the battle to get clear reception amidst the howling and chatter of thousands of amateurs and larger stations, many of whom freely roamed the air. The cult of "DX'ing," trying to receive the most distant stations possible, remained strong for years. As one newly converted radio fan wrote in 1924, the various programs interested him very little:

> In radio it is not the substance of communication without
> wires, but the fact of it that enthralls. It is a sport, in which
> your wits, learning, and resourcefulness are matched against
> the endless perversity of the elements. It is not a matter, as you
> may suppose, of buying a set and thereafter tuning in upon
> what your fancy dictates.... Someday, perhaps, I shall take
> an interest in radio programs. But at my present stage they
> are merely the tedium between call letters.[25]

But that portion of the audience most engrossed by the content of broadcasting, with its potential for "providing entertainment, spreading culture, developing high standards of morality and promoting national unity," soon eclipsed the part intoxicated with radio as a pure medium. A significant part of the new mass audience began demanding regulation of the small stations and amateurs. "Already," one writer reported in 1922, "those listening to the concerts and reports sent out from the big broadcasting stations have suddenly found themselves being bombarded by chatter from some sputtering little transmitting device in the town in which they are located." Argued another, "Broadcasting has turned the nation into a town meeting. But there is no chairman and no parliamentary law. This will bring about anarchy in the ether."[26]

Precisely how to structure the new service, along with the allied question of who would pay for it, dominated discussions of broadcasting's future. Everyone agreed that, after the large manufacturing companies had sold as many sets as possible and after the press had squeezed all possible circulation and advertising out of the radio boom, these two sources of financing would dry up. Various schemes proposed in these years can be grouped under two main headings, government and private. Government control over radio, underwritten by a tax upon or licensing of receiving sets, would require a federal commission to regulate broadcasting as a public utility. A more limited plan involved setting aside a fixed percentage of available wavelengths for a federal broadcasting chain. An alternative form of government control might proceed on the municipal or state levels; in fact, some of the most stable early stations were built by cities and state universities.

Even among those opposed to government involvement, there was no consensus. Acute discord reigned within the corporate alliance of the industry. David Sarnoff, head of RCA, led those who favored creation of a common fund by radio manufacturers and dealers. In Sarnoff's view, "the problem of broadcasting is fundamentally at the transmitting end"; he held the most centralized and monopolistic vision of all. In 1924 Sarnoff proposed that the radio cartel build perhaps six "super power broadcast stations" to blanket the entire country. He argued that "the industry itself has the responsibility of maintaining and supporting suitable broadcast stations so that the sets which are sold to the public and bought by them may not represent a refrigerator without ice." On the other hand, A T & T sought to make broadcasting an exclusive service of the Bell system, on the model of the telephone. In 1923 A. H. Griswold, A T & T vice-president for radio matters, suggested that in each local community leaders form a broadcast association: "For that association we would erect, own, and operate a broadcasting station; they to provide all the programs; they to give the public what the 'public' desires but we to have the latest facilities known to the art. . . . the fact remains that it is a telephone job, that we are a telephone people, that we can do it better than anybody else."[27]

The plan that finally emerged as the basis for American broadcasting charged not the audience but the advertisers who wanted to reach it. Toll broadcasting, the hiring of radio facilities by advertisers, began as an experiment of A T & T; in 1922 it started "selling time" to advertisers for its station WEAF in New York City. By exploiting certain key technological advantages, WEAF made toll broadcasting a boon for both advertisers and the station. Using its extensive web of telephone long lines, A T & T hooked up WEAF with a number of other stations around the country to create the first network broadcasting. Remote broadcasting of such affairs as the 1924 political conventions and various sports events made WEAF the most important radio station of the early period. The use of the Bell system's telephone wires for network and remote broadcasting made clear the tremendous power of the only nationwide system of wires designed for the transmission of speech.

As A T & T pressed its advantage, toll broadcasting flourished: sponsors advertised directly or indirectly, footing the bill for the "Everready Hour," the "Ipana Troubadors," the "Taystee Loafers," and other shows. A T & T refused to provide wires for commercial broadcasts by nonaffiliated stations; it also refused wires to broadcasters who had not bought their equipment from Western Electric (the vast majority) or who had failed to obtain a patent license from A T & T. Stations denied the use of A T & T long lines, including those of its patent allies, struggled with inferior telegraph wires as a substitute for network and remote hookups.[28]

Toll broadcasting received support from the Department of Commerce, which gave its blessing to the WEAF experiment and provided the station with a coveted clear channel. Herbert Hoover, sensitive to the extensive criticism of radio advertising in the press, adopted a public face directly at odds with his radio policies as secretary of commerce. In speeches and interviews Hoover reiterated the theme that it was "inconceivable that we should allow so great a possibility for service and for news and for entertainment and education, for vital commercial purposes to be drowned in advertising chatter." Pressed in 1924 to explain how broadcasting could be permanently financed, Hoover was still unsure of the answer. But he insisted that if broadcasters tried to sell "some brand of shoes or anything else over the radio you'll have no radio audience. People won't stand for that. It would kill the radio industry as quickly as anything you can think of."

But at the Washington radio conferences and in the day-to-day decisions at the Department of Commerce, Hoover relied heavily on the advice of the large radio companies in technical matters, and he favored commercial broadcasters over others. The department also permitted the sale of stations and their assigned wavelengths, which in effect made a radio channel private property. This undermined the original concept of the government granting a temporary license to a broadcaster, and it belied Hoover's call to "establish public right over the ether roads."[29]

Hoover may have felt the need to wear a mask in public on the subject of radio, but the advertisers themselves did not. The triumph of commercial broadcasting represented a substantial victory for the ideology of consumption in American life. With the accelerated mass production of consumer goods, advertising began playing a greatly expanded role in American business during the 1920s.

Advertisers sold not merely products but a way of life: happiness through buying, personal fulfillment from the purchase. Radio advertising did not become a truly significant fraction of total advertising expenditures until the 1930s, but the swiftness and thoroughness with which commercial broadcasting emerged as the model for radio surely reflected the cultural and economic force of the advertising ethic.

Advertising men aggressively and confidently reduced the new medium of communication to an extension of their trade. They recognized radio's extraordinary power to carry them into the intimate circle of family life at home. "What a glorious opportunity for the advertising man to spread his sales propaganda," exulted Edgar Felix, an early radio merchandising consultant, in 1927. "Here was a countless audience, sympathetic, pleasure seeking, enthusiastic, curious, interested, approachable in the privacy of their own homes." Harry P. Davis of Westinghouse argued that "broadcast advertising is modernity's medium of business expression. It made industry articulate. American business men, because of radio, are provided with a latch key to nearly every home in the United States."

Frank A. Arnold, director of development for the National Broadcasting Company, called broadcasting the "Fourth Dimension of Advertising," an addition to the three traditional advertising media of newspapers, magazines, and outdoor displays. Arnold elaborated the image of radio advertising as a sort of psychological burglar in the home. The fourth dimension allowed business men to invade psychic space previously unreachable.

> For years the national advertiser and his agency had been dreaming of the time to come when there would be evolved some great family medium which should reach the home and the adult members of the family in their moments of relaxation, bringing to them the editorial and advertising message. . . . Then came radio broadcasting, utilizing the very air we breathe, and with electricity as its vehicle entering the homes of the nation through doors and windows, no matter how tightly barred, and delivering its message audibly through the loudspeaker wherever placed. . . . In the midst of the family circle, in moments of relaxation, the voice of radio brings to the audience its program of entertainment or its message of advertising.

In 1929 Frank Presbrey, a historian of advertising, projected future television broadcasting in which "the department store counter will be radioed right into the home. . . . It is conceivable. . . . that at a certain hour each morning a department store salesman will unroll bolts of fabrics or place other articles before a camera and with colored motion picture and microphone give a selling talk to several hundred thousand women who have seated themselves before the radio in their homes and tuned in for the daily store news."[30]

By the late 1920s, three crucial developments in the radio world rationalized the advertiser's conception of broadcasting as a medium of commercial publicity. Broadcasting had made the original agreements of the patent allies obsolete; in 1926 they redefined their roles in the radio world. The key of the new accord was the decision of A T & T to abandon broadcasting directly and to sell its station WEAF to RCA. In exchange, RCA, GE, and Westinghouse set up the National Broadcasting Company, devoted exclusively to broadcasting, and contracted to lease the A T & T web of wires. NBC, with this powerful corporate backing, prepared to offer national radio broadcasting over two networks based in New York. GE and Westinghouse would continue to manufacture radio hardware and operate some stations; RCA would also operate several stations and would continue to market GE and Westinghouse equipment. A T & T won RCA's assurance that it would drop plans to build an independent long lines system.[31]

On the government level, Congress finally passed a comprehensive radio act in 1927, but only when forced to do so by legal rulings that challenged the Commerce Department's regulatory powers. In the fall of 1926, acting upon an opinion of the attorney general, Secretary Hoover continued to grant licenses but ceased to assign wavelengths, power, or time-sharing schedules. Stations became free to use whatever channel they wished, and the resulting shambles forced congressional action. The 1927 radio act established a temporary Federal Radio Commission to provide specific meaning for the vague language of the new law.[32]

Finally, changes in the market for receivers increased the popularity of radio as a center for family entertainment, thus transforming the nature of radio listening. In the early 1920s manufacturers built receivers mainly to achieve the greatest distance in stations. Beginning in 1925, however, they began to pay more attention to tone quality and appearance; a radio became a piece of furniture designed to please the entire family. Standardization of parts eliminated the struggle with a confusing hodgepodge of components from different manufacturers. And in 1928 radio dealers started to offer sets powered by electric current.[33]

The growth of radio broadcasting in the 1920s created a giant industry in less than a decade. By 1930 more than six hundred stations were broadcasting to more than twelve million radio homes, about 40 percent of the total number of American families. In that year dealers sold nearly four million radios, as the total number of sets in use reached thirteen million. The transition to commercial broadcasting proceeded quickly. In 1925 the largest block of stations (235, or 43 percent of the total) engaged in commercial broadcasting, and these included the majority of the more powerful stations.[34]

By the close of the decade, all of the elements that characterize the American system of broadcasting could be found in radio: the alliance of advertisers and commercial broadcasters, who dominated programming over national networks; an oligopoly of manufacturers making radio equipment; a weak, administrative type of federal regulation; and the widespread diffusion of receivers in American homes, where they served increasingly as centers for family life. In the 1930s discussions of radio's meaning shifted focus from radio technology to the content of radio messages now carried regularly to the ethereal hearth.

★

The partnership of advertisers and commercial broadcasters placed important limits and restraints on radio programming. During the Great Depression, perhaps the gravest crisis ever faced by the nation's political and economic systems, commercial broadcasting certainly restricted the range of political debate allowed over the air. For critics disenchanted with continual corporate paeans to broadcasting as a public service, the deep contradictions within American radio became baldly evident during the turbulent thirties. Yet corporate hegemony in programming and transmission was not so pervasive that it could create content out of thin air. During radio's "golden age," broadcast entertainment and news developed a peculiarly hybrid character that reflected a persistent cultural tension: the demands of the profit motive versus the residual power of traditional forms of popular culture. Radio content had to conform to definite political and cultural parameters imposed by the broadcasting structure. But it also contained important reminders of those utopian urges, the possibilities of conquering vast social and spatial distances, which had accompanied wireless technology and early broadcasting.

The economic crisis, instead of hampering radio, actually accelerated its expansion in a variety of ways. Programming benefited enormously from the influx of talent that had been forced out of a depressed entertainment world. Vaudeville, the recording industry, and ethnic and legitimate theaters all suffered from the depression, driving legions of performers into broadcasting. The well-financed national networks competed in the signing of new talent and offered an attractive outlet to advertisers seeking a national audience. (The Columbia Broadcasting System, financed at different times in its infancy by the Columbia Phonograph Company and Paramount Pictures, emerged in 1928 to join the NBC webs as a third national network.) More and more individual stations, desperate for funds, turned to commercial broadcasting and network affiliation as a means of survival. Affiliates of the two NBC networks paid for the sustaining (unsponsored) programs they accepted; NBC reimbursed these stations for the sponsored network programs they accepted. CBS evolved a different plan whereby the network offered its entire sustaining schedule free to affiliates in exchange for an option on any part of the station's schedule for sponsored network programs. In this way CBS could sell time to a network sponsor with no uncertainty as to acceptance by the individual stations; this plan helped CBS prosper, enabling it to compete with its older NBC rivals.[35]

Programming now achieved a regularity and professionalism absent in the first years of broadcasting, making it much easier for a listener to identify a program with its sponsor. Companies with national distribution paid thousands of dollars an hour to networks; by 1939 annual radio advertising totaled $171 million, with $83 million going over the national networks. Food and beverages, drugs, tobacco, and automotive products led in the use of radio advertising. Although network affiliates represented a minority of stations, NBC and CBS soon owned or controlled nearly every high-power station and clear channel. In 1937 NBC and CBS owned or controlled 210 of the 685 total stations, but these accounted for more than 88 percent of the total wattage power of American broadcasting.

In the government realm, a weak regulatory agency continued to favor commercial broadcasters. The Federal Radio Commission remained in power on a year-to-year basis until the creation of a permanent Federal Communications Commission in 1934. The 1927 radio act had established "public interest, convenience, and necessity," a phrase borrowed from public utility legislation, as the standard for licensing. The FRC consistently chose not to view advertisers as a special interest. It gave preference to commercial stations while discouraging what it termed "propaganda stations," particularly those run by labor and educational organizations. The

FRC thus reduced the "public interest, convenience, and necessity" phrase to mean the needs of the commercial broadcasters.[36]

Commercial broadcasting installed the listener as a consumer of radio, not as its customer. Only the sponsors and their advertising agencies enjoyed a direct relationship to the broadcasters. The agencies produced nearly all sponsored network shows, usually out of autonomous radio departments. As one pioneer in broadcast advertising described the trend, the agencies merely rented the facilities of the station from the broadcasters. The agencies "are planning the programs, engaging the artists, and writing the announcements, just as they prepare plans, copy, and art for printed advertisements." The commercial broadcaster had to figure out how to capture the widest possible audience for the sponsor. As Frank Arnold of NBC noted in 1931, "the air is full of experiments that are being tried in order to find the answer to the question, 'What constitutes the universal program?'"[37]

Broadcasting, a variety of critics charged, had made a fundamental error by abdicating control of programming. The ad agency had but one interest—satisfying its client. Thus, "any lingering idealism concerning the larger significance of the broadcasting medium vanished." The audience might express its will only negatively; it had no direct input into programming. As Mitchell Dawson pointed out, the broadcasters "must further remember their heterogeneous audience with its innumerable minority groups, ready to rise up and howl at the least offense. . . . No commercial station can afford to alienate any part of the public, as its profits depend upon showing a favorable response from as large an audience as possible." James Rorty, a former ad writer turned socialist, voiced a common sentiment of commercial radio's critics. The trouble with radio reflected the troubles of the American economy. "The ether," he wrote in 1931, "has become a great mirror in which the social, political, and cultural anomalies of our 'business man's civilization' are grotesquely magnified."[38]

Political censorship, both flagrant and subtle, characterized commercial radio from the beginning. In 1926 H. V. Kaltenborn, a journalist turned radio commentator, described his first broadcasting experience. He noted a trend that assumed greater significance in the thirties: "In point of fact the radio has been extremely timid about permitting the broadcasting of anything that contravenes the established order. Its influence has gone towards stabilization rather than change. The best broadcasting stations everywhere are owned by large corporations whose dependence on the good-will of the public authorities and the public at large makes them extremely unwilling to risk giving offense. . . . As radio is now controlled, it objects to that which provokes and stimulates independent thinking as 'too controversial.'"

Where a network or station required a script before a talk, it might demand changes or simply cancel. Political candidates from minority parties frequently could not even buy time for campaign talks. Critiques of public utilities or banks, subjects such as pacifism, and virtually any unorthodox economic view brought down the hand of censorship. If one relied on radio for news in the 1930s, one might learn very little about a critical movement of the period, namely, the upsurge in organized labor. The most powerful station in the country, WLW in Cincinnati (broadcasting at 500,000 watts in the mid-1930s), followed an explicit policy stating: "No reference to strikes is to be made on any news bulletin broadcast over our station." NBC often canceled programs that might undermine "public confidence and faith"; yet it proudly pointed to William Green as chairman of its Advisory Council Committee on Labor. Green, representing the most conservative elements in the labor movement, praised NBC for its response to the depression: "If distressed human beings are helped to forget their physical and mental troubles even temporarily, the psychology of community life is strengthened and a spirit of social unrest which must ever be regarded as a menace to national well being is allayed."[39]

What radio needed most of all, critics agreed, was competition; the most common prescription for curing radio's ills was not government takeover but a separate government-run network, such as England's British Broadcasting Corporation. Control of programs on this type of network might be more democratically determined by the audience or its representatives. The most vocal and active groups attacking the network advertising agency axis united around the call for "educational broadcasting." Unlike their experience with the motion picture, educational institutions had played a meaningful role in early radio broadcasting. By the 1930s, however, their stations had lost most of their influence and licenses. The National Committee on Education by Radio, an umbrella group of militant reformers, vigorously lobbied for legislation that would set aside 15 percent of all radio channels for broadcasting by educational institutions. But the commercial broadcasting interests bitterly and successfully opposed their efforts.[40]

Even if the educators or proponents of a federal network had been successful, it is doubtful that they could have offset the influence of the commercial broadcasters. Unlike any previous medium of communication, commercial radio formed a perpetual part of everyday life during the 1930s. Through entertainment and news programs, it became a household necessity by linking the private sphere with the world "out there." The exigencies of advertising demanded that programming present an aura of constant newness, yet the content relied heavily upon traditional cultural forms. Table 4 offers a rough outline of network radio programming at the start and close of the 1930s. Besides highlighting the gross increase in total network programming, it enables one to take a closer look at the most important developments in radio as a cultural form.[41]

Variety shows, especially when hosted by comedians, became the first important style of network radio. Relying heavily on the vaudeville format, these shows remained very popular throughout the decade; many of the stars continued the form on television. The master of ceremonies, who was either a comedian (Eddie Cantor, Ed Wynn, Fred Allen, George Jessel) or a singer (Al Jolson, Rudy Vallee, Kate Smith), served as a focal point for activity and as a means of easy identification with a sponsor's product. Nearly all the variety stars had long experience in vaudeville or the legitimate stage; the use of a studio audience recreated the human interaction so necessary in vaudeville. Ethnic and regional stereotypes and dialect stories, long a part of vaudeville and burlesque, easily made the transition to radio. But because one could not see the performer, sight gags were naturally impossible, so a premium was placed on one-line jokes and the give-and-take between comedian and straight man.

Comedy gave radio its first truly national hit, the "Amos n' Andy Show," which swept the country in 1928. Both Freeman Gosden and Charles Correll had spent many years on the minstrel and carnival circuit before entering radio; the Amos and Andy figures were direct descendents of pre–Civil War minstrel show characters. Andy, the pompous, domineering pseudointellectual, greatly resembled the minstrel interlocutor, whose job was to direct and control the simple, unsophisticated "endman," represented by Amos. Gosden and Correll went beyond a mere recreation of blackface stereotypes; they successfully adapted the minstrel tradition to radio. Using only their two voices, they managed to create scores of different characters and situations; they invented, in fact, a whole new world eagerly shared by millions of listeners. The show's re-

Table 4
Evening and Daytime Network Radio Programming

Type of Show	Evening				Daytime			
	1931 (310)	% of Total	1940 (453)	% of Total	1931 (152)	% of Total	1940 (538)	% of Total
Variety	43	14	80	18	8	5	46	9
Amateur			4					
Children's					8		4	
Comedy	9		32					
Country			12					
General	16		16				42	
Mixed	18		16					
Music	174	56	115	25	34	22	56	10
Concert	62		28		4		10	
Musical Variety	75		59					
Popular	37		24		30		46	
Records			4					
Drama	47	15	103	23	14	9	349	65
Comedy	18		21				5	
Documentary			4		10		19	
General			14		4			
Light	20		24					
Serial							305	
Thriller	9		40				20	
Talk	46	15	155	34	96	63	87	16
Forum	5		13					
General	14		38		96		68	
Human Interest			10				4	
News and Comment	13		56				10	
Quiz and Panel			30					
Religion	14		5				5	
Sports			3					

Note: Figures give the number of quarter hours of evening and daytime programming per week on the national radio networks during the seasons indicated. Total number of quarter hours appears in parentheses.

liance on situational jokes as well as one-liners also pointed toward a new form of humor well fitted to broadcasting: the serialized situation comedy.[42]

Music shows declined sharply during the 1930s, dropping from more than a half to a quarter of network evening programming. Live music of all kinds, particularly jazz and light classical music, had been the staple of radio in the 1920s. After World War II, musical shows once again became the backbone of radio, this time in the form of the disc jockey playing phonograph records. This later development accompanied the decline of network radio and a renaissance in local programming; in a sense it revived the conditions of the 1920s when music had been king.

Although the figures in Table 4 show a drastic shrinking of the time devoted to musical programs, they cannot measure the enormous influence of the medium on American musical forms. Radio did more than any other medium to publicize and commercialize previously isolated kinds of American folk music, such as country and western and blues. For both artist and audience, radio broke down the formidable geographical and racial barriers that had separated the various rich veins of American folk music. Radio accelerated the process that produced an incredibly fruitful cross-fertilization of all types of American musics.

In the field of drama, the spectacular growth of the daytime serial, or "soap opera," proved the single most important programming phenomenon of the decade. Aimed primarily at women working in the home, these serials alone constituted nearly 60 percent of all network daytime shows by 1940. The soaps usually revolved around a strong, warm character ("Ma Perkins," "Just Plain Bill," "Helen Trent," "Clara Lou and Em") who provided advice and strength to a host of weak and indecisive friends and relations. Action counted very little; development of character was all-important here. The trick was to continually draw out situations so there was just enough suspense to win over the allegiance of listeners.

A contemporary study found that the average soap opera fan tuned in regularly to 6.6 different series. After interviewing a hundred fans, Herta Herzog concluded that "the stories have become an integral part of the lives of many listeners," providing not only temporary emotional release, but "a model of reality by which one is taught how to think and how to act." In a sense, nothing really happened on the soaps, at least nothing so crucial that it prevented people from tuning in if they had missed an episode or two.[43]

So-called psychological thrillers ("Suspense," "Inner Sanctum," "The Shadow"), which emphasized crime, action, and suspense, became popular on evening radio in this period. The sophisticated use of music and special sound effects sharpened their impact, fully exploiting radio as a dramatic medium.

In the late 1930s serious drama bloomed for a short time; in fact, it developed almost as an afterthought. CBS began the unsponsored Columbia Workshop in 1936 as a filler for unsold time, a by-product of commercial success. Independent of the ad agency nexus, CBS developed an impressive series of dramatic programs that probably marked the aesthetic high point of radio drama. Original verse dramas written for radio by Archibald MacLeish, Norman Corwin, and Arch Oboler and adaptations by Orson Welles's Mercury Theater of the Air contributed to a creative ferment since unequaled in radio. MacLeish's "Fall of the City," a parable about fascism, and Welles's famous "War of the Worlds" broadcast proved both the extraordinary power of radio to induce suspension of belief and its ability to deal with the current issues of the day. MacLeish envisioned the rebirth of American poetry through radio: "The ear accepts, accepts and believes, accepts and creates. The ear is the poet's perfect audience, his only true audience. And it is radio and only radio which can give him public access to this perfect friend." In relation to total programming, however, these dramas were mere experiments that yielded brief aesthetic dividends. They were not commercially strong enough to establish a lasting tradition of original radio drama.[44]

By the end of the decade, radio news emerged as an independent force that made full and sometimes stunning use of the medium's capacity for direct and immediate coverage of events. Network news and commentary shows more than tripled in frequency, comprising about 14 percent of all network evening programs in 1940. According to a *Fortune* survey made in 1939, 70 percent of Americans relied on the radio as their prime source of news and 58 percent thought it more accurate than that supplied by the press.[45]

The relationship between the press and the radio had not been a simple, adversary one. Ever since the birth of broadcasting, the interaction had been symbiotic: radio interests used the press to publicize the new medium by advertising extensively in papers; scores of publishers began radio stations to publicize their papers; the United Press news service and client papers cooperated with the WEAF network in the gathering of 1924 election returns. Throughout the early 1930s, publishers remained divided about a policy toward radio. The most rancorous issue was whether the AP should offer regular news stories to radio stations. In 1933, alarmed by the creation of CBS's Columbia News Service, publishers called a meeting of representatives from the networks, major news services, and stations. They reached an informal accord in early 1934: the Press-Radio Bureau would furnish radio stations with brief daily bulletins of not more than thirty words each in exchange for a pledge from the networks to withdraw from news gathering.

But the agreement soon collapsed under the pressure of new and independent news agencies such as the Radio News Association and Transradio Press Service. These proponents of audible journalism prospered, selling news to independent stations dissatisfied with the straitjacket of the Press-Radio Bureau. The success of these agencies revealed a widespread desire for more news by radio; the Press-Radio Bureau folded when the established news agencies began selling news to stations and the networks fashioned their own news-gathering departments.[46]

The complex political and economic issues raised by the depression, the New Deal, and the impending European crisis created a news hunger among Americans. One response to this came in the form of the radio news commentator, someone who specialized in analyzing the background of general news situations. These commentators successfully attracted sponsors and, like the variety show hosts, provided easy identification with a product.

Written especially for the medium, radio news reports had a much sharper sense of urgency and immediacy to them. For example, compare the two leads below, both prepared by the UP in April of 1939 for a story concerning the European political situation. The first was for newspapers:

> London, April 26—(UP)—Prime Minister Neville Chamberlain announced today that Great Britain had decided to conscript all men between the ages of 20 and 21 for six months of military training.
>
> Conscription, he said, would be provided in a bill to be introduced by the government in the House of Commons. In addition, he said, the bill would empower the government to call up any and all reserves.
>
> The announcement in Commons was Chamberlain's reply to Fuehrer Adolph Hitler's speech on Friday, and a warning to the world that Britain is prepared to fight aggression.

Next, the lead for the radio version:

> Great Britain cast off centuries of tradition today in a desperate move to preserve the delicately balanced peace of Europe.
>
> Prime Minister Chamberlain announced England will expand her army by compulsory military service. A bill will be introduced at once to conscript all men between 20 and 21 years of age for six months training.

> Chamberlain's decision is a dramatic eleventh hour attempt
> to force Hitler to tone down his Reichstag speech. But reports
> from Berlin indicate it will fail.[47]

The high point of radio news came with the Munich crisis. Network commentators in Europe provided unprecedented round-the-clock, live coverage of the situation. Listeners heard the live voices of Hitler, Chamberlain, and other principals, while commentators in New York offered instant analysis.[48]

Perhaps the most important news show for the future was the "March of Time," which was begun in 1931 as a publicity vehicle for the new *Time* magazine. Billed as a review of the week's news, "March of Time" really presented a re-creation of key news events, complete with well-known radio actors impersonating Huey Long, Mussolini, Roosevelt, and other famous personalities. There had never been anything like it. As with the later "March of Time" newsreels, the combining of news reports with dramatic devices foreshadowed the polished techniques of television news. "March of Time" provided broadcasting's most explicit fusion of news and entertainment, of fact and fantasy. It transformed the great public issues of the day into one more hearthside drama.

Less than fifty years after the first wireless explorations, radio broadcasting stood at the very center of American society, an integral part of economic, political, and cultural processes. In its mature state, radio succeeded not in fulfilling the utopian visions first aroused by wireless technology, but in appropriating those urges for advertising interests. The ideology of consumption reiterated a basic message that what one had was never enough. It created a need for products largely through an appeal to a mythical past—lost community, lost intimacy, lost self-assurance. Consumer goods promised to make one happy by returning what had vanished. Commercial broadcasting wedded the advertiser's message to older popular cultural forms made historically specific for the new home environment of radio.

Those evincing more utopian attitudes toward wireless technology, indeed, toward all new means of communication, never troubled themselves much over the larger social context within which all technologies evolve. But these attitudes are worth recalling in any attempt to correct the present distortions between private transmission and public reception.

PART TWO

Theorists of Modern Communication

CHAPTER 4

Toward a New Community? Modern Communication in the Social Thought of Charles Horton Cooley, John Dewey, and Robert E. Park

Beginning with the telegraph, each successive new medium of communication has triggered a rush of prediction and speculation about its meaning for American life. In the 1890s, a trio of American thinkers began the first comprehensive reckoning with modern communication in toto as a force in the social process. Charles Horton Cooley, John Dewey, and Robert Park each ascribed enormous significance to the sum of recent advances in media technology, and each placed the implications he saw at the center of his larger social thought. Together, they construed modern communication essentially as an agent for restoring a broad moral and political consensus to America, a consensus they believed to have been threatened by the wrenching disruptions of the nineteenth century: industrialization, urbanization, and immigration.

A web of biographical and intellectual threads connected these theorists. Born between 1859 and 1864, all three hailed from a stable, small town, liberal Protestant milieu. As a young philosophy instructor at the University of Michigan, Dewey greatly influenced the formative interests of the other two as students. To Park and

Cooley, who later blazed two quite divergent trails in American sociology, Dewey transmitted a deep sense of society as an organism. Society was thus subject to natural laws and might be studied through the application of Darwin's genetic method. Both Park and Cooley later recalled being impressed by Dewey's critique of Herbert Spencer's version of the organic analogy of society. In Dewey's formulation, society existed for more than the benefit of its individual members. And his emphasis on the role of communication in reconciling individual freedom with social responsibility helped shape Park's and Cooley's own elaborations of communication as a crucial category for sociological analysis.

Although the three would later consider the effects of nonprint media such as motion pictures and radio, the revolution in late nineteenth-century journalism originally turned their thoughts to communication. Between 1880 and 1900, newspapers reached the stage of large organization and technical advance with which we are familiar today. Specialization in editorial functions, rationalized cooperative news gathering, the perfection of photoengraving, high-speed presses, and an upsurge in national advertising made this period a watershed in the history of American journalism. The widely copied "new journalism" of Joseph Pulitzer coupled reforming crusades with an emphasis on human interest stories and sensational accounts of violence, sex, and scandal. William Randolph Hearst and his imitators made less of a pretense of reform; they concentrated instead on attracting circulation through the most gaudy and lurid techniques. New and cheap magazines also mushroomed in this era, using lavish illustrations and popular fiction to compete against the older, more staid journals.

Dewey hoped to "transform philosophy somewhat by introducing a little newspaper business into it." He collaborated with Park and others in an abortive attempt to start a new kind of newspaper, one that would apply the techniques of modern journalism to publicize the latest discoveries made in social science. After failing in the venture, Dewey continued to proselytize the ideal of publicizing results of scientific and philosophic inquiry in the news media. Park shuttled between careers as a city reporter, press agent, and university sociologist. He turned from journalism to graduate work at Harvard and Berlin in order to study the philosophical aspects of how printed facts affected the public. Cooley, personally more aloof from the new journalism, nonetheless found in contemporary media developments a catalyst for his own more introspective examination of the role of communication in the social order.

Given their common backgrounds and affinitive sensibilities, it is not surprising that Cooley, Dewey, and Park shared certain unresolved tensions in their generally sanguine estimation of modern communication's prospects. All three thinkers consistently expressed a preference for what Park called the "referential" function of the media—the communication of ideas and facts—and they thus focused on the great potential of modern communication to extend what Dewey termed "organized intelligence" to the public. But a persistent anxiety about the "expressive" function of the media— the communication of sentiments and feelings—accompanied this more expansive point of view. They hoped that broadly based public opinion, rooted in the wide diffusion of organized intelligence, could counteract the modern *gesellschaft*, but feared that the expressive side of the new media would reinforce it. They thus recoiled from the new popular culture engendered by modern media, treating it only insofar as they perceived it adding to the superficiality and strain of modern life.

This generation of thinkers established the study of modern communication as a new field of inquiry. At the same time they identified the new media themselves as potentially critical solvents for the social problems facing America. But they preferred speculation on how the new media might improve American life to the study of how those media actually developed and operated during their lifetime.

★

"A true sociology," Charles Horton Cooley confided to his journal in 1902, "is systematic autobiography. The whole organization and progress of society exists in the mind, and I and others like me can understand it only as we learn what it means to us."[1] Not only does this remark reveal a good deal about Cooley's contribution to American social thought, but it highlights the need to understand how his private life shaped his thinking. Cooley was part of that growing wing in the young discipline of sociology intent upon criticizing the emphases on heredity and individualism to the exclusion of sociocultural influences. In the sociological theory of Herbert Spencer, Cooley saw a critical gap between a commitment to individual freedom and an insight into the organic nature of society. In his own work, Cooley sought to fill that space by exploring the question of how people are socialized. One can isolate three major themes in his writing: the organic unity of self and society; society as a mental phenomenon; and the doctrine of "primary groups." Out of these he built his faith in the beneficial powers of modern communication;

but private qualms about the new media sometimes poked through the expansive optimism of this quintessential Progressive.

Cooley was born in 1864 in Ann Arbor, Michigan, the fourth child of six in a Congregational family originally from western New York. That year Thomas McIntyre Cooley, the boy's father, became a justice of the Michigan Supreme Court, capping a brilliant legal career. Ambitious, intense, and fiercely competitive, the elder Cooley rose from a poor rural background to the very top of his profession. Young Charles, passive and withdrawn, found himself early alienated from his overbearing father. We learn from his journals and correspondence that he suffered miserable health between the ages of eight and twenty. Plagued by chronic constipation, a speech impediment, and acute shyness, Cooley found comfort in a jealously guarded inner life.

Years later he wondered if this inner life was the cause of his physical troubles. "All through my early life the discrepancy between my ambitions and my actual state was great and often painful. . . . My intenser life was always a dream-life. I did a little, read a great deal, and fancied infinitely. I seemed to spend nearly all of my hours either in stress or in apathy; very few in enjoyment." His youthful meditations and daydreams soon took the form of a journal, which he kept fairly regularly for over forty years. He observed in his old age that these writings were no genial record, but "a strenuous attempt to grasp and control my life." Further, he believed his sociology to be "the continuation, enlargement and verification of my journals."[2]

Due to his poor health, Cooley took seven years to finish his undergraduate degree at Michigan. His parents' comfortable financial status enabled him to take long trips across the country and to Europe. By the time he graduated with a degree in engineering in 1890, Cooley had held a variety of jobs, including that of statistician for the Interstate Commerce Commission (ICC) and the Bureau of the Census in Washington, D.C. Still, at age twenty-six, he had no set calling in mind. Worried about pleasing his parents and making a success of himself, he went through that earnest and painful soul-searching common for so many young middle-class Victorians. He knew he wanted to be "a scholar in righteousness," but he was unsure of the specific field. In the summer of 1890 he wrote that "I am one of those whose part is to be a patient separater of grains of truth. . . . I am to be a truth finder and truth keeper and I want fo fit myself better for my work. I wish more intellectual integrity, a more systematic and thorough habit of thinking."[3]

That fall Cooley returned to Ann Arbor to begin graduate work in the nascent field of sociology. "I imagine," Cooley later recalled, "that nearly all of us who took up sociology between 1870, say, and 1890 did so at the instigation of Spencer." Originally, Cooley found two related aspects of Herbert Spencer's writings particularly exciting: the analogy of society to an organism and the notion that "a society is but a collective name for a number of individuals." In *The Principles of Sociology* (1876), Spencer argued, by noting several parallels, that societies greatly resemble the organic world. Both societies and organisms exhibit growth throughout their lives, as well as progressive differentiation of structure and function. "As soon as a social combination acquires some permanence, there begin action and reaction between the society as a whole and each member of it, such that either affects the nature of the other. The control exercised by the aggregate over its units is one tendency ever to mould their activities and sentiments and ideas into congruity with social requirements; and these activities, sentiments, and ideas, in so far as they are changed by changing circumstances, tend to re-mould the society into congruity with themselves."

But Cooley found Spencer's explanation of precisely how individual and society interact inadequate. Spencer, Cooley later wrote, offered no idea of "a continuing social life, having an organization and history of its own, in which sentiments are gradually developed, and from which they are derived by the individual." According to Cooley, Spencer's concept of process was not social, but biological (emphasizing inheritance) and individual. It therefore could not explain the development of human personality, nor embrace the complex ways in which self and society reinforced each other. The bulk of Cooley's sociological theory and work in social psychology concerned itself with fleshing out the intricate and multifaceted relationship of the individual to society.[4]

Significantly, the ideas of John Dewey, a young instructor at Michigan during Cooley's student days, first turned him toward a critique of Spencer. Cooley attended his lectures in political philosophy and ethics in 1893 and 1894, where Dewey "maintained that society was an organism in a deeper sense than Spencer had perceived." At this point in his career, Dewey had already contributed to the development of a new psychology by emphasizing the mutual interplay between organism and environment, an interplay mediated by the mind. In his *Outlines of a Critical Theory of Ethics* (1891), he translated this into a conception of "the moral life as growth in freedom, as the individual finds and conforms to the law of his social placing." Cooley drank all this in, impressed by Dewey's personal character as well as his alternative to Spencer's version of social process.[5]

After completing his Ph.D. at Michigan in 1894, Cooley began to formulate a mature sociology of his own. For the rest of his quiet, uneventful life he remained at Ann Arbor despite numerous offers to go elsewhere. Aloof from university politics, forever shy with other people, Cooley felt strongly "what Goethe calls the joy of dwelling in one's self." Until his death in 1929, he was content with working out a sociology that reflected his reclusive, introverted personality.

His interest in communication began early. Cooley's doctoral thesis, inappropriately titled "The Theory of Transportation" (1894), argued that evolving modern society implied "unification of aim, specialization of activities in view of a common purpose, a growing interdependence among the parts of society." In American industry, in the cities, in all social life Cooley saw a movement toward unity that was guided by a critical mechanism: "Communication in the widest sense of the word; communication of ideas, of physical commodities between one time and another and one place and another. These are the threads that hold society together; upon them all unity depends." Transportation, the ostensible subject of the thesis, was the material means of communication, likened to the circulatory system of the body. The emphasis on transportation probably stemmed from Cooley's earlier statistical work at the ICC. But it was the mechanism of "psychical communication," parallel to that of the human nervous system, that Cooley really cared about. As he later recalled, he soon switched his interest: "I could not fail to reflect also on the psychic mechanism, embracing all sorts of language and the means of its transmission and record, whose function was analogous to that of transportation and even more intimately concerned with the social process."[6]

He pursued the import of communication proper (i.e., "psychical communication") in an article on "The Process of Social Change" (1897). Mankind's ascendancy over other creatures was associated with a flexibility of nature; the process of social change, a peculiarly human category, rested upon the imitative, sympathetic, and intellectual faculties. Cooley held that the recent trends of psychological and sociological studies moved toward the conclusion that the social factor in shaping individual conduct and character was far greater than had been perceived earlier. The contours of social change depended upon the evolution of social environment, "and the existing system of communication determines the reach of the environment. . . . Society is a matter of the incidence of men on one another; and since this incidence is a matter of communication, the history of the latter is the foundation of all history." The mechanisms of communication included "gesture, speech, writing, printing, mails, telephones, telegraphs, photography, and the techniques of the arts and sciences—all the ways through which thought and feeling can pass from man to man."

In the history of communication Cooley thought he saw a way to organize all history and the moral progress he felt sure accompanied it. Particularly in the past fifty years, Cooley asserted, society had moved significantly toward becoming a cooperative whole by means of the extension of knowledge and sympathy coincident with the latest improvements in communication. "Nowadays one is not less dependent upon social influences than formerly, but he is less dependent upon the particular ones that happen to be near by. . . . A million environments solicit him; there is eager competition in place of monopoly." New means of communication made all influences quicker in transmission and more accessible to a larger proportion of people. The process of social change, Cooley concluded, came about "through the competition of influences and the propagation of opportune innovations in thought and action," as determined by the state of communication.[7]

At the time he wrote this article, Cooley identified in his journal what seemed to him to be the crucial component of his own temperament. "An omnipresent and constraining element in my character is a need for symmetry and wholeness in what I do and think. I cannot keep up an interest in fragments, even quite large ones. I must unite them with the whole or let them alone. The feeling of disunity is a cause of constant restlessness and discontent." Indeed, at the core of his three major works lay the attempt to interpret all of life and society as an organic whole; "that is, a complex of forms or processes each of which is living and growing by interaction with the others, the whole being so unified that what takes place in one part affects all the rest."[8]

In his first book, *Human Nature and the Social Order* (1902), Cooley freely acknowledged his debt to William James and James Mark Baldwin. He sought a more detailed and fuller exposition of James's doctrine of "the social self," and of Baldwin's "dialectic of personal growth."[9] Cooley drew extensively on observations of his own children and a wide range of literary and historical sources; he marshaled all of these in an elaborate refutation of the Spencerian notion of the fully autonomous, independent individual. Cooley showed how conscience, emotions such as sympathy and hostility, leadership qualities, indeed, the entire human personality developed through a social give-and-take process.

Cooley located the data for his sociological research in the mind. "The immediate social reality is the personal idea. . . . In order to have society, it is evidently necessary that persons should get together somewhere; and they get together only as personal ideas in the mind." Thus, for Cooley, persons and society must be studied primarily in the imagination: "The imaginations which people have of one another are the solid facts of society, and . . . to observe and interpret these must be a chief aim of sociology." His idea of the "looking-glass self" grew from a belief that the self, from infancy, came into being only through constant intercourse with others. Our self-images are shaped by other people's images of us. "Each to each a looking glass/Reflects the other that doth pass."[10]

To this mentalist perspective on society Cooley attached an original symbol to explain the actual socialization process: the primary group. He defined primary groups as those "characterized by intimate face-to-face association and cooperation. They are primary in several senses, but chiefly that they are fundamental in forming the social nature and ideals of the individual." The family, children's play groups, the neighborhood, and community groups of elders Cooley thought to be basically alike in all societies. Such groups were universal repositories of "primary ideals"; traits such as fellowship, loyalty, lawfulness, and individual freedom flourished in them.[11]

Given Cooley's organicism and his conception of society as the collective aspect of personal thought, it is clear why communication proved such a critical category. In his early work of the 1890s, Cooley concentrated on the historical dynamic of communication, locating in it the motor for the entire engine of social change over time. His later writing, notably *Social Organization* (1909) and *Social Process* (1918), dwelled on utopian future prospects. He held to a very broad definition of communication as "the mechanism through which human relations exist and develop—all the symbols of the mind, together with the means of conveying them through space and preserving them in time." But his attention shifted to modern communication, which he viewed as a vehicle for social salvation.

Cooley believed that the epoch of modern communication ushered in by the nineteenth century made the possibility of a truly democratic community in America real. Four factors distinguished it: "Expressiveness, or the range of ideas and feeling it is competent to carry. Permanence of record, or the overcoming of time. Swiftness, or the overcoming of space. Diffusion, or access to all classes of men." What gesture and speech insured in the primary group, modern means of communication would guarantee for the whole society. By transforming the psychology of modern life, by increasing the power of human nature to "express itself in social wholes," these new forms paved the way for a more humane society and an era of moral progress. "They make it possible," Cooley wrote confidently, "for society to be organized more and more on the higher faculties of man, on intelligence and sympathy, rather than on authority, caste, and routine. They mean freedom, outlook, indefinite possibility."[12]

Cooley, the classic small-town Progressive, thus saw in the "recent marvelous improvement of communicative machinery" a means for projecting his ideal milieu on to the whole nation. He envisioned a society in which the individual is self-conscious and devoted to his work, yet he feels himself and that work as part of a larger and joyous whole. "If we have not yet an organic society in this sense, we have at least the mechanical conditions that must underly it."[13]

In all his work on communication, Cooley could more easily linger on its evolution or future glories than on its operation in the present. Cooley's journal, for example, shows him struggling to square his communication theories with the surrounding reality. He eagerly followed newspaper reports on the war with Spain through the spring and early summer of 1898. "I revel in the accounts of the battles, only wishing they were more equal, and so more exciting and glamorous." But by the end of July, he no longer enjoyed it: "I feel vulgarized by taking in and sharing newspaper thought and feeling about the war. For this and other reasons I seem to myself weak, mean, and ineffective. . . . I am sick of the war and of reading newspapers."

He continually berated himself for wasting time with newspapers and periodicals, which he felt magnified his own feelings of "sensuality, vanity, and triviality." Although he took several magazines, he dismissed most periodical literature as "a phenomenon of imitation and suggestion; the writers are interesting rather as an aggregate than as individuals." Referring to them, he found appalling the ease with which "in imagination we vicariously live in carnage and violence. It is a fact in reading of violent and outrageous deeds, not excepting the harrying of women, I instinctively feel with the aggressor, entering into his blood thirstiness and lust rather than into the feelings of the victim." To soothe himself, Cooley set his own work apart from the realm of periodical literature. "The vivacity which characterizes successful newspaper and magazine writing affects me like the crude shine of varnish. It catches the eye but does not satisfy contemplation. . . . It is unlikely that the sort of work I strive to do should please the readers of a popular magazine." He thus hoped that his own ambitions would not have to be realized through the popular media that so unsettled him. "I want fame and want it badly," he admitted, "but I want the real thing, to live in the minds of the wise, not popular vogue."[14]

Cooley attributed a contemporary climate of strain and anxiety to modern media, and he made a tentative explanation for it. The enlargement of social environment through the media produced "a more rapid and multitudinous flow of personal images, sentiments, and impulses." For many persons this brought "an over-excitation which weakens or breaks down character." Cooley frequently described this problem in the pathological terms common to early sociological studies: suicide, insanity, nervous prostration, drug abuse. A less serious effect, "very generally produced upon all except the strongest minds, appears to be a sort of superficiality of imagination, a dissipation of impulse, which watches the stream of personal imagery go like a procession, but lacks the power to organize and direct it." As a guard against mental exhaustion and dissipation from this flotsam of images, Cooley underlined the need to build one's moral strength. The Victorian stress upon character and self-control was Cooley's line of defense. The vocabulary of pathology, as well as the vigilance he proposed, revealed that Cooley felt more comfortable with the abstract entity of modern communication than with its omnipresent, insistent reality.[15]

At best, Cooley could only wonder about the worth of the new popular culture arising with the waves of modern media. He found it difficult to reconcile the faith in modern communication with his lifelong devotion to art. "I am more in love with the idea of art," he wrote in 1927, "than with any or all forms of it." In his consciously neoclassical aesthetic he celebrated art that expressed ideals and was painfully aware of what he viewed as the contemporary literary and artistic weakness. "It is, to put the matter otherwise, a *loud* time. The newspapers, the advertising, the general insistence of suggestion, have an effect of din, so that one feels that he must raise his voice to be heard, and the whispers of the gods are hard to catch." He lamented a "certain breathlessness and lack of assured power" in the body of modern art created by confused artists. He sampled motion pictures, popular fiction, phonograph records, and later the radio. But although he could study them, he could not enjoy these forms.[16]

Cooley acknowledged that the new popular culture still fulfilled an urgent need even if it did not include the noblest forms of art. "A best seller or a motion picture appealing to the superficial and undisciplined sentiment of a million people is not the art we look for though it may be better than none at all." Like that of Jane Addams, his version of a popular culture included a call for a "livelier community spirit" in all towns and neighborhoods. This community spirit would balance the larger common culture flowing outside "the channels of public guidance and formal institutions, working upon us through newspapers, popular literature, the drama, motion pictures, and the like." He could not imagine any "broad and rich growth of democracy without a corresponding development of popular art," and thought it too easy to simply deprecate "the poor taste of the masses." Yet the restraints of the genteel tradition made it impossible for Cooley to appreciate the flowering of popular culture brought on by the new media of his day. He missed out on the art of Chaplin and Keaton, on ragtime and jazz, on the popular fiction of writers like Jack London.

Near the end of his life, Cooley fell back on his old belief that things would surely improve. He wrote in his journal in 1926:

> What is new in our time is the immense growth of the organs of superficial thought and feeling in the cheap press, moving pictures, radio and the like. (Perhaps) the superficial life is more insistent than ever before, but it is also more varied, not so confusing. . . . Our mental life is more animated and various, more widely unified than that of our ancestors and also, perhaps less deeply channeled, has less repose. But I see no ground for saying that we are less competent to deal with the greater problems of life.[17]

Cooley always returned to the safety of inevitable progress. He readily admitted that "the reality of progress is a matter of faith, not of demonstration." Since progress was a moral category, the question of whether it took place was one of moral judgment. This belief, coupled with a conception of society bordering on the solipsistic, make Cooley seem quaint, even irrelevant, today. Yet his transcendent faith in the psychical unity of self and society places him squarely in the Emersonian tradition of American thought. Cooley closely resembles the Emerson intent on dissolving all barriers between the self and the oversoul, the Emerson who described the world as "this shadow of the soul, or *other me*."[18]

His intoxication with the possibilities of modern communication blinded Cooley to the severe reality of how the American media developed both during and before his lifetime. He never explored the process by which inventions and mechanical advances in communication were transformed into, or were products of, complex institutions. He could never connect his disgust with the babel of commercialism to the economic structure of the press and broadcasting. He chose not to consider the trends toward corporate centralization of the new media nor to examine how these trends affected local, community-based cultural activities. Cooley could never resolve the ironic contradiction implicit in his position on modern communication, that somehow "mechanical conditions" might prove the future basis for a truly "organic society."

Nonetheless, Cooley made the first successful attempts to explain how new communications media alter behavior and culture. Years later, empirical researchers returned to Cooley's concept of the primary group to help demonstrate the mediations between modern communication and the individual. They found that the social context of family and friends, play group and peer group, belied the once widely held model of modern media somehow directly and brutally assaulting the passive individual. Today this complex interaction is by no means perfectly understood, but Cooley made the first serious efforts to fathom it.

★

If modern communication stood at the very center of Cooley's thinking, it appeared as a tangent in the work of John Dewey. Against the backdrop of Dewey's long and prolific career, it may seem a minor theme indeed. Yet the nature and uses of communication remained a conspicuous concern in Dewey's professional and personal life from his early days at the University of Michigan through the 1930s. Throughout Dewey's career a creative tension caused him to alternate between political and philosophical solutions for social problems. Dewey's thinking on communication mirrored this larger, unresolved conflict. Particularly at those times when social issues most preoccupied him, Dewey was excited by the reforming potential of modern communication. What implications did new media hold for the nature of inquiry and for the political and social uses to which it might be put? How could "organized intelligence," made public through new media, help create a "great community" in America?

But there was another side to his thinking on communication. As part of his metaphysical and aesthetic speculations, Dewey also produced a subtle and suggestive explication of the moral meaning of the communicative process. Although Dewey never thoroughly and successfully integrated the political and ethical emphases in any one work, he continually played the two approaches against each other in his communication theories.

Born in 1859, raised in Burlington, Vermont, Dewey's was a stable and comfortable home. The driving force in his family was his mother, Lucina Rich Dewey, a pious evangelical Protestant. He seems to have been a quiet and reserved child, yet early possessed of a strong sense of self. After graduating from the University of Vermont, Dewey spent several years teaching high school, but during that time read widely in philosophy and psychology.[19]

In an autobiographical essay written at age seventy, Dewey recalled his early attraction to Hegelian philosophy when a graduate student at Johns Hopkins. He likened this interest to a conversion experience; in the light of the closeness of theological and philosophical studies in the late nineteenth century, the metaphor is not farfetched. Although the new, professionally oriented graduate school at Hopkins helped destroy the old ideal of the university as essentially a place for character building, the personal issues of religious faith and the search for a calling were still very much on Dewey's mind. Under the tutelage of George S. Morris, Dewey found in the Hegelian philosophy a fulfilling wholeness, quite like Cooley's discovery of "organicism": "It supplied a demand for unification that was doubtless an intense emotional craving, and yet was a hunger that only an intellectualized subject-matter could satisfy.... Hegel's synthesis of subject and object, matter and spirit, the divine and the human, was, however, no mere intellectual formula; it operated as an immense release, a liberation."[20]

Between 1884 and 1894 Dewey taught at the University of Michigan, and he began making notable contributions in several areas of philosophy: psychology, ethics, and epistemology. At first (as reflected in his 1887 book, *Psychology*) he sought a fusion of "physiological psychology" with the Hegelian idealism that served as the official creed of the Michigan philosophy department. But under the influence of James and Darwin, Dewey soon began to move toward his later instrumentalism. From James's "objective psychology" he learned that mind is not an entity separate from its environment, but an objective process through which the organism interacts with the world around it. From Darwinian biology Dewey applied the notion of adaptive species to ideas; he ultimately defined a method of inquiry aimed primarily at adjusting the human species to its surroundings. While at Michigan, however, Dewey still operated within the categories and vocabulary of idealism and concerned himself chiefly with ethical problems. In his writings on ethics Dewey arrived at a theory of experimental idealism, which was based on the premise that "true ideals are the *working hypotheses* of action." His search for a scientific system of ethics foreshadowed the later, more elaborate instrumentalism: "Moral theory, then, is the analytic perception of the conditions and relations in hand in a given act,—it is the action *in idea.*"[21]

During this period, Dewey started to translate philosophical problems into social ones, as the line between ethical and political questions blurred. Central to this development was Dewey's new concern with "organized intelligence," a concern culminating in his fascinating though aborted attempt at publishing a new kind of newspaper, "Thought News." In the early 1890s Dewey fell under the sway of Franklin Ford, a remarkable, somewhat shadowy figure who served as midwife to his emerging social conscience.

Little is known about Ford himself, a dynamic but quixotic man who was adept at attracting small groups of people to his grandiose schemes. Ford worked as a newspaperman in New York during the 1880s, writing for the commercial journal *Bradstreet's*. He felt frustrated by the paper's steady offering of financial gossip, editorials, and advertising. He hoped to turn it into a research bureau available to investors who would pay experts to investigate business conditions. Ford quit *Bradstreet's* in 1887 and began to wander across the country, visiting various news centers and newspapers in order to win others over to his plan. He arrived in Ann Arbor sometime in 1888 and found a receptive ear in Dewey. During the next four years, according to Dewey, the two studied "as a practical question the social bearings of intelligence and its distribution." Ford developed and codified his ideas, apparently with Dewey's aid, in the 1892 pamphlet, *Draft of Action*.

A curious mixture of press reform, syndicalism, and half-baked socialism, the *Draft* set forth Ford's somewhat opaque vision. His underlying premise held that new means of communication (printing press, telegraph, and locomotive) made it possible to treat news as a commodity. Ford proposed that philosophers, social scientists, and reformers also enter the "business of dealing in intelligence," using the same technological means as *Bradstreet's* or the Associated Press. Ford argued that the road to social union, the method for creating a new and more just society, "lies through the organization, the socializing of intelligence. . . . Unless intelligence be unified here, unless a single mind can be secured from Maine to California, the nation in the moral sense must go to pieces."[22]

Many years later, Robert Park, whom Dewey introduced to Ford, recalled the fervor and reforming zeal that Ford inspired in Dewey and a coterie of others. Park recollected:

> There was a group of us who believed that the newspaper, by the mere fact of reporting, with philosophic insight and scientific accuracy, the trends of current events, was destined to bring about profound and immediate changes. It was nothing short of a revolution, silent and continuous, that we were looking forward to, once the newspaper had reached the point where it was able and willing to report political and social events with the same accuracy that it was then reporting the stock market and ball games.[23]

Ford proposed creating a giant, centralized intelligence triangle to coordinate the new ordering of intelligence. The News Association, the parent concern, would publish several general newspapers: a national political paper, "The Newsbook"; smaller local dailies, "The Town"; and special advertising journals, "The Daily Want." As Ford's feverish prose described it: "These three journals are together the organs of the State in the social region, through these all incoming facts are rendered in the light of the general interest. In place of writing about sociology, so-called, we proceed to publish the sociological newspaper; that is, recognizing the social organism as attained in fact we set about reporting the state thereof. The principle of socialism is division of labor. This gained in the mental region, through the organization of intelligence, socialism is here." These newspapers would "out sensationalize" the contemporary press by presenting a more startling sensation: "The social fact is the sensational thing. News is the new thing. In truth the only sensation is a new idea. We are thus at the gateway of the highest sensations—those relating to the integrity of the organized social body and in turn to the welfare of the individual."[24]

A second agency, the Class News Company, would gather and sell facts relevant to distinct classes or social groups. Ford suggested starting weeklies and dailies such as "Grain," "Fruit," and "Chemical News." Finally, a third bureau, modestly called Fords, would sell intelligence to individuals, banks, or corporations on demand. This three-pronged news structure would be the practical outcome of the organization of inquiry. Ford wrote, "We are at the center of a new birth in letters—the advance of inquiry to the daily fact, to the social whole in movement. In place of the merely individual litera-ture now in its decadence, we secure new readings from the book of life. The new literature is the report of America, of what she has done."[25]

Ford's strange plan deserves to be classed with the scores of utopian cure-alls and eccentric remedies for America's ills that cropped up in this era. But Dewey found Ford intriguing on several levels. In correspondence with William James, he described his encounter with Ford as "a wonderful personal experience." He ex-citedly recounted to James what he learned from his conversations with Ford on

> the social bearings of intelligence and its distribution: What
> I have got out of it is, first, the perception of the true or practi-
> cal bearing of idealism—that philosophy has been the asser-
> tion of the unity of intelligence and the external world *in idea*
> or subjectively, while if true in idea it must finally secure
> the condition of its subjective expression. And secondly, I be-
> lieve that a tremendous movement is impending, when the
> intellectual forces which have been gathering since the Rena-
> scence and Reformation, shall demand complete free movement,
> and, by getting their physical leverage in the telegraph and
> printing press, shall, through free inquiry in a centralized way,
> demand the authority of all other so-called authorities.[26]

In other words, here was an opportunity to translate the "Abso-lute Reason" of idealism into a useful tool in today's world. Scientific inquiry, combined with the enormous physical potential of modern communication, could dramatically improve the social order. Or, as Dewey declared in his *Outlines of a Critical Theory of Ethics* (1891), in which he freely acknowledged his debt to Ford: "The duty of the present is the socializing of intelligence—the realizing of its bearing upon social practice."[27]

Dewey's letter to James solicited interest in what Dewey termed Ford's "theoretical discovery" and his "practical project." The latter, conceived as the opening shot in the intelligence revolution, was "Thought News—A Journal of Inquiry and a Record of Fact." In the spring of 1892, Ford and Dewey laid plans for launching their paper, creating a stir on the campus and in the local press. A circular written by the two men in March described the project:

> This will be a newspaper and will aim to perform the function of newspaper. . . . It is believed there is room, in the flood of opinion, for one journal which shall not go beyond the fact; which shall report thought rather than dress it up in the garments of the past; which instead of dwelling at length upon the merely individual processes that accompany the facts, shall set forth the facts themselves; which shall not discuss philosophic ideas per se but use them as tools in interpreting the movements of thought; which shall treat questions of science, letters, state, school and church as parts of the one moving life of man and hence of common interest, and not relegate them to departments of merely technical interest; which shall report new investigations and discoveries in their net outcome instead of in their overloaded gross bulk; which shall note new contributions to thought, whether by book or magazine, from the standpoint of the news in them, and not from that of patron or censor.[28]

They planned to bring the paper out at least once a month, beginning that April.

Ford clearly had more of a stake in the enterprise, seeing in it the realization of an old political dream. Yet it was the highly visible Dewey who caught the flak from an angry local press, which was annoyed about the criticism of existing newspapers. Ford talked effusively about "Thought News": "The statement that society is an organism was made long ago and accepted as a statement. It remains now to point to the fact, the visible, tangible thing, to show the idea in motion. . . . That is what Thought News will attempt to do."[29] But a lead editorial in the *Detroit Tribune* attacked Dewey: "The not altogether clear prospectus of Professor John Dewey's 'Thought News' will contain news already covered by the newspapers, and twenty to one . . . its thought will be exclusively that of its editors."[30]

Dewey, upset by Ford's boasts and reactions to them, retreated in a follow-up interview headlined "He's Planned No Revolution." He claimed to be taken aback by the grandiose meaning some of his followers invested in his newspaper project. "Thought News," he said, was not designed to revolutionize journalism. "Instead of trying to change the newspaper business by introducing philosophy into it, the idea is to transform philosophy somewhat by introducing a little newspaper business into it."[31]

After this interview, Ford must have seen that the two had come to a parting of the ways; we have no record of any further contact between Dewey and Ford. No issue of "Thought News" ever appeared. Many years later Dewey recalled that "it was an over enthusiastic project which we had not the means nor the time—and doubtless not the ability to carry through . . . the *idea* was advanced for those days, but it was too advanced for the maturity of those who had the idea in mind."[32]

Ford's spell over Dewey thus ended, right at the point where Dewey himself undoubtedly realized that he was temperamentally unsuited for direct involvement in journalism. His first priority was philosophy. In the 1920s and 1930s Dewey returned to a consideration of the political and social implications of modern communication. By this time, however, Dewey had taken up the problem of communication in the context of his metaphysics as well. In this aspect of his thought Dewey extended and explained the durable tradition in American thought that has ascribed spiritual meaning to new communications technologies.

The tension between the process of communication as an intimate ritual and communication viewed in terms of technical, material advance was expressed in this famous passage from *Democracy and Education* (1915): "Society not only continues to exist *by* transmission, *by* communication, but it may fairly be said to exist *in* transmission, *in* communication. There is more than a verbal tie between the words common, community, and communication. Men live in a community in virtue of the things they have in common; and communication is the way in which they come to possess things in common."[33]

In the 1890s Dewey's fascination with communication centered on those modern techniques that improved speed, power, and efficiency, and he was enthusiastic over their potential for aiding scientific inquiry. But in later years he also invested with nearly mystical qualities the capacity of communication to induce participation and sharing. "Of all affairs," he claimed in *Experience and Nature* (1925), "communication is the most wonderful . . . that the fruit of communication should be participation, sharing, is a wonder by the side of which transubstantiation pales." It literally transformed and enlarged the parties partaking in it, making experience a common possession.[34]

Communication was "uniquely instrumental and uniquely final." Here one finds one of the clearest examples of Dewey's stubborn insistence on the intimacy between means and ends, on the integral linkage of theory to practice. Communication "is instrumental as liberating us from the otherwise overwhelming pressure of events and enabling us to live in a world of things that have meaning. It is final as a sharing in the objects and arts precious to a community, a sharing whereby meanings are enhanced, deepened, and solidified in the sense of communion." When both halves of the communication equation are actualized in experience, "there exists an intelligence which is the method and reward of the common life, and a society worthy to command affection, admiration, and loyalty."[35]

In *Art as Experience* (1934), Dewey merely hinted at an analysis of the common ground shared by ritual, aesthetics, and modern communication: the popular arts. He unfortunately missed a chance to combine the lovely insights of that book with the view of communication as ritual and to extend these to an area where they might have proved quite fruitful. In the book, Dewey attempted to recover the continuity between aesthetic experience and the events of everyday life. He saw works of art as "the only media of complete and unhindered communication between man and man." In a world of gulfs and walls they came closest to creating a true sense of participation. Art was the paramount expression of communication as shared ritual. Theories that set art upon a pedestal and removed it to some ethereal ideal realm destroyed this relationship and prevented better understanding of aesthetic experience.

The result, Dewey observed, was an elevation of the more vigorous popular arts. "The arts which today have most vitality for the average person are things he does not take to be art; for instance, the movie, jazzed music, the comic strip. . . . For when what he knows as art is relegated to the museum and gallery, the unconquerable impulse toward experiences enjoyable in themselves finds such outlet as the daily environment provides."[36] Dewey did not deepen his analysis of the popular arts, those created, transformed, or merely popularized by the new communications media. But these arts, shaped by the demands of mass production and commercialism, but firmly rooted in the oldest communal forms of work, music, theater, folktale, and dance, bore out Dewey's aesthetic theory. Because of their ubiquity, easy access, and links to the shared past, they provide us with some of our most notable and essential art, art that, at its best, greatly enlarges the community of experience in everyday life.

Yet Dewey had not abandoned his consideration of the ties between political reform and modern communication; in fact, he developed it more fully. Like many in this period, he advocated a wider role for experts in the political arena; but unlike some, he never saw them as a panacea for political ills. He criticized writers like Walter Lippmann who restricted the phrase "organized intelligence" to mean the establishment of "expert organizations" for making facts intelligible to decision makers. In *Public Opinion* (1922), Lippmann attacked the traditional democratic theory of public opinion and the notion of the "omnicompetent citizen." He argued that modern communication had created ubiquitous "pseudo environments" that thwarted the ability of the average citizen to make political judgments based on facts. He placed his trust in the interposition of experts between the public and the world at large; only "statisticians, accountants, auditors, industrial counsellors, engineers of many species, scientific managers, personnel administrators" could make intelligible "an invisible and most stupendously difficult environment."[37]

Dewey, in reviewing Lippmann's influential work, rejected the replacing of the public with a small coterie of informed administrators: "There remains the possibility of treating news events in the light of a continuing study and record of underlying conditions. The union of social science, access to facts, and the art of literary presentation is not an easy thing to achieve. But its attainment seems to me the only genuine solution of the problem of an intelligent direction of social life. . . . The enlightenment of public opinion still seems to me to have priority over the enlightenment of officials and directors."

Thirty years after the "Thought News" adventure, Dewey still hoped for a new kind of press: one that would combine modern means of communication, social science techniques, and artistic presentation to provide a continuous, systematic, and effective exposition of social and political movements. Such a press would be an important check on the various expert organizations rapidly becoming a key part of modern government. As in the 1890s, he argued that it could conceivably compete with the sensational press: "This is an artistic as well as an intellectual problem, for it supposes not only a scientific organization for discovering, recording and interpreting all conduct having a public bearing, but also methods which make presentation of the results of inquiry arresting and weighty."[38]

A fuller treatment of these questions came in *The Public and Its*

Problems (1927), Dewey's most ambitious statement on the relations between political affairs, modern communication, and methods of inquiry. A public is the by-product of social activity between individuals ("conjoint behavior"), and a state is the organization of a public, by means of officials, for the protection of these shared interests. The scope of the state's activities, Dewey asserted, ought not to be predetermined by any political philosophy (such as "natural rights" or "inalienable sacred authority"), but rather by critical experiment. Democratic theory in particular, which was based on a celebration of the individual—a concept already in eclipse when the theory was formed—was obsolete, or at least in dire need of repair. For the machine age had "enormously expanded, multiplied, intensified, and complicated the scope of the indirect consequences" of conjoint behavior, forming "such immense and consolidated unions in action, on an impersonal rather than a community basis, that the resultant public cannot identify and distinguish itself." There was too much public, a public too diffused and scattered.

Once this was recognized, Dewey continued, the crucial question became how to transform the great society into a great community. Society possessed the physical agents of communication as never before, but the thought and aspirations congruous with them were not communicated and hence were not common. Somehow perfect ways of communicating meanings must be devised: "Our Babel is not one of tongues but of the signs and symbols without which shared experience is impossible." We could restore the public only by discovering the signs and symbols to go with modern means of communication. A genuinely shared interest in the consequences of interdependent activities could then spur desire and effort and thereby direct action.

Clearly, the physical means of communication—telegraph, telephone, radio, rapid mail delivery, and the printing press—had far outrun "the intellectual phase of inquiry and organization of its results." By this time Dewey seemed less sanguine about the ease with which these two phases would reinforce one another. He nevertheless restated his old vision of a reconstructed press, which would fuse social science to an aesthetically presented daily newspaper: "The highest and most difficult kind of inquiry, and subtle, delicate, vivid and responsive art of communication must take possession of the physical machinery of transmission and circulation and breathe life into it." Nor could he dismiss the face-to-face intimacy of Cooley's primary groups. "The Great Community, in the sense of free and full intercommunication, is conceivable. But it can never possess all

the qualities which make a local community." The local neighborhood environment would add oral communication to that of the
printed word. The small community and the larger organized intelligence must complement one another for a truly liberating social
intelligence.[39]

Dewey provided us with a rich and multilayered paradigm for
communication. As inspiring as the model may be, however, it is
unfortunate that Dewey could go no further in analyzing the forces
of modern communication emerging in his own lifetime. One looks
vainly to Dewey for a plain sense, or even hints, as to just how we
might transform privately owned media of communication into truly
common carriers. This omission reflected a bigger internal conflict
in Dewey's thought: a lifelong ambivalence toward social planning.
The urge in Dewey to dissolve any distance between theory and
practice led to a political failure of nerve, a refusal to address the
reality of social and economic conflict in the present.[40]

In the realm of news Dewey acknowledged the private control of
the press, which made it an enterprise for private profit. During the
Great Depression he noted how too often the banner of freedom of
the press merely served "the power of the business entrepreneur to
carry his own business in his own way for the sake of private profit."
When considering the radio, Dewey simply praised the impending
equilibrium between ear and eye. Since "in all social matters the
mass of people are guided through hearing rather than by sight," he
believed the radio would go a long way toward improving the education of society. However, he failed to discuss the role of commercial
advertising in the evolution of American broadcasting. He could
only state weakly that the radio, "even when in private hands, is
affected with a profound public interest."[41]

Of all the early theoretical visions of modern communication,
Dewey's had the greatest scope. Like Cooley, he expressed great hope
for the potential of new media to reconstitute neighborhood community values in a complex industrial society. Dewey firmly believed that the traditional sense of political and moral obligation
might be recovered if organized intelligence and scientific inquiry
could be made public. But as he retreated from the thorny political
problem of how to transform the physical machinery of transmission
and circulation, Dewey increasingly took refuge in a more comfortable identity: a philosopher of communication, absorbed in the
metaphysical complexities of the communicative process.

★

Robert Park, one of the young Dewey's most ardent disciples at
Michigan, himself nurtured a whole generation of scholars as the
most influential member of the "Chicago School" of sociology. Unlike
Cooley, he alternated between academic life and other careers. Although Park held no university position until he was fifty, he contributed fresh approaches to the sociology of the city, race relations,
and communication. By his own few influential writings and by
guiding the work of many students, Park held substantial sway over
American sociology between the two world wars. His writing combined an understanding gained from long experience as a journalist
and a thorough grounding in the philosophy of James
and Dewey, and an immersion in the works of European social
theorists, especially German thinkers. The resulting blend produced a variation of the uniquely American outlook on the importance of modern communication for creating and preserving social
consensus. Although Cooley and Dewey voiced a similar outlook,
Park's perspective also included knotty ironic twists that reflected
both his more cosmopolitan experiences and the dualities at the
center of his larger social theory.

Born in Pennsylvania in 1864, the same year as Cooley, Park soon
moved with his family to rural Minnesota, where his father became
a leading merchant on the Minnesota frontier. Young Park preferred
to spend his time with the Norwegian and Swedish immigrants on
the other side of town. A lifelong interest in immigrant cultures
surely must have begun with his boyhood hero worship of local
Scandinavians. In his own home Park felt closest to his mother; he
recalled that he was "an awkward, sentimental, and romantic boy."
Over the objection of his father, who wanted the boy to stay with the
family business, Park left home to enter the University of Minnesota. But his meager frontier schooling had not prepared him for
college life. Resolving to improve his study habits, he tried the
university once again, this time entering Michigan in 1883.[42]

At Ann Arbor, Park took six courses with Dewey and responded to
his embryonic instrumentalism, to "the notion that thought and
knowledge were to be regarded as incidents of and instruments of
action." Graduating in 1887, Park chose journalism as a career,
eager for the life of an "intellectual vagabond." He worked as a
reporter for eleven years in Minneapolis, Detroit, New York, and
Chicago. He covered the police beat; investigated epidemics, alco-
holism, the drug trade, and crime rings; and generally had his eyes

opened to the seamy underside of urban life. A small-town boy, Park brought an intense, almost voyeuristic curiosity about city ways to his reportorial task. As he tramped the streets, he developed a sharp sense of observation; but he did not possess a reforming temperament like that of his New York acquaintance and colleague, Jacob Riis.

Still, Park's prolonged exposure to the lower depths made him wonder how a different sort of journalism might actually improve social conditions. Around 1890 Dewey introduced Park to Franklin Ford, who greatly impressed the young journalist. Park became a devoted member of Ford's circle, and he later recalled the "Thought News" episode as the most important factor shaping his mind prior to his involvement with Booker T. Washington. Park was attracted to the notion of a new kind of journalism, one that would seek a clearer understanding of the deep forces that caused the urban pathology he saw firsthand; such a journalism could provide the knowledge that must precede any social action to correct it.[43]

After "Thought News" failed to get off the ground, Park continued his journalism career until 1898. By then, a hunger for a more theoretical comprehension of public opinion replaced any reforming tendencies he may have possessed. Park went to Harvard to study philosophy, aiming "to gain insight into the nature and function of the kind of knowledge we call news. Besides, I wanted to gain a fundamental point of view from which I could describe the behavior of society, under the influence of news, in the precise and universal language of science." He took an M.A. degree, studying philosophy and psychology with James, Royce, and Santayana. He then traveled to Germany, where he received his only formal instruction in sociology under George Simmel at Berlin. Before returning to the United States in 1903 to complete his Ph.D. degree, he also studied the new science of "collective psychology" under Wilhelm Windelband at Heidelberg.[44]

Park's dissertation, "The Crowd and the Public" (1904), offered the first groping toward an American theory of collective behavior and public opinion. Park, writing in German and in the tradition of European "crowd psychology," nonetheless managed to infuse an American perspective into an old problem. He analyzed and accepted the nature and social setting of the crowd, as defined by LeBon, Sighele, and other conservative European social theorists. The crowd, which was distinguished by a highly emotional, irrational, and intolerant "psychic current," represented the lowest form of "common consciousness." Park posed the public as another form of protean collective behavior, one characterized by people involved in rational discourse. Park minimized the gap between crowd and public, emphasizing their similarities as embryonic stages in the social process: "Whenever a new interest asserts itself amid those already existing, a crowd or a public simultaneously develops, and through this union of groups, or certain individuals among them, a new social form for the new interest is created. . . . Neither the crowd nor the public recognizes itself as a whole, nor do they attempt to determine their own action. No regulation, conscious control, or self-consciousness exists."

But the two differed in their respective modes of interaction. The crowd was based on feeling, empathy, and instinct; the public, on thinking and reason. Park proposed the public as an alternative form of collective behavior, thereby setting himself apart from the conservative European sociological tradition within which he was working. The modern world, he seemed to be saying, offered more than the crowd as an alternative category to traditional community. Still, although modern communication had made possible the extension and refinement of public opinion, Park thought it had so far failed to achieve this in fact.

Journalism, rather than instructing and directing public opinion, too often simply proved a mechanism for "controlling collective attention." The opinion formed in this manner resembled "the judgement derived from the unreflective perception," that is, an opinion formed "directly and simultaneously as information is received." At the end of his book, Park asserted that he meant to make only a formal distinction between the two, not a value judgment. But it seems a ritual denial. Indeed, Park's separation of the public from other, less attractive forms of collective behavior marked the beginning of an important American tradition later developed in the thought of Dewey, C. Wright Mills, and others.[45]

Completion of his Ph.D. made Park restless once again. He planned a return to newspaper work, but instead took up public relations duties for the Congo Reform Association. Through this job Park met Booker T. Washington, and for nine years he served as Washington's personal secretary. Park doubled as press agent and research coordinator at Tuskeegee, and he spent years roaming the South studying black life and race relations. In 1914 W. I. Thomas, the Chicago sociologist, invited Park to join the sociology department at that school. Finally settled as a university sociologist at the age of fifty, Park concentrated on defining the parameters and methodology of a fledgling science. He concerned himself mostly with the problem of how to study society as a whole—what were its timeless, formal processes? To his students he delegated the specific studies focusing on social problems.

In the *Introduction to the Science of Sociology* (written with E. W. Burgess, 1921), the most influential sociology text between the wars, Park defined the field as "the science of collective behavior"; he added that "social control is the central fact and the central problem of society." Park posited four ascending ideal social processes from which the social order emerged. Competition, the most elementary and biological form of interaction, results in an economic order. Conflict represented the next highest phase, where competitors consciously identify one another as rivals or enemies. Accommodation meant a cessation of hostilities, when "conflict disappears as overt reaction, although it remains latent as a potential force." Finally, assimilation is a complex process of interpenetration and fusion in which "persons and groups acquire the memories, sentiments, and attitudes of other persons and groups, and, by sharing their experience, are incorporated with them in a common cultural life."[46]

Park and his students used the city as a laboratory for testing hypotheses, seeing in it a microcosm of all social evolution and the locus of social disorganization. Park advanced the idea of "human ecology" and applied the biological concept of a symbiotic ecological community to man. He used the notion of a "biotic order," especially in tracing the spatial patterns of cities, to better understand the social process distinctive to humans. But the "moral order," the social relations not specifically derived from the struggle for survival, most intrigued him.[47]

Just as competition was the fundamental organizing principle of the biotic community, ensuring differentiation and individuation, communication was the basic form of interaction in human society. From Cooley, Park took the idea of identifying the historical enlargement of communication forms, from speech through broadcasting, with all social growth. And he frequently cited Dewey on the nature of the communicative process. He thus combined Cooley's and Dewey's definitions of communication: "It is a social-psychological process by which one individual is enabled to assume, in some sense and to some degree, the attitudes and the point of view of another; it is the process by which a rational and moral order among men is substituted for one that is merely physiological and instinctive."[48] But Park made a more thorough analysis than Cooley or Dewey of how modern communication had really evolved.

He pioneered in the study of the press as a social and cultural institution, particularly as it related to urban growth and immigration.

Park located the most profound changes in the modern newspaper at those points where its emphasis shifted dramatically from editorials to news. The first such shift occurred with the rise of the "penny press" in the 1830s and 1840s; since that time, "the struggle for existence has been a struggle for circulation." The "yellow press" marked another great epoch in newspaper evolution. Closely linked to the dramatic urban boom of the late nineteenth century, these papers erased the once sharp line dividing news and fiction. The rise of the human interest story changed the nature of news itself, investing in it a symbolic and universal flavor transcending time and place. Park himself had written news to appeal to fundamental passions, "a kind of popular literature for the entertainment and instruction of the proletarian public of the cities."[48]

Immigrants swelled the circulation of easy-to-read yellow journals and tabloids, but they also created a separate, vital press of their own. Park surveyed dozens of Yiddish, Polish, Japanese, Italian, and other foreign-language papers and found that they helped establish reading habits among those who did not read in the old country. Arguing against their suppression or control by native Americans, Park stressed their role in preserving ethnic cultures and exposing readers to a more cosmopolitan outlook through the native tongue. The foreign-language press thus served to "breed new loyalties from the old heritages," easing immigrants into American life.[49]

Near the very end of his life, in his seventies, Park returned to the more philosophical questions that he had pondered in the 1890s. He reflected on "news as a form of knowledge" in its own right and on the power of the modern media to unify society in times of crisis. Beginning with William James's discrimination between "knowledge of acquaintance" (informal) and "knowledge about" (rational, systematic), Park set out to find the place of news on the spectrum of knowledge. The basically transient qualities of news defined it as an ephemeral element, but one critical to the formation of public opinion and political activity in general. Its publication lent legitimacy to current events. As a form of knowledge, news contributed to history, sociology, literature, and folklore. Modern means of communication, particularly radio, expanded the scope, speed, and number of news reports. Thus, in contemporary life "the role of news has assumed increased rather than diminished importance as compared with some other forms of knowledge, history, for example. The changes in recent years have been so rapid and drastic that the modern world seems to have lost its historical perspective, and we appear to be living from day to day in what I have described as a 'specious present.'"[50]

Referring to the European crisis in 1941, Park argued that the press must go beyond merely orienting the public to issues; it must "bring into existence a collective will and a political power which, as it mobilizes the community to act, tends to terminate discussion." The circulation of news became urgent during such crises as Munich and the fall of France. Park must have been thinking of the inevitable entrance of America into the war when he noted, "The task of organizing, or energizing, and above all, of animating with a common will and a common purpose vast armies and whole people is an incredibly complicated but, with modern means of communication, not impossible task."[51]

The news represented only one of two main functions of communication. Park delineated two ideal types of communication, the "referential" and the "expressive." In the referential function, ideas and facts are communicated; in the expressive function, sentiments, attitudes, and emotions are manifest. Communication as a whole made possible the unity, consensus, and integrity of the social group. It modified and qualified competition, creating a moral order that imposed limits on the biotic. Communication was an integrating and socializing principle; competition, a principle of individuation. But communication could and frequently did exacerbate competition by bringing into contact isolated cultures. Yet Park argued that it could in the long run ease the resultant social tensions by bringing greater intimacy and understanding and by substituting a moral order for a biotic one through a process of cultural interaction. Also, "The obvious conditions which facilitate or obstruct these processes are mainly physical and in modern times they have been progressively overcome by means of technical devices like the alphabet, printing press, radio, etc."[52]

But Park ascribed most of the positive attributes to the referential side of communication. The expressive manifestations of modern media troubled Park even more profoundly than they did Cooley or Dewey. He considered the symbolic and expressive forms of communication clearly inferior to the referential sorts, not even acknowledging, as had Cooley and Dewey, that they spoke to an urgent thirst for art experience. Park thought that the cinema and periodical fiction were "demoralizing" forces that tended to undermine traditional reins of social control. He often used phrases such as "subversive cultural influence" and "social disorganization" when discussing the expressive side of communication. Like the critics of early motion pictures, he assailed the drift of modern leisure, which was increasingly organized around the new media. "This restlessness and thirst for adventure is, for the most part, barren and illusory, because it is uncreative. . . . It is in the improvident use of our leisure, I suspect, that the greatest wastes in American life occur."[53]

There was a real irony in Park's inability to see how his theoretical principle of cultural interaction through communication operated in American life, precisely through the expressive function. American popular culture has been continually and powerfully revitalized by the entry of previously alien and isolated cultural groups and forms through modern media. Black and rural white musics, ethnic theatrical traditions, European émigré film producers and directors, countercultural writers and cartoonists—these are only a few examples of marginal cultures that have produced tidal waves in the American mainstream because they were diffused by modern communication. That these cultures themselves have all been significantly altered by the process only supports Park's dialectical model of communication; communication promotes tolerance, assimilation, and even intimacy after an initial phase of conflict.

After Park had given up journalism and his hopes of reforming it, he characterized the sociologist as "a kind of super reporter," on the trail of what Franklin Ford had called "the Big News." The usage was perhaps more than metaphorical. Park, due to his lifelong preoccupation with and commitment to the news, shrank from seriously considering the expressive functions of modern communication except insofar as they contaminated the referential. Despite his awareness that the boundary between the two was blurring, Park retained his intellectual faith in the consensual power and historical significance of news as a form of knowledge.

★

Cooley, Dewey, and Park all brought variations of a Progressive sensibility to bear on their speculations concerning modern communication as a social force. A generally confident and optimistic outlook stood behind the subjunctive mood in which they approached the topic. Underlying the question of what the media could become was the broad assumption that they would promote unity and a democratically achieved consensus in American public life. The unease that these men felt about the expressive aspects of new media was a persistent but minor theme in their work. The darker side of modern communication's potential was in the cultural sphere. All three sensed a sharp challenge to the traditional ideals of culture from new media, but rather than fully explore it, they merely noted the possibility nervously. Indeed, the overall failure to examine the ways in which media technologies and institutions actually developed in their lifetime limited their contributions to the understanding of media.

This weakness was most glaring in Cooley, perhaps because his larger social thought was so close to being a theology. Cooley originally entered the field of sociology because he was attracted to the enormity of its subject matter. In the late nineteenth century, sociology offered an alluring opportunity for defining unities and wholes in the modern world, a task earlier performed mainly by religion. It seems safe to assume that had he been born earlier, Cooley, like many others who took up the "calling" of sociology in that period, might have entered the clergy. Ultimately, his secular philosophy retained a strongly religious flavor. In his most important work, *Social Organization*, he tried to define the title concept as "the differentiated unity of mental or social life, present in the simplest intercourse but capable of infinite growth and adaptation." It would be useless, he demurred, to attempt a more elaborate definition. "We have only to open our eyes to *see* organization; and if we cannot do that no definition will help us."[54] Cooley's faith in the future role of modern communication rested on the same presumption that informed this ecstatic sociological vision.

Both Dewey and Park exhibited a more dynamic intellectual development than Cooley. Their fascination with the new media originally centered on the intriguing connection they saw between the modern press and advances in knowledge. Greater accuracy in news, they believed, could be linked to a progressively better grasp of basic social processes. The diffusion of the latest intellectual discoveries through modern media would vastly improve the level of intelligent public discourse, thereby insuring political consensus through the free movement of ideas. Dewey clung most tenaciously to an informed public opinion as the basis for political reform and for achieving the "Great Community." But he offered no clues for reconstructing media institutions to achieve that end. In later years, Dewey added investigations into the metaphysical nature of the communications process itself, stressing its affinity to ritual and communion. It is this part of Dewey's inquiry into communication that remains most valuable today as a means of understanding the potent appeal of modern media.

Park, the one with the most personal experience in the media and the man who did the most research into their history and operation, was the least expansive of the three. Unlike Dewey, he seems to have virtually abandoned the early concern with the larger audience as he shifted his energies to the academic arena. As an entrepreneur of research at Chicago, Park encouraged the kind of narrowly defined, empirical studies that now characterize modern sociology. Yet he never encouraged that sort of research into modern communication. Even as he looked to the creation of an empirically based sociology, Park always remained the ex-newspaperman. His mentor Dewey had entered into the "Thought News" venture with a desire to "transform philosophy somewhat by introducing a little newspaper business into it." Park, by contrast, was most interested in bringing some sort of philosophical and historical understanding to his old profession.

During the next generation, communication studies moved decisively toward empirical research. The focus on how media actually operated in American society, especially their effects on individual behavior, replaced the older speculative interest in their potential. By the late 1930s, this new approach to modern media gained full force. Yet the neglect of the moral concerns originally voiced by the Progressive generation led to severe contradictions in the development and application of the behavioral approach to communications research. For if the pioneer theorists had not adequately examined how the media actually operated, the behavioral approach ultimately suffered from its virtually uncritical relationship to the needs and demands of the media that helped spawn it.

CHAPTER 5

The Rise of Empirical Media Study: Communications Research as Behavioral Science, 1930–1960

By the late 1930s an aggressively empirical spirit, stressing new and increasingly sophisticated research techniques, characterized the study of modern communication in America. The shift from the philosophical approach and subjunctive mood of the Progressive media theorists coincided with a larger trend toward empirical analysis within American social science. The emergence of communications research as a new and hybrid field of the social sciences represented an attempt to unify various fledgling strategies for examining the impact of modern media. The empirical study of media and their audiences—relying upon observation, experiment, and induction to verify hypotheses—has been generally guided by a phrase coined around 1940 by pioneers in the field: "Who says what to whom and with what effect?" Emphasis on the evaluation of the scientifically measurable behavioral effects of modern communication provided intellectual pollen for the cross-fertilization of methodologies, disciplines, and institutions in communications research.

In the course of doing what one might term the "normal science" in this field, American social scientists have added greatly to our knowledge of the operations and functions of modern media and their behavioral effects on audiences. However, important theoretical contributions derived from the accumulation of empirical studies often tended to downplay the impact of modern communication; this reflected the difficulties found in ascribing direct behavioral effects to media exposure. By relying heavily on marketing and polling research and laboratory experiments for its data, the science of communication effectively eliminated from the discourse broader questions involving social control and aesthetics. By the late 1940s, however, certain dissents from the empirical tradition and the behavioral paradigm were voiced by thinkers concerned with these neglected issues. It might now be useful to examine in detail the origins and development of this empirical approach. One can delineate four areas of research that ultimately led to the separate and self-conscious field of communications research.

Propaganda analysis emerged as a significant new activity after the armistice. During the Great War propaganda had become a massive scientific endeavor, a sophisticated art critical to the military efforts of all the combatants. Utilizing the latest forms of modern communication, nations made propaganda a regular feature of governing—a tendency that continued after the war's end. Propaganda acquired a sinister connotation; it meant partisan appeal based on half-truths and devious manipulation of communications channels. A postwar wave of autobiographies, exposés, and popular articles helped further a belief in the deceitful power of propaganda and the ease with which modern media could be insidiously controlled in its service. The scholarly studies of propaganda generally took these fears as their starting point.

For example, Harold Lasswell's pioneer work, *Propaganda Technique in the World War* (1927), began by noting: "We live among more people than ever who are puzzled, uneasy, or vexed at the unknown cunning which seems to have duped and degraded them. It is often an object of vituperation, and therefore, of interest, discussion, and, finally, of study." Lasswell sought to classify the mechanisms, tactics, and strategies of propaganda, which he defined as "the control of opinion by significant symbols . . . by stories, rumors, reports, pictures, and other forms of social communication." Other propaganda studies in these years also directed attention to how the modern media operated and how they could be abused for propaganda purposes in various countries, particularly during wartime.[1]

Public opinion research, a related but somewhat broader field than propaganda analysis, also flourished in this period. Walter Lippmann, particularly in his influential *Public Opinion* (1922) and *The Phantom Public* (1925), shared with the propaganda analysts a concern that people acted increasingly not upon their knowledge of the real world but in response to the ubiquitous "pseudo-environments" communicated through the modern media. Lippmann attacked the notion of the "omnicompetent citizen," the idea that each person must acquire an informed opinion about all public affairs. He viewed this notion as the heart of classical democratic theory. But democracy in its original form "never seriously faced the problem which arises because the pictures inside people's heads do not automatically correspond with the world outside." Lippmann performed some of the first analyses of the American press: its operations, its economic base, and the nature of censorship and stereotypes in newspapers and motion pictures. In short, he revealed why "the picture inside so often misleads men in their dealings with the world outside." Ultimately, Lippmann made an elaborate political argument for "an independent, expert organization for making the unseen facts intelligible to those who have to make the decisions." This was also a plea for replacing the press with the social scientist, who would organize and interpret public opinion according to a coordinated and objective analysis of this incredibly problematic environment.[2]

The founding of *Public Opinion Quarterly* in 1937 demonstrated the growth and interdisciplinary nature of the new field. In the foreword to its first issue, the editors stated the objectives of the new journal in terms close to those in Lippmann's earlier call:

> A new situation has arisen throughout the world, created
> by the spread of literacy among the people and the miracu-
> lous improvement of the means of communication. Always the
> opinions of relatively small publics have been a prime force
> in political life, but now, for the first time in history, we are
> confronted nearly everywhere by mass opinion as the final de-
> terminant of political and economic action. . . . Scholarship is
> developing new possibilities of scientific approach as a means of
> verifying hypotheses and of introducing greater precision of
> thought and treatment.[3]

A third new avenue of inquiry used a social psychological approach in studying modern media. The most comprehensive of these early attempts was the Payne Fund study of the effects of motion pictures on children and adolescents. Under the direction of W. W. Charters, the Payne Fund sponsored a series of twelve coordinated studies performed in the early 1930s. In his *Motion Pictures and Youth* (1934), Charters summarized the significant findings of the studies and laid out the overall design in terms of a rather mechanistic formula: general influence × content × attendance = total influence. "If, in short, the general influence of motion pictures is ascertained, if the content is known and the number of visits of children has been computed, the total influence of the picture will be in general a product of these three factors." Each study, published separately, tackled one part of the equation: attendance, content of films, retention of information, effects upon sleep and health, relationship to juvenile delinquency, emotional effects, and so forth. The studies employed four basic research techniques: physiological experiments such as the testing of effects on sleep and health; written tests measuring attitudes and beliefs; rating scales comparing film content with accepted moral standards of the larger society; interviews and movie "autobiographies" to determine film impact on conduct.

The studies all pointed to the importance of individual differences in assessing the effects of movies: differences in social and economic background, education, home life, neighborhood, sex, and age. Nevertheless, several positive correlations were identified; the most noteworthy of these linked frequent movie attendance with truancy, delinquency, and general antisocial conduct. In all but one of the studies, Charters reported, the influence of motion pictures is "clearly apparent as cause or effect or as an aggravation of precedent conditions." In the most controversial of the studies, *Movies and Conduct* (1934), sociologist Herbert Blumer collected and analyzed movie "autobiographies" written by children. He concluded that films effectively operated through "emotional possession" of the young fan, getting "such a strong grip on him that even his effort to rid himself of it by reasoning with himself may prove of little avail." All of the researchers were careful to note the complexity of the situation and the difficulty of singling out movies from other cultural influences. Still, through popularization and selective quotation in books and articles, the Payne Fund studies provided ammunition for vigorous attacks on movies and the movie industry. The political wrangling over how to interpret the Payne Fund studies eventually overshadowed the actual findings themselves.[4]

The fourth and perhaps most important relevant field was marketing research. In the early twentieth century, publishers, advertisers, and manufacturers had begun to make surveys of consumers to analyze buying habits and the effectiveness of advertising. By the 1920s independent market surveying organizations had taken over a large part of the task, contracting their services to whomever was willing to pay. Market research did much to refine sampling techniques, and by the 1930s these methods were used widely in polling political preferences as well as those of consumers.

The growth of commercial radio broadcasting greatly accelerated the advance of marketing research. Unlike newspapers or magazines, radio reached an unseen mass audience that was unmeasurable in terms of periodical circulation. It somehow had to prove its worth to advertisers. Marketing techniques were extensively utilized in gathering the basic demographics of the mushrooming radio audience: who listened, when, what did they buy. Program ratings, based on scientific samplings by telephone surveys and later by A. C. Nielsen's "audimeter" (directly attached to the set), increasingly dictated advertising rates and program content itself. Nielsen himself began his career as a market researcher for food and drug retailers. Subscriptions from networks, broadcast advertisers, individual stations, ad agencies, and talent firms supported the various rating services.[5]

Each of these four empirically oriented fields—propaganda analysis, public opinion analysis, social psychology, and marketing research—brought a different perspective to bear on their common denominator. The "agencies of mass impression," as they were termed by the 1933 President's Research Committee on Recent Social Trends, were "those through which large numbers of individuals may simultaneously receive the same communication and be correspondingly influenced."[6] Newspapers and periodicals, motion pictures, and radio broadcasting were all mass media in this sense, although that particular term did not gain widespread use until the 1940s.

By the late 1930s, social scientists increasingly viewed this common denominator as a subject matter around which a new research field ought to be organized. The idea of communications research as a unified area of study attracted them for several reasons. It offered an excellent opportunity for empirically studying questions of behavioral and attitudinal change in new settings. Ample funding sources and a large volume of easily quantifiable data were readily available from the media industries themselves. In addition, the relations of media to public policy became a pressing research task as well, particularly with the impending war crisis.

The joining of the needs of behavioral science and private policy makers was most effectively accomplished in the substantial work of Paul F. Lazarsfeld, a Viennese psychologist who resettled in the United States in 1935. Five years later, the relationship between public policy and the behavioral approach to communications research was spelled out by a group of social scientists in an influential memorandum on "Research in Mass Communication." An examination of Lazarsfeld's early career and the 1940 memo reveals precisely how communications research coalesced and how the behavioral model triumphed as a guide for the new discipline.

★

One of the central figures in twentieth-century social science, particularly in the growth of empirical social research, Paul F. Lazarsfeld was an Austrian Jew born in Vienna in 1901. He took a doctorate in applied mathematics at the University of Vienna, and he began teaching psychology and statistics there in 1925. In 1927 Lazarsfeld organized an affiliated research institute that was designed to apply psychological research to social and economic problems. Over the next few years he directed a wide variety of studies on such topics as the occupational choices of youth, life in a village decimated by unemployment, analyses of local voting patterns, and marketing surveys. Early in his career Lazarsfeld had defined his own special interest largely in terms of methodological goals—the combining of statistical analysis with descriptions of entire choice processes. This methodological thread tied together the plethora of subjects examined at the Vienna Research Institute.[7]

Yet Lazarsfeld also saw himself as working within a European humanistic tradition, the analysis of "action" (*Handlung*). This approach was particularly strong among his mentors in the psychology department at the University of Vienna. It proposed to organize psychology around the study of action, namely, how people make choices between available alternatives. It differed from contemporary radical behaviorism in that it required some reference to individual consciousness in the explanation of why people act the way they do. In Europe, three research emphases developed within the study of action. One sought to identify the broad set of goals or motivations present at the start of any act. A second focused on the specific intentions emerging from these goals and on the ways in which they were successfully transformed. Finally, there was the study of the various influences that seemed to push an act forward to its final consummation.[8]

By the early 1930s Lazarsfeld increasingly directed his own work and that of the research institute toward marketing studies. He had two motives. Market research provided much-needed sources of income for his struggling institute. Furthermore, in market research and its study of "the action of a purchase" Lazarsfeld saw a great opportunity to pursue his methodological interests within a framework of the *Handlung* tradition of psychology.

In his early and widely read publications concerning market research, Lazarsfeld had two audiences in mind. To businessmen and
marketing analysts he sought to demonstrate that the "psychological analysis of action is the master technique in market research." It
offered the most rational strategy, he argued, for improving the
knowledge needed to forecast and control consumer behavior. By
plotting the "psychological coordinates of a purchase" and by identifying the development of the motives, situations, and influences
surrounding buying, Lazarsfeld carefully schematized the act of
purchasing in diagrams and charts. The master technique, which
provided a systematic view of how market behavior is motivated
and how buying decisions are arrived at, constituted "a valuable aid
in finding one's way around midst the thousand and one questions of
specific procedures and interpretations in market research." To psychologists, his second audience, Lazarsfeld touted the raw material
of market surveys as a fertile field of data for the development of
theoretical constructs. Market research could be used to illuminate
the subtleties of psychological processes, particularly in the area of
motivation.[9]

Lazarsfeld first traveled to America in 1933 as a European Rockefeller fellow. For two years he toured the United States, busily establishing contacts in the marketing world, among academic psychologists and sociologists, and with the earliest political pollsters. His
primary aim was to get American research organizations and business firms to subsidize the research institute in Vienna, to which he
planned a return. But by 1935 the deteriorating political situation
in his native Austria forced Lazarsfeld to resettle in America. After
a brief attempt to recreate his research institute at the University of
Newark, Lazarsfeld was appointed in 1937 to head the newly created Princeton Office of Radio Research, which was funded by the
Rockefeller Foundation. By 1939 Lazarsfeld and the project moved
to Columbia; there he became a professor of sociology and turned
the radio project into the Bureau of Applied Social Research.

Lazarsfeld's early years in America involved a good deal of im-
provisation and job shuttling. But his reputation and experience as
a managerial scholar, one who was able to coordinate and adminis-
trate numerous studies in a research bureau, helped him make a
relatively smooth transition compared with that of many other
émigré scholars. In his memoir Lazarsfeld described what he
thought his chief contribution had been: "the expansion of social
research institutes in American universities and the development of
a research style which prevails in many of them." The empirical

study of action required a staff of collaborators trained to collect and analyze data wherever a research opportunity offered itself. Lazarsfeld essentially invented the Newark Research Center in 1935 because, as he wrote a colleague, "I wanted to direct a rather great variety of studies, so that I was sure from year to year my methodological experience could increase—and that is, as you know, my main interest in research." When offered the directorship of the pioneering Princeton Office of Radio Research in 1937, he jumped at the chance because "radio is a topic around which actually any kind of research method can be tried out and can be applied satisfactorily." Lazarsfeld thus brought his methodological concerns and the research institute structure to bear on the first comprehensive studies of radio in America. More than anyone else, he shaped the field of communications research in the next decade.[10]

The aim of the radio project was left purposely vague by the Rockefeller Foundation: to study the effect of radio on society. The two associate directors of the project, psychologist Hadley Cantril and CBS researcher Frank Stanton (later network president), singled out a series of more specific problems to concentrate on: the role of radio in the lives of different types of listeners, the psychological value of radio, and the various reasons why people liked it. Their original plan called largely for laboratory experiments of the kind performed in Cantril's and Gordon Allport's *The Psychology of Radio* (1935).[11] But once Lazarsfeld took over, he turned the project into a much broader sort of enterprise. Over the next few years he directed scores of studies that analyzed radio content and the demographics of the radio audience. He relied mainly on program ratings, polling surveys, and network research departments for data; but he used them not merely to compare the drawing power of shows, but also to examine social differences among listeners and to correlate tastes with social stratification. Comparative studies of radio and print audiences moved Lazarsfeld toward the concept of a general science of communications research. A large number of commercial contracts with networks, publishers, and marketing firms supplied the project with supplemental funding and important sources of data.

The Princeton radio project produced several key summary publications. These were designed to convince the Rockefeller Foundation that the project had some direction amidst the myriad of studies it was churning out. In early 1939 Lazarsfeld edited a special issue of the *Journal of Applied Psychology*, which pulled together a number of radio studies done by the project. As in his earlier writings on psychology and marketing, Lazarsfeld addressed two audiences. One comprised those who wished to increase the effectiveness of radio: advertisers, educators, entertainers, molders of public opinion. They all faced, he thought, a standard set of problems: how to get their message across the air and accepted by the audience. And psychologists, in order to get their full share of the new research, would have to show that their inventory of indexes, questionnaires, tests, and experimental setups were useful to those who wanted to use radio more effectively.

Lazarsfeld's own concern with methodological questions remained paramount; radio research might provide the crucial link among various subjects: "We should not be surprised if a discipline of 'action research' should evolve one day, bringing out more clearly the great methodological similarity of many studies which now are not connected because they are done under different headings, such as criminology, market research, or accident prevention." The short studies included in the special issue dealt mainly with creating measurement devices. "Index Problems," for example, examined the composition of indexes of "radio mindedness" and the charting of attitudes toward popular songs and advertising; "Program Research" offered ways of measuring the efficacy of advertising; "Questionnaire Techniques" treated the construction of viable questionnaires.[12]

A second special issue of the journal, appearing in late 1940, was organized around similar lines. "Radio," Lazarsfeld wrote, "has now made the whole nation an experimental situation. A rather centrally controlled industry provides a variety of stimuli, the reactions to which can be studied and compared in all groups of the population." Furthermore, Lazarsfeld argued, the profusion of radio studies in the past few years touched on areas other than broadcasting. "Radio research will not long remain isolated, but will merge into the larger strain of communications research . . . a trend toward fusion of funds and research institutions will occur. . . . The applied psychologist is the natural coordinator of these efforts with competitive commercial purposes but allied scientific aims."[13]

Lazarsfeld's *Radio and the Printed Page* (1940), based on studies done by the radio project, marked a key step toward the consolidation of the field. Breaking down the radio audience by demographic, income, and educational categories, the book compared the listening and reading audiences. Lower-income strata of the population were seldom reached by either the printed page or the so-called serious or educational broadcasts. Radio disseminated information to the broad masses, but not via educational programs. Reliance on radio over print for news correlated directly with lower educational and income levels. In the final chapter Lazarsfeld offered some larger generalizations on the social consequences of radio, noting that "you have the picture of radio as a stupendous technical advance with a strongly conservative tendency in all social matters." Generally, radio avoided depressing material that might call for social criticism, catered to the prejudices of its audience to prevent alienation, and steered clear of controversy and specialized program fare. "Broadcasting in America," Lazarsfeld reminded the reader, "is done to sell merchandise; and most of the other possible effects of radio become submerged in a strange kind of social mechanism which brings the commercial effect to its strongest expression."[14]

The commercial needs of modern media, and of the radio industry in particular, encouraged the trend toward a unified field of communications research. The demands of public policy significantly reinforced this tendency. Because of the impending international crisis, an understanding of the relationship of modern communications to society was critical for achieving political consensus. Toward this end, a diverse group of scholars, meeting under the auspices of the Rockefeller Foundation, produced a lengthy memorandum outlining the case for "Research in Mass Communication." Written in 1940, the document was meant for private circulation only, but it is historically significant as a review of the "state of the art"and as an accurate forecast of the developments in the field.[15]

If America was to adapt to a changing world, that adaptation could be achieved only with public consent. To secure that consent, the memo argued, would require an unprecedented knowledge of the public mind and of how it could be influenced in relation to public affairs. Research measuring what effects mass communications have or can have would have particular relevance to public policy. "Techniques for the study of communication have long since been developed and applied in the fields of market research, advertising, propaganda, publicity, and public relations. Studies using these techniques produce facts of great importance for *private* policy. The techniques themselves are transferable and should be used to support *public* policy."

The memorandum reduced the subject of communications research to a paradigm of four interrogative categories: who, said what, to whom, and with what effect. The last of these categories seemed most crucial: "With what psychological effect brief in span or lasting in its influence? With what effect in individual behavior, or . . . effects that manifest themselves in changed ways of living or even in the institutions of society?" In 1940 there was a need for specific studies that attempted to answer these questions in respect to given communications or a series of them; these answers would "have a practical utility in the use of mass communication and in their wise control in the public interest."

The five major techniques available for research were those that had already been applied successfully in other areas, especially that of market research. These included the poll, or short interview; the panel, or repeated interviewing of the same respondents over time; the intensive interview; community studies; and systematic content analysis. After elucidating each of these research procedures, the memorandum called for a national institute for research in communication, an organization that would provide for "the planning, direction, and supervision of research, and for the coordination of any single project with other related projects."[16]

Such a thorough integration of research in mass communication was never realized, even during wartime. But the four questions scheme—who says what to whom with what effect—became the dominant paradigm defining the scope and problems of American communications research. The behavioral science of communication became restricted to a rather narrow model that explained communication as essentially a process of persuasion. The omission of "why" from the series of questions reflected an unwillingness to investigate issues concerning which social groups controlled the messages communicated through the media. The emphasis on practical applications of communications research to policy problems made such issues somewhat irrelevant. A basic acceptance of the organization and commercial basis of the American media was an obvious given for most researchers working in this tradition. For those who criticized how the media were structured, the problematic "why" would have to be addressed. Indeed, the neglect of the "why" factor eventually led to an abandonment of the dominant research model by a small but vocal minority.

Nevertheless, throughout the war and into the postwar era, the four questions model was the most influential guide to communications research. Content analysis of the media (what) and research into audience structure and interests (to whom) continued to become more sophisticated and to link more closely private and public policy decisions. The war caused intense concern about the persuasive powers of the mass media, their potential for directly altering opinions, attitudes, and behavior. This was the essence of the effects aspect of the paradigm, and it continued to be the central question in the field during the postwar era. By 1960, American social scientists reached a theoretical consensus, based on the empirical work of the preceding generation, on how the "effects" of mass communication operated in American society.

★

World War II brought a sense of urgency that resulted in the pump priming of federal funding for empirical research on the mass media. In the broad mobilization of public opinion to support the war effort, modern communication, which now included the mature film and broadcasting industries, was a far more ubiquitous and insistent presence in American life than it had been in 1917. In the push to further understand how modern media affected social and political life, the war effort effectively dissolved any remaining institutional barriers to research in universities, marketing and polling firms, and the media themselves. Indeed, the government itself became a major center of communications research. Many of the resulting content analyses and audience studies concerned specifically war-related problems, such as the nature and performance of German propaganda, the British communications system in wartime, and the means by which the U.S. Office of War Information bolstered civilian morale. Other studies suggested ways of making commercial media fare—radio daytime serials, for example—more relevant to the military struggle.[17]

Content analyses and audience studies progressed in nonmilitary contexts as well. Empirical research continued to perfect the description of the audience in its social setting; it mapped out key features of behavior and attitudes as they related to income, sex, age, and occupation. A new general approach to audience research emerged in these years, namely, the examination of the "uses and gratifications" of media content. This involved analyzing the consumption of media content as it was subjectively interpreted by audience members. This type of analysis utilized intensive interviews to supplement more general questionnaires.

The close relationship between university-based empirical research and the policy needs of the media industries grew even stronger during the 1940s. For example, NBC reexamined its morning program schedule in 1944 in order to determine how a modified program policy might attract a larger audience. The Bureau of Applied Social Research (BASR) performed a series of studies designed to develop "listener typologies." Classifying different listener types by distinguishing psychological characteristics, the NBC-BASR study identified what gratifications listeners derived from their various listening patterns. The study concluded with a list of conditions upon which program policy modifications could be most successfully made.[18]

Concentration on the persuasive effects of mass media yielded perhaps the key legacy of the war effort. The major new research strategy that emerged in this work was the so-called experimental approach. A group of studies testing the effects of army orientation films—the "Why We Fight" series—created rigorously controlled laboratory procedures quite different from the survey and field techniques prevailing in the prewar years. Conducted by the War Department's Information and Education Division, this research was restricted to the analysis of the effects of the films on their audience. "The principal criteria of 'effectiveness' used in evaluating these films were whether they succeeded in imparting information, in changing opinions in the direction of the interpretations presented, and in increasing men's motivation to serve." Researchers found that these films had marked effects on the men's knowledge of factual material concerning the events leading up to the war. Opinion changes, however, were less frequent and generally less marked than changes in factual knowledge. Finally, the films had no effect on items prepared to measure motivation for service as soldiers, and increased motivation was the ultimate objective of the orientation program.[19]

Experimental investigations begun during the war spawned a whole new direction in empirical research, one that emphasized the isolation of basic psychological variables determining the effects of persuasive communication. In contrast to applied research, experimental researchers sought to develop "scientific propositions which specify the conditions under which the effectiveness of one or another type of persuasive communication is increased or decreased." This conscious separation of basic from applied research reflected the larger concern of experimental psychologists, whose goal was a better theoretical understanding of the higher mental processes. "Such research, involving psychological experiments in a communication setting, can contribute to our understanding of the processes of memory, thought, motivation, and social influence.[20]

In the experimental approach, the study of media effects became wrenched from the social context of everyday life. Yet new survey techniques for studying the problem of media and persuasion in more naturalistic settings appeared at the same time. Rather than exploring the psychological process of persuasion in a controlled experimental situation, the refined survey approach revealed the complexities of the persuasion process as it operated in society. The first breakthrough along these lines was Paul L. Lazarsfeld, Bernard Berelson, and Hazel Gaudet's *The People's Choice* (1944). Basing their research on repeated interviews with a group of six hundred respondents, the authors hoped to discover precisely how mass media influenced political attitudes in a presidential campaign. However, when questioned about exposure to campaign communications, panel members mentioned small political discussions more frequently than radio or print. These unexpected responses led the researchers to construct the classic "two-step flow" model of communication effects.

The study revealed that personal relationships were potentially more influential in moving people to their decisions, particularly for those who changed their position during the campaign or made up their minds late. Influence and information "often flow from the radio and print to the opinion leaders and from these to the less active sections of the population." These results proved quite surprising because the design of the study, guided by the picture of an atomized and fragmented mass audience, did not anticipate the power of personal influence. In the postwar years, the two-step flow hypothesis inspired a succession of studies that examined small group mediation between mass and individual communication.[21]

The most comprehensive and significant of these was Elihu Katz and Paul F. Lazarsfeld's *Personal Influence* (1955). Part I offered a theoretical review of a new direction in the study of mass media effects: "The traditional image of the mass persuasion process must make room for 'people' as intervening factors between the stimuli of the media and the resultant opinions, decisions, and actions." The authors held that knowledge of interpersonal relations ("sociometric connections") among people in groups was the new frontier for a basic understanding of media effects. Part II presented the results of studies concerning the flow of personal influence in the daily lives of eight hundred women from Decatur, Illinois.

Significantly, the authors originally formulated their research design in answer to a marketing survey request by a national news magazine. It included examinations of household marketing habits, fashion tastes in dresses and cosmetics, attendance at movies, and the formation of opinions in local political affairs. The study identified opinion leaders in these areas; these individuals were cross-indexed according to gregariousness, place in life cycle, and social status. The Decatur study highlighted statistical refinement in its effort to trace the "flow of influence" and to compare the relative authority of mass media and people on decision making. The implications for communications research and theory, argued Katz and Lazarsfeld, were clear. Respondents must be studied in the group context, for "knowledge of an individual's interpersonal environment is basic to an understanding of his exposure and reaction to the mass media."[22]

The new stress on personal influence in understanding media effects constituted a rediscovery of the primary group concept originated by Charles Horton Cooley. The recovery of this tradition took place in the context of several other social scientific research projects begun in the 1930s. The Hawthorne studies of factory workers were the most famous of these.[23] In communications research, the role ascribed to interpersonal relations as a critical buffer between the mass media and their audiences recalled Cooley's insistence on the primacy of face-to-face relationships in all social processes. In fact, it challenged the very concept of the mass audience itself. In an important review of communications research and the concept of the "mass" done in 1953, Eliot Friedson argued that media use should not be regarded as purely individual and unstructured behavior; it was usually a group activity involving family, friends, and the local community. He used audience research data to show that selection of media content is governed largely by social habit and that most attendance occurred in groups. The mass media, Friedson asserted, are typically "absorbed into the pattern of local life, becoming only some of a number of focal points around which leisure activities have been organized by the members of the group."[24]

Beyond the question of mass audience, the accumulated evidence of empirical communications research played a central role in the larger postwar debate over the nature and reality of mass society. Critics of the so-called theory of mass society placed behind their argument the weight of both the survey and experimental traditions in communications research. A thorough discussion of the mass society controversy cannot be undertaken here, but it is important to note that the whole notion of a theory of mass society was something of an artificial and spurious construct, an intellectual straw man created by its opponents.

Leon Bramson, a sociologist who critically traced the history and influence of mass society theory in American and European social thought, revealed this, perhaps unwittingly, when he described the "typical" theorist of mass society: "The blend of romanticism, existentialism, Marxism, and psychoanalysis which forms the basis of his world perspective give him a certain shadowy picture." Bramson and other critics, such as Edward Shils and Daniel Bell, lumped together an extraordinarily diverse group of thinkers as mass society theorists: Jose Ortega y Gassett, Karl Mannheim, C. Wright Mills, Hannah Arendt, Erich Fromm, Herbert Marcuse, Wilhelm Reich, and Dwight McDonald, to mention only a few. What united these theorists, according to Bramson, was "their preference for a hierarchically ordered society; their hostility to individualist liberalism; stress on the costs of social mobility, and on the infiltration of the cultural minorities; and the extra-scientific character of some of their judgements." In *The Political Context of Sociology* (1961), Bramson took the mass society theorists to task for something most of them certainly would have denied: "My quarrel is with their contention that their theory is the result of a purely scientific analysis, with their presumed scientific judgement of the relation between mass society and totalitarianism, and by implication, of the results of industrialization and democratization."[25]

Having created an artificially monolithic theory of mass society, Bramson and other critics offered the findings of the empirical tradition of American communications research as the "scientific" evidence to disprove it. The key fact emerging from the empirical tradition, argued Bramson, was "a rejection of the image of the isolated, anonymous, detached individual-in-the-mass, in favor of an individual who receives the messages of the mass media within a social context."

In their lengthy article "America, Mass Society, and Mass Media" (1960), Raymond and Alice Bauer elaborated this theme too, suggesting that several major premises of the theory of mass society had been challenged by the results of communications research: that modern mass society resulted in a breakdown of primary groups, thus minimizing the influence of informal communication compared to mass media; that the audience for mass media was atomized, isolated, anonymous, and detached; that the mass media themselves were omnipotent, capable of manipulating the attitudes and behavior of the isolated individuals in the mass. In fact, the Bauers asserted, despite "a plethora of intriguing titles, speculative generalizations, and an excellent body of laboratory research, there is little empirical evidence of the effect of mass media in American society as a whole." They concluded:

> Up to this point there is a vast amount of data indicating that personal characteristics influence communications exposure, but little if any firm data indicating that mass communications,

under field conditions, influence personal characteristics. Considering the state of our present knowledge, the reasonable conclusion to reach in any given instance (in the absence of specific information to the contrary) is that any correlation between communications behavior and the personal characteristics of the people involved is a result of selective exposure, rather than evidence for the effects of communications.[26]

By 1960 the urge to present a theoretically coherent set of propositions on media effects found its most comprehensive and authoritative expression in Joseph T. Klapper's *Effects of Mass Communication*. Klapper offered a series of "emerging generalizations" that were based on an exhaustive review of empirical research dealing with the measurable effects on individuals. The most important of these proposed the following: "(1) Mass communication *ordinarily* does not serve as a necessary and sufficient cause of audience effects, but rather functions among and through a nexus of mediating factors and influences; (2) these mediating factors are such that they typically render mass communication a contributory agent, but not the sole cause, in the process of reinforcing the existing conditions." Klapper advocated a new orientation for communications research, the "phenomenistic approach": "It is in essence a shift away from the tendency to regard mass communication as a necessary and sufficient cause of audience effects toward a view of the media as influences, working amid other influences, in a total situation."[27]

The "still distant goal of empirically documented theory," Klapper argued, could be reached only by continuing research that took into account the roles of the many influences involved in any communication situation. This was a theme echoed by all those who viewed communications research as a slowly maturing behavioral science. Only by raising the scientific standards of research to greater heights of precision and rigor could social scientists elucidate cause-and-effect sequences in communication. "The job of the 'science of communication,'" argued the Bauers, "is to identify the crucial variables in the communication process and determine the patterns of interaction of each on the other."[28]

Numerous intricate and even elegant multivariate models of the communications process have flourished since 1960, all with the aim of guiding communications research toward becoming a "true" behavioral science. The socialization model, functional analysis, mass media and social systems, and the uses and gratifications approach represent only a few of these.[29] The enormous growth of television has provided a whole new source of data and encouraged more elaborate research procedures. But the newer research seeking to measure the effects of television on human behavior has restated and reformulated many of the traditional concerns: effects of crime and violence, effects on children, audience passivity and escape, and demographic variables in audience gratification.[30]

The casting of communications research as a behavioral science—a science aimed at establishing laws of human behavior in society in accordance with empirical findings—remains a potent force today, as evidenced by the multitude of studies being carried on in this tradition. But by the late 1940s, important dissenters began to emerge on the American intellectual scene. Their critiques of the behavioral approach, both implicit and explicit, offered alternatives and substantial correctives to the scientific pretensions of the mainstream.

★

When film analysis split off as a self-consciously independent field of study, it implicitly challenged the methods and aims of the behavioral approach to communications research. It set movies apart from the content of the other forms of mass communication, investing in them an artistic integrity that demanded creation of a critical language. But the ruling metaphors of that language were still linked closely to showing how films reflected the society that produced them. Rather than quantitatively measuring the effects of films on audience behavior, postwar studies sought to explain how movies revealed deep and persistent patterns in the collective unconscious of a society or historical era. The most influential of these drew heavily upon psychoanalysis and cultural anthropology for their critical tools.

Siegfried Kracauer's psychological history of German film, *From Caligari to Hitler* (1947), served as the prototype for this type of study. Kracauer, a German émigré, contended that analysis of German films exposed "deep psychological dispositions predominant in Germany from 1918 to 1935" and yielded valuable clues to how Hitler was able to assume power. He argued that the films of a nation revealed its mental life in a more direct way than other media, for two reasons: they were collective productions and they addressed themselves and appealed to the anonymous multitudes.

"What films reflect are not so much explicit credos as psychological dispositions—those deep layers of collective mentality which extend more or less below the dimension of consciousness. . . . What counts is not so much the statistically measurable popularity of films as the popularity of their pictorial and narrative motifs. Persistent reiteration of these motifs mark them as outward projections of inner urges." Kracauer claimed not to be putting national character above history, but to be tracing "the psychological pattern of a people at a particular time." However, his book often slipped into grand claims connecting traits shown on the screen to the struggle within "the German collective soul"; the central conflict mirrored in movies was the urge to chaos versus the urge to authority. Despite these extravagances, Kracauer's work was redeemed by some extremely acute aesthetic analyses of individual German films and by his interpretation of thematic developments over time. Kracauer also made valuable studies of Nazi propaganda films made during the war.[31]

In the best work of those who followed in this tradition, the larger claims for film revelation were toned down. Barbara Deming, wartime film curator for the Library of Congress, was strongly influenced by Kracauer and applied his method to American films of the 1940s. "It is not as mirrors reflect us but, rather, as our dreams do, that movies most truly reveal the times," argued Deming. She proposed deciphering "the dream that all of us have been buying at the box office, to cut through to the real nature of the identification we have experienced there." *Running Away From Myself* (1950) drew a collective dream portrait that focused on the common plight of film heroes of the forties. To Deming these heroes represented variations on a deep crisis in faith that reflected popular anxieties of the period. "The hero who sees nothing to fight for; the hero who despairs of making a life for himself; the hero who achieves success but finds it empty; and the malcontent who breaks with the old life, only to find himself nowhere—each mourns a vision of happiness that eludes him." These obsessive dream patterns—nightmares, really—were identified in both wartime and peacetime movies of the decade.[32]

Martha Wolfenstein and Nathan Leites's *Movies: A Psychological Study* (1950) advanced perhaps the most expressly psychoanalytic approach to film studies. They analyzed manifest and latent dream content to obtain hints of deeply lying, less articulate aspirations, fears, and wishes. "The common day dreams of a culture are in part the sources, in part the products of its popular myths, stories, plays, and films." The authors looked at "contemporary American films to see . . . the recurrent day dreams which enter into the consciousness of millions of movie goers." Their cross-cultural comparison of the treatment of certain major relationships—between lovers, parents and children, and killers and victims—embraced British, French, and American films.

The major plot configurations in American movies, they concluded, underlined the importance of winning against external hazards. The psychological projection and denial of false appearances framed the forbidden fantasies that characterized American films. "In a false appearance the heroine is promiscuous, the hero is a murderer, the young couple carry on an illicit affair, two men friends share the favors of a woman. This device makes it possible for us to eat our cake and have it, since we can enjoy the suggested wish-fulfillments without empathic guilt; we know that the characters with whom we identify have not done anything." The underlying premise of American films, Wolfenstein and Leites argued, is that one need not feel guilty for mere wishes. Heroes emerge from the shadow of false appearances; all that really changes is other people's perception of them.[33]

While the postwar maturing of film studies represented an implied critique of the dominant communications research model, other more explicit questionings found expression during these years. Doubts regarding the limits of empirical research were rarely voiced by American social scientists, but two prominent exceptions were Robert Lynd and C. Wright Mills. Lynd, one of the cosigners of the 1940 memorandum on "Research in Mass Communication," defended empiricism in the social sciences at the same time that he warned of its seductive quality. His description, in 1939, of the dangers of unchecked empiricism was particularly prophetic for communication studies: "To carry it on one usually places oneself inside the going system, accepts temporarily its values and goals, and sets to work at gathering data and charting trends. . . . Time is long, the data are never all in, the situation is changing, and, as the 'objective' analyst finds more in the situation to record, he tends to be drawn deeper within the net of assumptions by which the institution he is studying professes to operate." Lynn held that the close empirical description of how things work or change, with accentuation on increased statistical refinement, often saves us "from having to ask troublesome questions: 'Where are our institutions taking us, and where do we want them to take us?'"[34]

In the same spirit, C. Wright Mills tried to take a step back from the prevailing methods of inquiry in sociology. He found ominous the modern shift from public to client in the social scientist's primary audience. A concomitant problem was the "bureaucratization of reflection," with research institutes threatening the intellectual place of the independent, critically minded social scientist. Significantly, Mills focused on Paul Lazarsfeld's work in his critique of "abstracted empiricism" as a research style. Mills disputed Lazarsfeld's conception of the sociologist's role as the methodologist, "the toolmaker," for all of the social sciences. In Lazarsfeld's view, the sociologist converted unorganized, individual social philosophers and observers into organized teams of full-fledged, empirical social scientists, who applied scientific procedures to new areas of research. But there was, in truth, no principle or theory that guided the selection of the subjects of these studies. "It is merely assumed," wrote Mills, "that if only The Method is used, such studies as result—scattered from Elmira to Zagreb to Shanghai—will add up finally to a 'full-fledged, organized' science of man and society. The practice, in the meantime, is to get on with the next study."

The range of social science was severely limited by confining the term *empirical* to mean abstracted, statistical information about a series of contemporary individuals. "Those in the grip of the methodological inhibition," Mills observed, "often refuse to say anything about modern society unless it has been through the fine little mill of the Statistical Ritual. . . . Much of such work, I am now convinced, has become the mere following of a ritual—which happens to have gained commercial and foundation value—rather than, in the words of its spokesman, 'a commitment to the hard demands of science.'"[35]

But the most developed critique of the empirical approach issued from the Frankfurt Institute of Social Research during its years of exile in America. This critique was an extension of the "critical theory" evolved by the Frankfurt group in the 1930s, and it was applied to the analysis of American mass culture in the 1940s and 1950s. The key figures here were Max Horkheimer, T. W. Adorno, and Leo Lowenthal. They subordinated questions about the impact of mass media as defined by the empirical tradition—issues of persuasive effects—to broader problems of consciousness: namely, issues of cultural value.

Critical theory insisted that the social totality must be taken into account in any analysis of one of its aspects. Otherwise, the result would be a distorted overemphasis of one facet of the whole, a "fetishization" in Marxist terms. Social research must interpret the present not only historically, but in terms of future potential as well. The separation of "is" and "ought," ostensibly characteristic of "value-free" bourgeois social science, was rejected by the Frankfurt institute. Critical theory did not seek truth for its own sake, but tried to bring about social change instead.

Although they advocated a holistic approach to social research, the Frankfurt theorists at the same time cautioned against a premature synthesis of contradictions. Hegelian "identity theory" had celebrated the unity of subject and object, but as the political events of their native Germany had grimly demonstrated, subject and object were still nonidentical. The Frankfurt thinkers feared that the historical moment for proletarian revolution had passed without being seized. They thus stressed the preservation of "negations," the critical social and cultural forces that managed to survive the dominant political order. The social totality was a dialectical one that included affirmative, status quo-oriented elements and their disharmonious, potentially subversive contraries. By the 1940s the Frankfurt group increasingly insisted upon the need for protecting those critical elements resisting the "affirmative culture"—the individual philosopher, the preservation of theory, and, crucially, the traditions of art and "high culture" threatened by the flood of mass culture.[36]

From the Frankfurt point of view, traditional empirical research into mass communication and mass culture was inadequate on two levels. First, it did not frame studies with the social totality in view. Second, its reduction of cultural questions to empirically verifiable categories was entirely inappropriate. Leo Lowenthal, pondering the historical perspectives of popular culture, outlined the dissatisfaction with the alleged objectivity of communications research. "Empirical social science has become a kind of applied asceticism. It stands clear of entanglements with foreign powers and thrives in an atmosphere of rigidly enforced neutrality. It refuses to enter the sphere of meaning. . . . Social research takes the phenomena of modern life, including mass media, at face value. It rejects the task of placing them in an historical and moral context."

Lowenthal asserted that the standard categories of effects, content analysis, and audience stratification derived largely from market research, "an instrument of expedient manipulation." Empirical communications research labored under the false hypothesis that the consumer's choice is the decisive social phenomenon from which one should begin further analysis. Critical research began from a different premise, Lowenthal noted. "We first ask: What are the functions of cultural communication within the total process of a society? Then we ask such specific questions as these: What passes the censorship of the socially powerful agencies? How are things produced under the dicta of formal and informal censorship?" In short, these were the sort of questions ignored by the behavioral model.[37]

T. W. Adorno's unhappy tenure with Lazarsfeld's Office of Radio Research illustrated concretely the methodological clash described by Lowenthal. In a series of papers done for the radio project in the 1930s, Adorno tried to explore such qualitative issues as the "false harmony" of much contemporary music, the perversion of symphonic music on the radio, and the aesthetic bankruptcy of American popular music. In seeking insights into the relationship between music, radio, and society, he found his ideas untranslatable into testable hypotheses. Adorno resisted the pressure to transform cultural phenomena into quantitative data. In considering such issues as the psychological regression of hearing and the fetishization of certain classical performers and works, it seemed to Adorno thoroughly misguided "to proceed from the subject's reactions as if they were a primary and final source of sociological knowledge." He later recalled, "When I was confronted with the demands to 'measure culture,' I reflected that culture might be precisely that condition that excludes a mentality capable of measuring it. . . . The task of translating my reflections into research terms was equivalent to squaring the circle."[38]

The Frankfurt influence could be detected in the vigorous postwar debate over the implications of mass culture, most notably in the work of David Riesman and Dwight Macdonald. But it is important to remember that the bulk of the exiles' work in this area remained untranslated into English until the 1960s. Horkheimer and Adorno's essay, "The Culture Industry" (1944), their most complete statement, was among these. Here one finds their most unrelenting attack on how modern media have become technological instruments extending political and economic domination to the cultural sphere, debasing art and regimenting individual consciousness. Lurking beneath their critique was the unstated certainty that the rise of modern mass culture was an effective stalking horse for fascism itself.[39]

It was through explicit linking of the cultural sphere to the realms of industry and politics that critical theory made its greatest impact upon the mass culture controversy in America. But the Frankfurt theorists' overwhelmingly pessimistic evaluation of mass culture and mass media was not without its own special irony, because in this case theirs was a decidedly undialectical point of view. They placed art and mass culture at opposite poles: one was the inspired product of autonomous individuals, a last refuge of civilization; the other was a phony, reified product administered from above for the purpose of domination. They left no room for any interplay between the authentic desires and utopian impulses of the masses and their expression in the content and use of the mass media. This was not merely undialectical, it ignored a great portion of American twentieth-century cultural history as well. Nonetheless, their understanding of media effects in the broadest possible terms of politics, culture, and consciousness (rediscovered and revived during the 1960s) provided a valuable theoretical alternative to the reigning empirical approach.

Research into the effects of mass media continues to thrive today. But the future of communications research as a unified behavioral science seems much more limited than originally envisioned by its pioneers. Perhaps it makes sense to speak of communications research as a science of "administrative research," as Paul Lazarsfeld referred to it in 1941. Lazarsfeld suggested that such research be "carried through in the service of some kind of administrative agency of public or private character."[40] As a subordinate to marketing and advertising, communications research indeed has reached a high level of precision and predictive power. As a result, it holds a central position within the decision-making processes of the media themselves, particularly broadcasting. But this science is surely inadequate for confronting the realms of value and meaning. Communication, even with the technological sophistication of modern media, remains a human activity—sensuous, infinitely varied, often ambiguous, stubbornly resistant to the kinds of laws found in the physical sciences.

This inadequacy becomes evident during attempts to inject "scientific findings" into the continuing debates over public policy for the media. The broadcasting industry, for example, must continually reaffirm the power of television to influence consumption behavior to its private customers, the commercial advertisers. This influence is, in fact, the fundamental assumption behind the American broadcasting structure. Yet on issues concerning the welfare of public consumers of television, such as the impact of violent programming on children, the industry stresses research literature that touts the negligible effects of the media. Public hearings on such questions as television violence or advertising aimed exclusively at children inevitably degenerate into a parade of scientific experts testifying for either the "exaggerated" or "proven" effects of the media.

Thinkers outside of the mainstream of American culture have looked for alternatives to the ruling behavioral model of communications research because it proved deficient for exploring the spheres of meaning and the relationship between communication and the social order. The Frankfurt school's fitful attempts in this direction reflected the deep alienation of cultural outsiders from American mass media and mass culture. A similar alienation prompted two Canadian thinkers, Harold Innis and Marshall McLuhan, to pursue theoretical studies into the nature of communications media. In their case, however, the brute reality of cultural imperialism, spearheaded by the proximity of American media, seemed to threaten their nation's very cultural identity. Innis and McLuhan, rejecting the behavioral model and eschewing the standard empirical techniques, advanced versions of the most holistic and radical media theory yet propounded.

CHAPTER 6

Metahistory, Mythology, and the Media: The American Thought of Harold Innis and Marshall McLuhan

For the most radical and elaborate American media theory, one must look to the work of two Canadians, Harold Adams Innis and Marshall McLuhan. They represent two wings of a body of speculation that locates the formal characteristics of communications media as the prime mover behind the historical process, social organizations, and changing sensory awareness. Innis's work on communication began at least in part as a conscious Canadian attack on the burgeoning American cultural and economic hegemony in the postwar world. This critical perspective was prominent in the works of the early McLuhan as well, although his negative appraisal of American civilization had somewhat different roots from that of Innis. As Canadians, both men were less constrained by the behavioral tradition of communication studies dominant in the United States. Innis, an economic historian, and McLuhan, a literary critic, came to communication studies late in their careers, and they brought with them fundamentally new ways of analyzing media.

Throughout their work the brute and seemingly irreversible fact of American power, particularly American technological power, served as a key referent. In the works of Innis and the early McLuhan, American media and American society loom as spectral threats to Canadian culture; in the mature works of McLuhan, they are exalted. Their writings reveal close affinities with several

American intellectual traditions. Strongly influenced by Thorstein Veblen's dichotomy of industry and business, Innis's forays into media theory near the end of his life may be viewed in part as an attempt to construct an intellectual bridge between technology and the price system.

McLuhan's later works and his enormous popular vogue remind us of the continuing powerful attraction of the "rhetoric of the technological sublime," as Leo Marx has phrased it. Both Innis and McLuhan espoused varieties of technological determinism strongly reminiscent of the work of Charles Horton Cooley and Robert Park. McLuhan's stress on media as the basis for organic unity recalls not only Cooley but also the popular excitement surrounding each new development in communications technology. Whereas so much of American social thought in the nineteenth and twentieth centuries has focused on the upheavals wrought by extraordinary advances in American material production, Innis and McLuhan sought tools in media studies for addressing the concurrent problems of consumption, leisure, and the industrialization of the mind.

Innis's work in communication remains largely unknown, except through his influence on McLuhan, and McLuhan's adaptation of Innis was a highly selective and distorted one. Though McLuhan was a self-proclaimed disciple of Innis, a vigorous and lonely voice against American media imperialism, his enduring legacy may well be his role in legitimizing the status quo of American communications industries and their advertisers. Innis's excursions into media theory were tentative and incomplete, yet full of rich suggestions for future research and analysis. McLuhan, despite protestations that he merely made "probes," fashioned a more closed and static theory of media than is generally realized.

The thought of both men needs to be evaluated historically, because it emerged from and was shaped by shifting intellectual, political, and moral perspectives. In McLuhan's case, however, it is somewhat difficult to separate his ideas from the historical phenomenon of his persona. As the most advanced communications theorists, both Innis and McLuhan must be assessed historically, but they must also be judged on the continuing relevance of their contributions to the understanding of present and future media.

★

On initial viewing, the career of Harold Adams Innis appears to encompass the work of two very different thinkers. The first Innis was a renowned economic historian and economic theorist, a central figure in the construction of a distinct Canadian political economy between the two world wars. This Innis combined prodigious research in primary materials, a thorough firsthand knowledge of Canadian geography, and imaginative synthesizing to produce a unified approach to Canadian history: the so-called staples thesis of economic growth. By contrast, the later Innis immersed himself in the history and political economy of communication from the ancient world through the present. His flights of speculation, as much philosophical as historical, required a full-scale redirection of thinking into uncharted territories. The later Innis is of primary concern here, but it is necessary to trace at least the outlines of his early work because several themes unite the economic and communications studies.

Born in 1894 in rural southern Ontario, Innis spent his early years on the small farm of his strict Baptist parents. Hoping that he would enter the ministry, his family scraped together money for schooling; young Innis not only refused to study for the ministry, but refused baptism as well. Nonetheless, throughout his life he retained the strong sense of individualism in matters of conscience and the deep belief in separation of church and state inculcated by his pious parents. He was hungry for education; at fourteen he began to commute twenty miles each way to attend the nearest collegiate institute. In 1912 he entered McMaster University in Toronto. For a time he also taught in remote prairie public schools in Manitoba, an educational pioneer getting a firsthand look at the Canadian West. After completing his B.A. degree in 1916, Innis immediately enlisted in the Canadian army and shipped out to the French front. He was badly wounded shortly thereafter and returned to Canada. He took his M.A. in economics at McMaster in 1918 and decided to plunge ahead for the doctorate at the University of Chicago. He completed his Ph.D. in 1920, writing a dissertation on the history of the Canadian Pacific Railway.[1]

At Chicago, Innis first encountered in absentia one of the key intellectual influences of his life: Thorstein Veblen. Although Veblen had left Chicago some years earlier, his towering presence lingered among the younger faculty. Innis was part of that younger generation of students profoundly moved by Veblen's iconoclastic attacks on the received doctrines of neoclassical economics. Innis's war experience left him something of an angry young man, dissatisfied with university life; it also intensified his Canadian nationalism and a belief that standard economics were thoroughly inadequate for explaining the Canadian situation. His intense involvement with a Veblen study group at Chicago exposed him to the full range of Veblen's exciting and heretical works.[2]

Veblen's assault on neoclassical economics challenged the notion that economic laws were universal: timeless and true for all places. He accused the neoclassical thinkers of constructing a mere "taxonomy" of economic concepts and never questioning the moral and political implications behind the current distribution of wealth. Veblen objected to the orthodox view that the economic situation possessed an intrinsic tendency toward "normal equilibrium" and was guided by the operation of the market place as rational coordinator of economic agents. For their psychology of human motivation, the neoclassicists relied on a simplistic "hedonist calculus" of rationalism: the assumption that men always act rationally to avoid pain and achieve happiness. In short, they took for granted the very things that Veblen thought needed to be explained.

Veblen sought to recast economics as an "evolutionary science" concerned with tracing the complex development of human institutions and habits over time. He paid particular attention to the stages of technological growth, which derived ultimately from the "instinct of workmanship." In Veblen's schema, advances in technology, from handicrafts through machine industry, produced more goods for the subsistence and comfort of men. The modern machine process operated under a systematic, disciplined, and reasoned procedure; it enforced these habits among those who worked with machines. Its parts were standardized and interdependent, adding up to an integrated and efficient method of production. But it was operated by businessmen whose aim was simply to make a profit measured in terms of prices. Toward that end, businessmen encouraged habits opposed to the rational workings of industrial production—conspicuous consumption, speculation, wasteful competition. The resulting contradictions precipitated severe depressions and kept the level of production far below its capacity in order to maximize profits.[3]

The young Innis was inspired by Veblen's departure from neoclassical orthodoxy and the alternative approaches he suggested. In 1929, the year of Veblen's death, Innis published an article in which he reviewed Veblen's work and suggested possible applications of his theories. Innis was strongly attracted to the scientific side of Veblen, the Veblen who "insisted upon the existence of laws of growth and decay of institutions and associations. . . . Veblen has waged a constructive warfare of emancipation against the tendency toward standardized static economics which becomes so dangerous on a continent with ever increasing numbers of students clamoring for textbooks on final economic theory."

At the center of Veblen's work Innis saw an elaborate argument documenting the impact of machine industry and the industrial revolution. He argued that Veblen's concern sprang from the post–Civil War environment in which the terrific efficiency of American machine industry gave rise to the problems of overproduction and conspicuous consumption. Veblen himself had "lived through one of the economic storms of new countries." A generation later, Canada endured the throes of an economic storm similar to that of Veblen's post–Civil War Middle West.

The Canadian Innis viewed with dismay the conflict between the inert economics of a long and highly industrialized country such as England and the needs of the recently industrialized nations. The key for understanding the dynamics of economic growth and the "wealth of nations" lay in analyzing the application of changing technologies to abundant resources. This was especially true for frontier areas such as Canada, which were relatively free from the constraints of obsolescent institutions. Specific economic histories of these nations had to be written and integrated with a dynamic economic theory. Innis spent the better part of his early career framing a Canadian economic history and growth theory along these Veblenian lines.[4]

When he began to teach at the University of Toronto in 1920, Innis found it necessary to start virtually from scratch in courses on Canadian economics and economic history. Over the next fifteen years he formulated his own approach to these subjects. The "staples thesis" showed how the modern Canadian nation had descended directly from colonial trade in staple commodities such as fish, fur, and lumber. In his classic *Fur Trade in Canada* (1930), Innis traced Canadian economic growth from the trade in beaver pelts in the sixteenth century through the formation in the 1870s of the giant Northwest Company, the geographical and economic forerunner of the Canadian nation itself. He advanced a general argument about the mutual demands exerted by economically advanced and under-developed civilizations:

> The fur trade was the line of contact between a relatively
> complex civilization and a much more simple civilization. The
> complex European culture had reached a stage industrially
> in which technological equipment essential to specialized pro-
> duction had been accumulated. Ships capable of undertaking

long ocean voyages, a manufacturing system which demanded
large quantities of raw materials, and a distributing organization which absorbed the finished products without difficulty
were typical products of European civilization. The heavy
overhead cost of long voyages limited the trade to commodities
which were highly valuable, to commodities demanded by the
more advanced types of manufacturing processes of that period,
and to commodities available on a large scale. The fur of the
beaver was preeminently suited to the demands of early trade.
[At the same time,] the pull of a relatively simple civilization
on the resources of a complex civilization may be regarded
as of paramount importance. No monopoly or organization
could withstand the demands of the Indian civilization of North
America for European goods. The task of continuously supplying goods to the Indian tribes of North America, of maintaining the depreciation of those goods, and replacing the
goods destroyed was overwhelming.[5]

Early North American development depended on water transport
from Europe. It accentuated dependence on European manufactured
products and on European markets for staple raw materials. The
most promising source of early trade had been coastal fishing, especially cod. Later, beaver replaced cod, bringing about interior
penetration and trade with the Indians. With the depletion of the
beaver, lumber became the leading staple. Following the rise of
machine industry, agricultural products (particularly wheat) and
minerals completed the staples cycle. After the fur trade study,
Innis wrote two other staple histories, *Settlement and the Mining
Frontier* (1936) and *The Cod Fisheries* (1940); he also projected a
fourth on the paper and pulp industry.

Innis believed he had thus explained the crux of the Canadian
historical experience. "The economic history of Canada has been
dominated by the discrepancy between the center and the margin of
western civilization. Energy has been directed toward the exploitation of staple products and the tendency has been cumulative. . . .
Agriculture, industry, transportation, trade, finance, and governmental activities tend to become subordinate to the production of
the staple for a more highly specialized manufacturing community."
The Dominion had emerged not in spite of geography but because of
it, along lines largely determined by the fur trade. The trade in
staples, characteristic of an economically weak country, placed
Canada at the mercy of highly industrialized areas—first western

Europe, later the United States. It had also been responsible for various peculiar tendencies in Canadian development: maintenance of close cultural connections with Europe, greater tolerance among her people, and a balance between government ownership and private enterprise.[6]

In the early 1930s Innis also turned his attention to the nature of the price system, the institutional structure that communicates a consensus about the relative value of goods and services. The severe dislocations of the depression forced political economists to focus on questions of current policy, particularly problems concerning greater government intervention in the Canadian economy. Innis argued that the price system was no universal, static order, as Adam Smith and the neoclassical economists had held. In Smith's time, perhaps, it had operated more efficiently and could explain more about the nature of economic relations. But historical study of the price system itself, its widely diverse tendencies varying with each nation's situation, was critical for more realistic appraisal of the economic malaise in the 1930s.

As Innis attempted to get behind the price system and to examine what made it differ in various times and places, he started to move away from strictly economic considerations. For he began to perceive that "the penetrative powers of the price system" were but one aspect of the penetrative powers of communication. He began a long and difficult trek into new and uncharted intellectual territories, reaching beyond standard economic approaches toward a new synthesis centering on the strategic importance of communication.[7]

By 1940 Innis drastically reoriented his reading and research, beginning an intensive study of the history of printing, journalism, advertising, censorship, and propaganda. He seems originally to have had in mind another staple book on the Canadian pulp and paper industry, but he never wrote it. Instead, he pursued the subject of communication as a factor hitherto virtually ignored by economists. "The character of the competition," he asserted, "varies with the communicability of knowledge. The sensitivity of economic life and the possibilities of disturbance to equilibrium are dependent to an important extent on the press."[8]

The first fruit of his work in this period was an article on "The Newspaper in Economic Development." The newspaper as an institution played a leading role in accelerating the speed of nineteenth-century communication and transportation; speed in the collection, production, and dissemination of information lay at the core of newspaper growth. The advent of the telegraph, which increased the supply of news and rationalized its gathering, made the press a far more efficient advertising medium. Power presses raised the space capacity of newspapers and, coupled with the demands for more advertising space, forced a conversion from relatively scarce rags to wood pulp as the new raw material for newsprint. As a result, American newspapers and paper companies launched an intensive drive to control the Canadian pulp and paper mills, thus forcing a sharp decline in the price of newsprint. Here Innis documented a classic case of "cyclonic" economic development. From the Canadian point of view, the expanding American press of the post–Civil War era possessed an economic dynamic of its own, which was editorially reinforced with demands for lower tariffs in this staple industry.

The newspaper, which exploited certain types of news and was subservient to advertisers, contributed significantly to the diffusion of the price system, both horizontally over space and vertically as "a spearhead in penetrating to lower incomes." As a trailblazer in techniques of mass production, distribution, and marketing, the newspaper proved to be a harbinger of department stores and the modern consumer economy. Between 1875 and 1925, a great increase in space for features and advertising accompanied the decline in space for news and opinion. Large-scale organizations built up goodwill through press advertising, and the oligopolistic position of the newspaper became closely allied to that of business firms. Large users of advertising concentrated on the creation of effective selling techniques, whereas newspapers were compelled to develop marketing research organizations.

But Innis ended his piece cryptically: "Finally, this paper is designed to emphasize the importance of a change in the concept of the dimension of time, and to argue that it cannot be regarded in a straight line but as a series of curves depending in part on technological advances. . . . The concepts of time and space must be made relative and elastic and the attention given by the social scientist to problems of space should be paralleled by attention to the problems of time."[9] With its insistence on immediacy and speed, both in published news and as an economic enterprise, the newspaper had severely altered our concepts of time and space. Here we find a prologue to Innis's theoretical work in communication.

In his final ten years, Innis moved beyond the discussion of communication as a motor force behind the market to an exploration of communication as the axis upon which all history turned. The word *exploration* is crucial because Innis's writing on communication, taken as a whole, is incomplete, repetitious, and thoroughly lacking in closure. It presents not a set system of doctrine, but a sweeping and suggestive metahistorical effort at understanding the development and decline of civilizations. Innis did enormous amounts of primary research and travel for his Canadian economic studies, but he relied almost totally on secondary sources to construct a history of communication from 4,000 B.C. to the mid-twentieth century.

Systems of communication, that is, modes of symbolic representation, were the technological extensions of mind and consciousness. They therefore held the key to grasping a civilization's values, sources of authority, and organization of knowledge. Obsessive as the communication writings appear, Innis did not offer a monocausal theory of historical change; he made frequent references to legal, political, economic, and religious institutions, as well as to geographical influences and various forms of technical change. But the lack of attention previously given to communication by social scientists as a whole required an intensive, close-up view of this neglected factor.

Innis's later work clearly bore the stamp of his Canadian treatises, although not as deeply as some have argued.[10] Even as he despaired of the state of modern political economy, he continued to rely on economic metaphors and categories of thought, such as "monopoly," "equilibrium," and "bias." He exchanged a staples approach to economic history for a staples approach to cultural history; instead of beaver, cod, lumber, and minerals, he now examined such communication staples as speech, writing, clay, papyrus, and printing. Just as he had studied the staples of Canadian history to comprehend its contemporary situation, he looked now to ancient forms of communication as an aid to understanding the implications of modern media. Innis's deep commitment to Canadian nationalism spurred him on as he became more alarmed by the latest imperial incursions into Canadian society, namely, the cultural imperialism of American advertising and broadcasting.[11] America had replaced France and Great Britain as the empire seeking to conquer Canada. The steady jumping back-and-forth between ancient empires and current events reveals that Innis used the past as a historical laboratory for the contemplation of modern dilemmas.

There is an overall sense of roughness and incompleteness about his later work. The style is often so impenetrably dense and eclectic that it exasperates and frustrates the reader. Sometime in the 1940s Innis wrote a thousand-page unfinished manuscript, "A History of Communication." It remained unpublished, though it served as the basis for much of the published material: *Empire and Communications* (1950), *The Bias of Communication* (1951), and *Changing Concepts of Time* (1952). These were essentially collections of oral presentations and essays rather than unified books. Nowhere does Innis present us with a coherent, clean statement of his position. He demands an adventurous reader who is willing to bring imagination and fortitude to bear on Innis's galaxy of insight and erudition.

★

According to Innis, the rise and fall of civilizations and the cultural changes within an individual civilization may be understood primarily as functions of the predominant media of communication. All civilizations exist by controlling areas of space and stretches of time. They can therefore be appraised in relation to territory and duration. The "bias of communication" is the spatial or temporal tendency in media that establishes the parameters for the dissemination of knowledge over space and time.

> Media that emphasize time are those that are durable in character, such as parchment, clay, and stone. The heavy materials are suited to the development of architecture and sculpture. Media that emphasize space are apt to be less durable and light in character, such as papyrus and paper. The latter are suited to wide areas in administration and trade.... Materials that emphasize time favor decentralization and hierarchical types of institutions, while those that emphasize space favor centralization and systems of government less hierarchical in character. Large scale political organizations such as empires must be considered from the standpoint of two dimensions, those of time and space, and persist by overcoming the bias of media which overemphasize either dimension.[12]

Monopolies of knowledge develop and decline partly in relation to the medium of communication on which they are built; these monopolies feature restriction to one medium, limitations on certain forms of knowledge, and tight control by a small power group. In cultural terms time represents a concern with history, tradition, and the growth of religious and hierarchical institutions. Space implies the growth of empire, expansion, concern with the present, and secular political authority. Temporal culture is one of faith, afterlife, ceremony, and the moral order. Spatial culture is secular, scientific, materialistic, and unbounded. Obviously, in any culture both sets of values are operative, one dominantly and one recessively. Innis saw the rise and fall of civilizations, especially empires, in terms of a dialectic between competing monopolies of knowledge based on the temporal or spatial bias.[13]

Only at rare intervals had a civilization managed to achieve a balance between time- and space-biased media, for example, classical Greece, Renaissance Italy, and Elizabethan England. Western civilization was now in terrible danger of disintegration because of its failure to confront the problems of duration. Innis set up a series of ideal dualisms or, more properly, continuums in the history of communication to illustrate the historical dialectic of monopolies of knowledge based on competing media. The experience of past civilizations clearly held a lesson for the present; the understanding of a civilization's media bias was necessary, if not sufficient, for the survival of that civilization.

The contrast between oral and written modes of communication provided a paradigm for all later media. An oral tradition is one of consensually shared standards and sacred beliefs. The achievement of Greek civilization, for example, reflected the power of the spoken word. "Continuous philosophic discussion aimed at truth. The life and movement of dialectic opposed the establishment of a finished system of dogma." Innis made no secret of his own bias toward the oral tradition and the necessity for recapturing some of its spirit, particularly in the modern university. "The oral dialectic is overwhelmingly significant where the subject matter is human action and feeling, and it is important in the discovery of new truth but of very little value in disseminating it. The oral discussion inherently involves personal contact and a consideration of the feelings of others, and it is in sharp contrast with the cruelty of mechanized communication and the tendencies which we have come to note in the modern world."[14]

The appearance of writing caused a shift away from the oral tradition and toward secular authority, with the resultant emphasis on spatial over temporal relations. Writing at first simply recorded the oral tradition, petrifying it and thus eliminating the essence of oral dialectic. In a culture based on written tradition, knowledge is based on the administrative and technical needs of the present and future empire, rather than on the traditional time-based codes of oral culture. In ancient Egypt and Babylonia small groups of priests originally established monopoly control over complex systems of writing such as hieroglyphics and cuneiform. These monopolies were gradually destroyed by simpler writing systems, which greatly enlarged the class of scribes and facilitated government administration over larger areas.

Development of a highly flexible phonetic alphabet, which first appeared among the commercial Phoenicians, further propelled the spatial bias. In Greece, the spread of papyrus and writing based on a phonetic alphabet at first brought a magnificent balance to Greek culture, culminating in tragedy and the writings of Plato. Eventually, however, writing contributed to the collapse of Greek civilization by widening the gap between city states and by ossifying the philosophical method of the oral tradition.

The Byzantine empire also developed on the basis of a blending between organizations reflecting different media biases, "that of papyrus in the development of an imperial bureaucracy in relation to a vast area and that of parchment in the development of an ecclesiastical hierarchy in relation to time."[15] Just at the point where a medium created a monopoly of knowledge, a new medium subversively broke through, usually on the outer fringes of a society. Parchment, biased toward time, was adapted by monasticism and contributed to the growth of a powerful ecclesiastical organization in western Europe. It invited competition from paper, which favored space. Italy's near monopoly of paper production in fourteenth- and fifteenth-century Europe coincided with its strength as a commercial center ("keeping books"), the emergence of professional writers, and the revival of learning.

Printing became the dominant medium of Western civilization and remained so pervasive that one can hardly comprehend the environment it created. Printing represented the birth of a machine process based on uniform repeatability; as such, it provided a model for subsequent developments of mass production and for the standardization of goods and knowledge. It reversed the Greek maxim "nothing in excess" by ushering in a civilization that might be described as "everything in excess." By the seventeenth century, it had successfully challenged the time bias of the medieval church, whose authority was based on parchment manuscript. Printing accelerated the spatial bias of paper and fostered the rise of nationalism, vernacular languages, and the extension of political bureaucracy.[16]

Printing achieved its most complete monopoly of knowledge in America. There, "the modern obsession with present-mindedness" stemming from printing's space bias found protection in the U.S. Constitution, which supported the rapid growth of the newspaper industry. "The overwhelming pressure of mechanization evident in the newspaper and the magazine has led to the creation of vast monopolies of communication. Their entrenched position involves a continuous, systematic, ruthless destruction of permanence essential to cultural activity. The emphasis on change is the only permanent characteristic."

The power of the American newspaper industry enabled it to monopolize the Canadian pulp and paper trade and to force low tariffs—this was economic monopoly. But a growing cultural monopoly troubled Innis as well. For the finished products derived from pulp and paper consisted largely of advertising and reading material exported back into Canada, a cultural bombardment that threatened Canadian national life. "Canadian publications supported by the advertising of products of American branch plants and forced to compete with American publications imitate them in format, style, and content. Canadian writers must adapt themselves to American standards. Our poets and painters are reduced to the status of sandwich men."

In its drive to conquer space and new markets, the press transformed our notions of time. Modern press associations turned news into a commodity, which could be sold in competition and monopolized like any other. "Lack of continuity in news is the inevitable result of dependence on advertisements for the sale of goods," hence the emphasis on excitement, sensationalism, and capriciousness in news. Innis's study of the press suggested that time had been spatialized into "a uniform and quantitative continuum" obscuring qualitative differences. "Advertisers build up monopolies of time to an important extent through the use of news. They are able to take full advantage of technological advances in communication and to place information before large numbers at the earliest possible moment. Market changes in the speed of communication have far reaching effects on monopolies over time because of their impact on the most sensitive elements of the economic system."[17]

Innis made only tentative attempts to extend his analysis into the realm of newer media such as radio and television. He suggested that radio, with its appeal to the ear, signaled a return to the consideration of problems of time, as reflected in the growth of government planning and the welfare state. He noted, for example, that Franklin D. Roosevelt, architect of the New Deal, depended heavily on the radio to win approval of his policies.[18] But radio presaged a return to oral tradition only in a shallow sense. If one extends Innis's thinking here, it appears that broadcasting was actually stepping up the spatial bias of the modern era. Radio and television receivers are

which suggested that this merely reflected the tendency of the universe toward entropy. From the physicist's point of view, "Man, as a conscious and constant, single natural force, seems to have no function except that of dissipating or degrading energy."[21]

For Innis, communication rather than energy served as the operative principle. Any final philosophy of history he might have worked out would surely have been closely intertwined with a philosophy of knowledge, namely, how changes in communication affect the way we think. Innis wondered if all the improvements in communication had in fact worked against man's understanding, particularly his understanding of the timeless problems of Western culture. The political economy in Adam Smith's *Wealth of Nations* embodied general and universal principles; such an approach deteriorated when it was subordinated to mathematical abstraction, science, and obsession with the price system and problems of the moment. The spatial bias of the modern press and the demands of advertising had turned economics and the social sciences toward specialization and fixation on short-run problems.

> Enormous compilations of statistics confront the social scientist. He is compelled to interpret them or to discover patterns or trends which will enable him to predict the future. With the use of elaborate calculating machines and of refinement in mathematical technique he can develop formulae to be used by industry and business and by governments in the formulation of policy. But elaboration assumes prediction for short periods of time. Work in the social sciences has become increasingly concerned with topical problems and social science departments become schools of journalism. The difficulty of handling the concept of time in economic theory and of developing a reconciliation between static and dynamic approaches is a reflection of the neglect of the time factor in Western civilization.[22]

"Industrialization of the mind" and "mechanized knowledge" threatened the traditional role of the university, making it subservient to the military, the vested interests of business, and the state bureaucracy. The university, where an individual once learned to assess problems in terms of time and space, to acquire a sense of balance and proportion, and to decide how much or how little information he needed, was rapidly declining.

Innis's concern paralleled that of Robert Park, who wrote an influential piece on physics and society in which he wondered if science, "in awakening the vast energies that are resident in the material world, brought into existence forces which science cannot hope to control?" Because of the destruction of the time bias, the problem for both the modern university and modern civilization was how to create moral forces to counterbalance the forces unleashed by the physical sciences.[23] Unlike Park, though, Innis did not regard modern communication as a means of achieving scientific reporting in the press. Nor did he share the Progressive hope that new media would contribute to an objective social science.

Innis held little expectation that twentieth-century civilization could escape the monopolies of knowledge built up through the bias of modern communication. He emphasized the "extraordinary, perhaps insuperable, difficulty of assessing the quality of a culture of which we are a part or of assessing the quality of a culture of which we are not a part." In the modern West, "we are perhaps too much a part of the civilization which followed the spread of the printing industry to be able to determine its characteristics." America, where the full impact of printing accrued through the Bill of Rights, now threatened the survival of that civilization. America's strongest tradition was her lack of tradition. The problem of getting outside of America's space-oriented bias appeared insoluble.[24]

The revulsion against mechanized knowledge, anguish over the decline in university life, and pleas for recapturing some of the oral tradition of the Greeks all echoed rather familiar sentiments held by a large fraction of twentieth-century intellectuals. Combined with the Canadian perspective on American power, Innis arrived at a most gloomy position by the end of his life. His greatest mission at that point seems to have been playing the prophet, reminding us of the fate of all empires (including America's) determined to blindly ignore the biases of their culture.

As a historian of communication, however, Innis may ultimately provide a clearer understanding of modern media, even though he warned of the difficulties of escaping their biases. One recalls that he began his communication studies by applying the tools of economic history to media and by treating media as he did economic staples. Intensive study of the physical characteristics of staple resources and of the technological changes and market influences that gave them economic significance served as the focal point for analyzing a total economic situation.

In one sense, Innis's work in communication represented an attempt to overcome the Veblenian dualism of business and industry and to locate the crucial link between these two tendencies of the modern economy. Advances in communication technology were closely tied to the pressure for market expansion, which was necessary for greater profits. Whereas Veblen concentrated on new technologies of production, Innis focused on advances in communication as new technologies for consumption. As America led the advance of industrial production, so it pioneered new technologies of consumption. Innis originally followed this approach in showing how the American press and advertising matrix directly impinged on the Canadian economy. And here was the takeoff point for his metahistorical flights.

As with his philosophical speculations on media, Innis's historical method holds rich possibilities as a guide to further research. The rise of broadcasting may again serve as an example. Although the technology of the modern newspaper emerged several centuries after the first printing press, that of broadcasting appeared only sixty years after James Clerk-Maxwell's mathematical prediction of electromagnetic waves. Wireless telegraphy and wireless telephony both developed with the crucial aid of corporate research facilities and government sponsorship. The demands of military strategy cannot be neglected in any history of radio *technique*. However, radio *technology*, a fully integrated and public system of communication, arrived after World War I in the form of radio broadcasting. From the first, radio broadcasting performed a marketing function; it originated as a stimulus to the sale of surplus radio equipment stockpiled by the large electrical corporations. But with the rise of commercial broadcasting in the mid-1920s, radio soon served this function for the entire economy. It produced no product as such, but greatly enlarged markets for all consumer goods.

The great geniuses of radio and television have been marketing geniuses. Broadcasting became the most space-biased of all modern media. It centralized and intensified the advertising and marketing functions performed by the nineteenth-century press. It accelerated the redefinition of time into pecuniary units. The penetration of radio and television into every household was unprecedented. Modern communication thus provided outlets for the greatest productive capacity (industry) ever, laying the foundation for the greatest marketing machinery (business) in history.

Innis's legacy, then, is a complex one reflecting the tension between the economic, moral, and metahistorical meanings of communication. His early pursuit of the economic implications of communication led him to interpret the media from the perspective of a moral critic of modern civilization. His historical researches were not enough, however; he felt compelled to consider communication outside its historical development, to probe the way new media altered our notions of time and space. The importance of confronting the many levels of Innis's contribution is reinforced when one considers the direction taken by his most prominent disciple, Marshall McLuhan. For with McLuhan, the subtleties of "Inniscence" disappeared into the mists of mythology.

★

Writing about Marshall McLuhan, one faces a bundle of paradoxes wrapped in a central contradiction. McLuhan speaks in at least two distinct voices; he is a Janus-like figure whose public adventures have contributed to the confusion surrounding the meaning of what he has to say. He wants desperately to elevate his media theory to the level of science. He insists that he is a clinically detached observer who scientifically analyzes the impact of communications media on the mind and society. At the same time, he proclaims that he is readily willing to discard anything that he has ever said, that he has no desire to defend past statements, and that he must rely on the method of "insight" since cause-and-effect reasoning is obsolete. This second McLuhan operates something like a Renaissance fool, punning and blustering along in a rollicking intellectual slapstick.

Not surprisingly, McLuhan's pretensions to scientific discourse and objectivity, as well as his encyclopedic and highly selective appeals to authorities from many fields of knowledge, leave him highly vulnerable to technical attacks from various quarters. There have already been numerous devastating critiques on nearly every facet of his theory.[25] He has certainly been discredited as a "scientist." Both his mature speculations and their wide popularity appear to have been singular phenomena of the 1960s. Only a short time later, much of his writing already has the quality of a period piece, curiously quaint and outdated.

Yet technical critiques of McLuhan are somewhat beside the point. How does one logically attack a court jester, a man who declares the end of linear logic? McLuhan's analysis of modern media has profoundly transformed our perceptions of twentieth-century life, particularly for the generation born after World War II. When the French coined the term *mcluhanisme*, they were referring not only to the man but also to a new cultural stance, a commitment to the serious examination of popular culture. If nothing else, McLuhan's efforts instilled an urgent awareness of the media environment as a basic force shaping the modern sensibility.

A post-McLuhan writer thus faces the vexing problem of severing himself from the intellectual milieu created by the subject itself, of somehow correcting what Innis might have termed the "McLuhan bias." This problem parallels McLuhan's own attempts to get outside of the media environment surrounding us in order to understand it. A historical approach to McLuhan may perhaps seem premature at this point, but it offers one route out of this impasse. McLuhan's spectacular notoriety during the 1960s resembled the arrival of a streaking meteor from outer space, and the public McLuhan did everything possible to reinforce the notion that he came from nowhere. In fact, he came from several places. Notwithstanding the claim that he had no point of view, very real (though shifting) moral, psychological, and political beliefs can be discerned throughout his development.

McLuhan's career may be roughly divided into three periods: his early years as a traditional literary critic, ending with the publication of his first book, *The Mechanical Bride* (1951); a transitional phase in the 1950s during which he adapted the work of Harold Innis, immersed himself in cultural anthropology, and edited the journal *Explorations*; and the mature stage of the 1960s, when he published his theories in *The Gutenberg Galaxy* (1962), *Understanding Media* (1964), and several lesser works.

For a very public figure, little is known about McLuhan's private life or early years. He has been deliberately vague and even misleading on the subject of his own biography. One can reconstruct only the bare outlines. He was born in 1911 in Edmonton, Alberta, the son of a Methodist insurance salesman and a Baptist actress. He studied engineering at the University of Manitoba, where he received his B.A. and M.A. degrees in 1933 and 1934. A growing zeal for English literature eclipsed his original desire to be an engineer. He enrolled at Trinity Hall in Cambridge University in 1935, completing an M.A. and eventually his Ph.D. in 1942; the subject of his doctoral dissertation was the Elizabethan writer and educator, Thomas Nashe. McLuhan began his career as a teacher at the University of Wisconsin in 1936. At some point in the late 1930s he converted to Roman Catholicism. He taught literature at two Catholic schools, St. Louis University (1937 to 1944) and Assumption University in Windsor, Ontario (1945 to 1946). After 1946 he served as professor of literature at the University of Toronto; in 1963 he became director of its Center for Culture and Technology.[26]

McLuhan pursued a sedate career as teacher and critic for some twenty years, publishing numerous pieces on a wide variety of writers from the medieval period through the modern era. At Cambridge, McLuhan was deeply influenced by the methodology and moral temper of the so-called New Critics, particularly I. A. Richards and F. R. Leavis. Richards, drawing on the latest work in behavioral psychology and philosophy, sought to construct a science of criticism by examining how literature produces certain psychological states. In works such as *Principles of Literary Criticism* (1925) and *Practical Criticism* (1929) he extended the scope of philosophical empiricism to embrace the logical structure of meaning itself. He insisted that a work's merit was separate from both the author's own intentions and from any biographical influences. Leavis, editor of the influential journal *Scrutiny*, emphasized criticism based on the unity and formal structure of the work itself—the text is all. He held that the critic must focus on the internal relationships between various parts of the text and must explicate all its layers of meaning, ambiguity, and paradox. Interpretation could only be accomplished through the structure of a work's own language; literary theory, philosophy, and history were irrelevant.

Politically and spiritually the New Criticism, and most of the writers associated with it, expressed deep antagonism to modern industrial civilization. It celebrated instead the lost organic unity of agrarian Christian culture. Significantly, McLuhan's first published essay in 1936 resounded with praise for G. K. Chesterton, "for seeking to re-establish agriculture and small property as the only free basis for a free culture." Chesterton's *What's Wrong With the World* (1910) apparently had an important role in McLuhan's Catholic conversion, an act that meshed neatly with his literary interests of that period.[27]

Through his own literary criticism, McLuhan expressed a personal variant of the Tory, neo-Catholic, antimodern tradition flourishing on both sides of the Atlantic. His vigorous promotion of modernist writers such as Pound, Eliot, Joyce, and Yeats derived largely from their critique of what Eliot labeled the "dissociation of sensibility," a feature of modern secular civilization. Yet McLuhan's essays on American writers and his reading of American history reveal most clearly the aesthetic, political, and moral position of these early years.

McLuhan posited an underlying split in the American mind and society, one that reflected an old struggle over the nature of education and learning. He championed the "Southern quality" in American letters, the passionate, historical, and tragic sense of life exemplified in the works of Poe, Twain, Faulkner, Cabell, Tate, and others. In McLuhan's view, southern culture stood as a modern manifestation of the Ciceronian ideal of "rational man reaching his noblest attainment in the expression of an eloquent wisdom." According to McLuhan, ever since Socrates used dialectics against the rhetoric of his sophist teachers, a continuing quarrel had raged over whether grammar and rhetoric on the one hand or dialectics on the other should prevail in organizing knowledge. The debate continued among medieval and Renaissance authorities, with the Schoolmen insisting that one part of the trivium be the superior method in theology (dialectics) and the humanists insisting on the others (grammar, rhetoric). As the quarrel heightened in seventeenth-century England, representatives of both parties migrated to America— the Schoolmen to New England and the quasi-humanist gentry to Virginia.

In America, McLuhan argued, the two radically opposed intellectual traditions developed on new soil and were geographically separated for the first time. Nourished by the agrarian estate life of the South, the Ciceronian ideal reached its flower in "the scholar statesman of encyclopedic knowledge, profound practical experience, and voluble social and public eloquence." It produced, among other things, the most creative tradition in American political thought, a tradition that stretched from Jefferson to Wilson. It advocated an agrarian society with every man as aristocrat and subordinated knowledge and action to a political good. On the other hand, the New England mind afforded a sharp contrast. Based on the Ramist application of dialectics to theological controversy, it embodied a thoroughly different tradition: "For this mind there is nothing which cannot be settled by *method*. It is the mind which weaves the intricacies of efficient production, 'scientific' scholarship, and business administration. It doesn't permit itself an inkling of what constitutes a social or political problem . . . simply because there is no method for tackling such problems." McLuhan thus reduced American history to an internal debate within the medieval trivium. Southern literature's stress on passion versus the northern concern with character, the Civil War, and the educational debate at Chicago over the "Great Books" program all reflected the intellectual struggle of the humanist against the technological specialist.[28]

McLuhan left no doubt where his own sympathies lay. His affinity with the southern Agrarian movement of the 1920s and 1930s is striking. McLuhan, the Catholic and provincial Canadian, joined John Crowe Ransom in celebrating the South as the true inheritor of the humanist tradition, "unique on this continent for having founded and defended a culture which was according to the European principles of culture."[29] In opposition to it, McLuhan lumped together northern business civilization, the gospel of progress, urban decadence, "social engineers," John Dewey, and a crude caricature of Marxism. Slavery was dismissed as merely the one main condition of aristocratic life present in the South and absent in the North. Although physically defeated in the Civil War, the South remained spiritually sound and was the best hope for the perpetuation of the Christian humanist tradition in North America.

In *The Mechanical Bride* (1951), his first full-scale analysis of modern media and popular culture, McLuhan combined the exegetic techniques of the New Criticism with the moral perspective expressed in the early literary essays. This was an important work in McLuhan's evolution. It was an attempt to apply a literary technique to a new subject matter in order to preserve the humanist values so central to his writing. *The Mechanical Bride* contains a sharp tension between McLuhan's clear desire to criticize the "collective trance" induced by modern communication (especially through advertising) and his movement toward a strategy of "suspended judgement," of considering the forms of media content on their own terms as aesthetic wholes.

In the preface he identified his method with that of Edgar Allan Poe's sailor in the story "Descent into the Maelstrom": "Poe's sailor saved himself by studying the action of the whirlpool and by cooperating with it. The present book likewise makes few attempts to attack the very considerable currents and pressures set up around us today by the mechanical agencies of the press, radio, movies, and advertising." McLuhan hoped to set the reader at the center of the media maelstrom for the purpose of an objective study:

> Poe's sailor says that when locked in by the whirling walls and the numerous objects which floated in that environment: 'I must have been delirious, for I even sought amusement in speculating upon the relative velocities of their several descents toward the foam below.' It was this amusement born of his rational detachment as a spectator of his own situation that gave him the thread which led him out of the Labyrinth. And it is in the same spirit that this book is offered as an amusement. Many who are accustomed to the note of moral indignation will mistake this amusement for mere indifference.[30]

McLuhan offered several dozen short meditations on a wide assortment of texts: advertisements, comic strips, radio shows, pulp characters, magazines, and recurring themes in the "folklore of industrial man." Like the psychoanalyst interpreting the dream images of his patient, McLuhan argued that everyday popular culture held a rich source of data for diagnosing the "collective trance" or "dream state" into which industrial society had fallen. Ads seemed to be "a kind of social ritual or magic that flatter and enhance us in our own eyes." American advertising consistently proclaimed freedom of choice as the foundation of the American way of life, but glossed over questions of power and control. "Let the people have freedom, and let others have the power. Especially the power to tell them that they are free and that they are consumed with the spirit of rivalry and success."

For McLuhan, "freedom, like taste, is an activity of perception and judgement based on a great range of particular acts and experiences—Whatever fosters mere passivity and submission is the enemy of this vital activity." He scoffed at merely "reforming" the media industries through changes in policies of entertainment and control. Instead he proposed to educate the individual sensibility and to break the hypnotic attraction of the media through the tough-minded evaluation of "unpleasant facts under the conditions of art and controlled observation." Popular culture was a valuable index of the guiding impulses and dominant drives in society precisely because it resembled the psychoanalytic data yielded by individuals or groups involuntarily, in moments of inattention. McLuhan tried to beat the ad agencies and market researchers at their own game by probing the collective unconscious to which they appealed.[31]

What are the central images and myths in this industrial folklore? An unrelenting diet of sex, death, and technological advance, ingeniously interwoven in cluster patterns designed to sell merchandise. We get the car as sex object, the female body reduced to dissociated mechanical parts, and the equation of sexuality with power. We read the ghoulish appeals to violent death in the press and pulps. Images of hectic speed, mayhem, violence, and instant death imply that sex is no longer the ultimate thrill. With the high-powered techniques of applied science, market research, and polling behind them, the modern ad agencies have usurped the ancient Ciceronian claim for eloquence as the way to power and influence. The "eloquence" of commerce today attempts to keep the consumer and citizen from ever questioning the naturalness of these cultural themes. "Far from being a conscious conspiracy, this is a nightmare dream from which we would do well to awaken at once."[32]

Finally, *The Mechanical Bride* was an argument for a new kind of education and a plea for the development of critical intellect by using the very sources that manipulated, exploited, and controlled the public with unprecedented power. During the 1940s McLuhan vigorously defended the "Great Books" program at Chicago and humanist programs of general studies.[33] With his first book, however, McLuhan argued that formal education of any type could not hope to compete with the unofficial education people received from the new media. "The classroom cannot compete with the glitter and the billion dollar success and prestige of this commercial education. Least of all with a commercial education program which is designed as entertainment and which by-passes the intelligence while operating directly on the will and the desires."

Like a modern-day Erasmus, McLuhan proposed a wholesale shake-up of our educational priorities. Robert Hutchins called the media barrage a "constant storm of triviality and propaganda that now beats upon the citizen"; McLuhan thought it could be controlled only by critical inspection. "Its baneful effects are at present entirely dependent on its being ignored." To McLuhan, the unofficial commercial culture reflected the true native culture of the industrial world. "And it is through the native culture, or not at all, that we effect contact with past cultures. For the quality of anybody's relations with the minds of the past is exactly and necessarily determined by the quality of his contemporary insights."[34]

The Mechanical Bride proffered an essentially literary study of media content, an explication of the literature of everyday life. It marked a real turning point in McLuhan's career, the beginning of his own descent into the maelstrom of media studies. Perhaps it is worth recalling that Poe's sailor, although able to save himself by means of an extraordinary curiosity, was powerless to save his two brothers on the ship. He escaped his fate only after he gave up hope. "I positively felt a wish to explore its depth, even at the sacrifice I was going to make; and my principle grief was that I should never be able to tell my old companions on shore about the mysteries I should see." Indeed, his old mates who eventually pulled him up out of the sea could not even recognize their friend—his hair now turned white, his whole countenance changed. They refused to believe his tale.

After this book, McLuhan moved away from the interpretation of modern myth toward the construction of his own mythology, and many of his old mates found it difficult to believe his tale. But two crucial influences helped shape his thinking at Toronto during the 1950s. One was his exposure to Harold Innis. The second was his involvement in the culture and communication seminar; its short-lived journal *Explorations* thoroughly immersed him in cultural anthropology. As a result, his work took a decisive turn toward the glorification of neoprimitivism and away from what he jeeringly began to call the "single point of view."

★

McLuhan borrowed from Innis the tools with which to extend an aesthetic doctrine into an all-encompassing theory of social change. Innis's historical and economic studies provided the intellectual legitimacy for McLuhan's grand leap from investigating the forms of transmitted messages to the forms of transmission themselves. Innis's extension of the analysis of economic staples to an exploration of communication forms and media biases paralleled the New Critical method that McLuhan absorbed at Cambridge: in a work of art the form is the content and the only valid criterion for judging a work. Or, as McLuhan wrote in an early piece on the relationship between economics and communication, "it is the formal characteristics of the medium, recurring in a variety of material situations, and not any particular 'message,' which constitutes the efficacy of its historical action."[35]

McLuhan declared in *The Gutenberg Galaxy* that Harold Innis was "the first person to hit upon the process of change as implicit in the forms of media technology. The present book is a footnote of explanation to his work."[36] This was a rather disingenuous accolade, but it squared with McLuhan's overall simplification and mystification of Innis's accomplishments. McLuhan read Innis's contribution to communication studies as a purely methodological one, pursued by a man with no motivation save the desire to break out of the "single point of view" and into the realm of "insight." For McLuhan, the single point of view characteristic of Innis's traditional historical work (and of all print culture) was a severely limited way of *looking at* something. Insight, however, was the sudden awareness of a complex process of interaction, the technique of discovering by juxtaposing multiple aspects of a situation.

McLuhan thus described the later Innis as inevitably adopting "a discontinuous style, an aphoristic, mental camera sort of procedure which was indispensable to his needs. . . . He juxtaposes one condensed observation with another, mounts one insight or image on another in quick succession to create a sense of the multiple relationships in process of undergoing rapid development from the impact of specific technological changes. . . . It is an ideogrammic prose, a complex mental cinema." Although this type of writing does appear in Innis, this passage is a more accurate account of McLuhan's own style. In McLuhan's paeans to Innis we catch a glimpse of his own self-image: "The later Innis had no position. He had become a roving mental eye, an intellectual radar screen on the alert for objective clues to the inner spirit or core of our times."[37]

McLuhan chose to ignore Innis's political and moral position on communication, his Canadian nationalism, and his critique of American media. He preferred to view Innis as a poet or artist, but at the same time he condescendingly lamented Innis's deficiencies in the use of artistic analysis. He compared Innis's patterns of insights to symbolist poetry and modern painting. That is to say, in order to avoid the lineality of print and to present a dynamic model of history, Innis presented a rapid montagelike shot of events, a mosaic structure of insights. The primacy of aesthetic categories in McLuhan's thought forced him into this narrow reading of Innis. Once again, it is difficult not to see McLuhan's own wish fulfillment in operation here.[38]

From 1953 to 1955 McLuhan chaired an ongoing interdisciplinary seminar on culture and communication at Toronto; the seminar was sponsored by the Ford Foundation. Along with anthropologist Edmund Carpenter, McLuhan started and edited *Explorations*, a lively quixotic journal designed to give seminar members an outlet. The purpose of this journal was to go beyond the literary concepts of media study, beyond the limitations of content analysis. Its basic premise held that changes in communication modified human sensibilities as well as human relations. Print technology, the basis of American educational and industrial establishments, was on the verge of being superseded by the electronic revolution in communication. By means of the journal, McLuhan and Carpenter hoped to develop an awareness of the role of print and literacy in shaping Western society and to investigate implications of the newer configurations of electronic media. Because literary and literacy biases were so deeply rooted, how could one step outside of them for objective explorations?[39]

The answer in large part was a radical shift toward studies of the language and communication systems in primitive societies. In one article, Dorothy Lee analyzed the speech of Trobriand islanders. She argued that no past or present tenses and no causal or teleological relationships existed in their language. They did not perceive lineal order as a value. They avoided seeing patterns as connected lines; lineal connection (cause and effect) was not automatically made in their language. Edmund Carpenter also found similar characteristics in the thought and speech of Aivilik Eskimos. In another article, Siegfried Giedion claimed that ancient cave paintings could not be understood from the space perspectives of today. These primitive artists saw things without any relation to the self. Their conception of space revealed the psychic realities confronting prehistoric man; their art does not seem rational to a twentieth-century individual because it lacks a sense of the horizontal and vertical.[40]

McLuhan and Carpenter postulated polarities between the sensory lives of preliterate and literate societies, between ear-oriented and eye-oriented cultures. In preliterate culture "acoustic space" prevailed; perception was keyed to the ear, but involved the simultaneous interplay of all senses. Tribal art served as a means of merging the individual and his environment, not as a means of training his perception of that environment. On the other hand, the "visual space" characteristic of literate man focused on the particular and abstracted it from a total situation; hence "seeing is believing." Both men held that the eye operates in isolation, perceiving a flat continuous world and favoring one thing at a time. The transition from spoken word to writing and printing elevated the sense of sight to a paramount place, truncating one sense from the cluster of human senses. This detachment allowed great power over the environment by fragmenting fields of perception. But the alienation from all senses except sight also produced emotional detachment, a declining ability to feel, express, and experience emotions.[41]

During the *Explorations* period, McLuhan moved toward an explicit analogy between preliterate and postliterate cultures. New forms of electronic media seemed to have reversed the sensory fragmentation of visual space, thus foreshadowing a psychic return to the tribal situation. Like art forms, they magically transformed the environment around us. In 1955 he wrote: "The new media are not bridges between man and nature; they are nature. . . . By surpassing writing, we have regained our Wholeness, not on a national or cultural, but cosmic plane. We have evoked a super-civilized sub-primitive man. . . . We are back in acoustic space. We begin again to structure the primordial feelings and emotions from which 3000 years of literacy divorced us."[42]

★

McLuhan's mature theory rests on a new version of the Christian myth, enabling McLuhan to concentrate on elaborating a psychology and ecology of modern media. For Eden, the Fall, and paradise regained, McLuhan substituted tribalism (oral culture), detribalization (phonetic alphabet and print), and retribalization (electronic media). Unlike Innis, who was interested mainly in the relationship between communication and social organization, McLuhan's argument primarily concerned the impact of media technology on the human sensorium.[43]

The Gutenberg Galaxy presented a protracted meditation on the sensory and cultural results of phonetic literacy and printing. Relying heavily on quotations from scientific authorities and literary favorites, McLuhan fleshed out the psychology merely hinted at in the *Explorations* period. Technological tools, such as the wheel or the alphabet, became mega-extensions of human sense organs or bodily functions. Each new media technology possessed the power to hypnotize because it isolated the senses, which in tribal man presumably existed in perfect symmetry. A division of faculties and a change in sense ratios occurred when any one sense or bodily function was externalized in technological form.

> Those who experience the first onset of a new technology, whether it be alphabet or radio, respond most emphatically because the new sense ratios, set up at once by the technological dilation of eye or ear, present men with a surprising new world, which evokes a vigorous new "closure," or novel pattern of interplay, among all of the senses together. But the initial shock gradually dissipates as the entire community absorbs the new habit of perception into all of its areas of work and association. But the real revolution is in this later and prolonged phase of "adjustment" of all personal and social life to the new model of perception set up by the new technology.[44]

The phonetic alphabet made the first critical break between eye and ear, between semantic meaning and visual code. Unlike pictographic or syllabic forms of writing, the phonetic alphabet assigned semantically meaningless letters to semantically meaningless sounds. By extending and intensifying the visual function, it diminished the roles of the other senses of hearing, touch, and taste in literate cultures. Following Innis, McLuhan pointed to the Greek myth of King Cadmus, who introduced the phonetic alphabet to Greece. He was said to have sown the dragon's teeth that later sprang up as armed men. The alphabet meant power and authority, especially because it provided a means of controlling military structures at a distance. Combined with papyrus, it spelled the end of priestly monopolies of knowledge and power and, by implication, the destruction of nonalphabetic cultures. "By the meaningless sign linked to the meaningless sound," McLuhan asserted, "we have built the shape and meaning of Western man."[45]

The invention of movable type completed the process of alienating man from his original tribal state of a participatory, "audile-tactile" way of life. "The invention of typography confirmed and extended the new visual stress of applied knowledge, providing the first repeatable commodity, the first assembly line, and the first mass production." As such, print differed markedly from the phonetic literacy expressed in written manuscripts. Compared to printed books, medieval manuscripts were of low definition; they were usually read out loud and thus required some interplay of the senses. The printed book mechanically intensified the effects of the phonetic alphabet, further fragmenting sensory life by heightening the visual bias. It made reading a more private and silent activity. The book's portability also contributed to a new cult of individualism. By turning the spoken language into a closed visual system, print created the uniform and centralizing conditions necessary for nationalism. When the assumptions of homogeneous repeatability were extended to other concerns of life, they "led gradually to all those forms of production and social organization from which the Western world derives many satisfactions and nearly all of its characteristic traits."[46]

The Gutenberg Galaxy is a great synthetic work, a tour de force of humanist scholarship. McLuhan's own contribution to it rested largely on his interpretations of Renaissance authors; he invariably reduced their works to sophisticated comments on the impact of print in their time. As artists, Shakespeare, Pope, Marlowe, Swift, Rabelais, and More were the only contemporaries capable of understanding the traumas brought on by the new print technology.

McLuhan saw the present age as a new Renaissance, a new sensory galaxy ushered in by electronic media that are capable of jolting our sensibilities as sharply as the printing press did earlier. The present is the "early part of an age for which the meaning of print culture is becoming as alien as the meaning of manuscript culture was to the eighteenth century." Ironically, America, which has the largest backlog of obsolete technology, now leads the transition into the electronic era. It thus suffers the most severe pains of conversion. "The new electric galaxy of events has already moved deeply into the Gutenberg galaxy. Even without collision, such coexistence of technologies and awareness brings trauma and tension to every living person. Our most ordinary and conventional attitudes seem suddenly twisted into gargoyles and grotesques. Familiar institutions and associations seem at times menacing and malignant."[47]

If *The Gutenberg Galaxy* stood as McLuhan's history of the disturbances ensuing from literacy and print, *Understanding Media* (1964) was his educational guide for easing the psychic conversion into the new age. In fact, the book first appeared as a mimeographed report, commissioned by the U.S. Office of Education, on how to teach the effects of media in secondary schools. It is the work that made McLuhan a household name and stirred the greatest controversy both in and outside of the schools. It is also his least substantial and most dated book. Its subtitle, "The Extensions of Man," reflects the increasing importance McLuhan placed on his psychology as well as on his role as a pioneering scientist.

According to McLuhan, the new electric technology is "organic and non-mechanical in tendency because it extends, not our eyes, but our central nervous systems as a planetary venture." He was by no means the first to employ the analogy between media and the central nervous system. While seeking a government subsidy for his research in electromagnetic telegraphy in 1838, Samuel Morse wrote in terms that uncannily presaged McLuhan. Six years before the completion of the first American telegraph line, Morse thought it not too visionary "to suppose that it would not be long ere the whole surface of this country would be channelled for those *nerves* which are to diffuse, with the speed of thought, a knowledge of all that is occurring throughout the land; making, in fact, one *neighborhood* of the whole country."[48] But McLuhan elevated this metaphor into a psychological and biological principle at the center of a rigid technological determinism.

The effects of media technology occur not on the conscious level of opinion and concepts, but on the subliminal level of sense ratios and patterns of perception. His famous phrase, "the medium is the message," refers to the change in scale or pace or pattern that any extension of communications technology introduces into human affairs. Each extension, however, brings with it a numbness or narcoticizing effect that blinds people to its real meaning. McLuhan claimed, "I am in the position of Louis Pasteur telling doctors that their greatest enemy was quite invisible, and quite unrecognized by them. Our conventional response to all media, namely that it is how they are used that counts, is the numb stance of the technological idiot. For the 'content' of a medium is like the juicy piece of meat carried by the burglar to distract the watchdog of the mind."[49]

which to make an image." Although McLuhan is correct in noting the difference between electromagnetic and film images, his argument is certainly not scientific. There is no evidence for his hypothesis; it is difficult to see any difference between the automatic, filling in of the television picture and the "persistence of vision" phenomenon that makes motion pictures possible. Each of these occurs automatically, without conscious thought by the viewer. In addition, the quality of the television image has improved enormously over the past fifteen years with color and the new solid-state and cable systems.

McLuhan's pseudoscientific description of television's sensory impact centered on the supposed tactility of the image. "The TV image requires each instant that we 'close' the spaces in the mesh by a convulsive sensuous participation that is profoundly kinetic and tactile, because tactility is the interplay of the senses, rather than the isolated contact of skin and object." For McLuhan, the sense of touch represented the sum of all human senses, the long lost *sensus communis* of the tribal man. Television is thus the practical means for recovering the shattered psychological unity in the modern world.[54]

In the last analysis, McLuhan offered us a trick of vision, not a true social theory. Either one sees it or one does not. Formerly, only the artist could accurately foresee and comprehend the violent psychic changes accompanying new media technology. Today, the instant speed of electric information permits easy recognition of the patterns of change. The transcendental leap is now possible for all. "If adjustment (economic, social, or personal) to information movement at electronic speed is quite impossible, we can always change our models and metaphors of organization, and escape into sheer understanding. Sequential analysis and adjustment natural to low speed information movement becomes irrelevant and useless even at telegraph speed. But as speed increases, the understanding in all kinds of structures and situations becomes relatively simple."

McLuhan substituted mythology for history by ignoring or distorting the real historical and sociological factors that shaped media institutions. "It is instructive to follow the embryonic stages of any new [media] growth," he wrote, "for during this period of development it is much misunderstood."[55] In his role as mythmaker, McLuhan argued deterministically that our media of communication had to evolve the way they did. His technological naturalism made media biological rather than social extensions of man. Although he purported to trace the cultural development of man through communications media, his history is curiously devoid of real people.

The obsession with his own image as a clinically detached scientist stemmed from his need to exploit the prestige enjoyed by scientific explanation in the modern era. Behind the flashy scientism, McLuhan actually transformed the history of communication into a seductive allegorical narrative, which preaches that we must first submit before we can be saved.

The plain fact that so much of McLuhan's later works already seems dated reveals him as a distinctive phenomenon of the 1960s. He may very well be remembered more for his analyses of content than those of form, even though he has repudiated *The Mechanical Bride* as obsolete since television. The great attention given to the generation gap, youth revolt, and university protest in *Understanding Media* and the later picture books (*The Medium is the Massage, Counterblast*) seems particularly naive today. His enormous popularity no doubt accounted for the ferocity of some of the attacks made upon him by the literary and university establishments; he reserved his greatest scorn in interviews for the traditional literary critics.

His vogue and the reaction to it clearly met a need. The sixties will be remembered, among other things, as the decade in which television came of age as the dominant medium of communication. Television had saturated America by 1960, with at least one set in virtually every home. Daily national network news arrived in 1963. McLuhan both reflected and encouraged the growth of media awareness in American society. He also identified correctly the extremely incestuous trend among the media themselves; an extraordinarily high percentage of media content consists of items concerning other media forms. Today, all entertainment, news, political events, and advertising coexist equally as multimedia affairs.

Along the way to his popular breakthrough, however, McLuhan smoothed out any of the critical edges he had exhibited in his thinking. He certainly abandoned the critical context that had been so crucial in the work of his alleged mentor, Harold Innis. Stripped from the public McLuhan were any Innisian vestiges of moral and political concern with American media imperialism, Canadian resistance, the power of advertising, or the growing hegemony of space over time bias in Western culture. In his focus on the primacy of forms of transmission, McLuhan borrowed freely from Innis; but with McLuhan, Innis's despairing warnings about the direction of new communications technologies were transformed into a celebration of the "inevitable."

McLuhan's glorification of television slid very easily into an apology for the corporate interests that controlled the medium. The McLuhan cult on Madison Avenue was very real in the sixties, as the advertising industry leaped to embrace a college professor who told ad men that they were creative artists. "People are looking all the time for an intellectual explanation of the work they are involved in," wrote one advertising executive in 1966. "They have for many years . . . revolted from the idea that advertising was mysterious, a sort of 'black art.' They wanted to know why and how it worked. I think in many ways McLuhan has had more to say for us to solve these problems than anybody previously."[56] McLuhan's frequent appearances on television helped turn him from knowledgeable sage into a mere pop idol grateful for the chance to glorify the medium giving him so much free exposure.

McLuhan's corporate multimedia newsletter, *Dew Line*, as well as his various consulting deals with advertising and media conglomerates, made it hard to swallow his continual public stance that he *personally* abhorred the changes he described. Yet one need not accept his personal mythology or his ties with the corporate world to acknowledge his contribution to a general shift in perception in American culture.

McLuhan's impact ought to be set in the context of the broader trend toward synchronic analyses of language, communication, myth, and expressive forms of all types. The post–World War II intellectual breakthroughs in structural anthropology, linguistics, and semiotics[57] all had certain affinities with the New Critical literary tradition in which McLuhan had originally been trained. Indeed, McLuhan himself may be viewed as a "medium" who popularized these approaches by applying their techniques to the analysis of American media fare. He made these esoteric disciplines relevant to the public imagination; in the process, he greatly enlarged the range of "legitimate" areas for cultural study.

McLuhan's penchant for exaggeration and outrage, for the pun and the probe, no doubt detracted from his status as a serious social theorist. The man who once appeared as a learned, obsessed, and even inspired prophet succeeded in getting just enough of his message across to be reduced to just another entertainer. His recent death made front-page news, putting him once again in the media spotlight from which he had receded. But the obituaries generally treated him as a quaint oddity from the mythological sixties, the quintessential product and creator of that media-haunted decade.

EPILOGUE

Dialectical Tensions in the American Media, Past and Future

We may think of the post-McLuhan era as one characterized by a deeper and more sophisticated consciousness of the enormous role played by modern communication in everyday life. But the semantic ambiguities once associated with the word *communication* now seem to have regrouped around that increasingly opaque term, *the media*. Much of the discourse about the media, in learned journals as well as informal conversation, suffers from fuzziness, lack of clarity, and a jumble of definitions. Think, for example, of the ways in which the noun *media* finds growing expression as an adjective, as in "media event," "media people," or "media hype."

Think, too, of the various usages of the noun form. The modern sense of the word dates, interestingly enough, from its use in advertising trade journals of the 1920s, as in the phrase "advertising media." But today the term is used interchangeably with the press or the journalistic profession, especially in the sense of investigative reporting. At the same time, *media* is often used to distinguish nonprint forms of communication, such as film and broadcasting, from print. It may connote the larger realms of entertainment and show business. Denunciations of the media as too liberal, too permissive, too conservative, or too manipulative invoke the term as a moral or political category. Most everyone engages in damning the media for glorifying, exaggerating, or even causing some particularly odious feature of modern life.

Confusion of the singular and plural forms, *medium* and *media*, surely reflects a popular perception of the incestuous relations among the various mass disseminators of words and images. Media content is remarkably reflexive; each medium is filled with material from and about other media. Over the past twenty years, a virtual fusion of the techniques, style, and subjects of entertainment programs and news programs has taken place. On the level of public awareness, this superheated reflexiveness takes some curious forms. Television rating wars between the networks are now treated as hard news; film and broadcasting executives enjoy an exalted status as celebrities, cult figures, and creative auteurs in their own right.

The bourgeois commercial nexus at the center of the American film, broadcasting, and press industries clearly encourages this situation. It also promotes the media as a total, unchanging, "natural" part of modern life. Indeed, the everywhere-ness, all-at-once-ness, and never-ending-ness of the media are powerful barriers to understanding, or even acknowledging, their history.

The diverse meanings evoked by the term *media* represent a linguistic legacy of the contradictory elements embedded in the history of all modern means of communication. For each medium is a matrix of institutional development, popular responses, and cultural content that ought to be understood as a product of dialectical tensions, of opposing forces and tendencies clashing and evolving over time, with things continually giving rise to their opposite. Broadly speaking, these contradictions have been expressed in terms of the tension between the progressive or utopian possibilities offered by new communications technologies and their disposition as instruments of domination and exploitation.

One finds parallels or refractions of this dialectic in the thought of American communications theorists. Within the tradition as a whole, Harold Innis and the later McLuhan represent opposite poles. Charles H. Cooley and John Dewey shared affinities with McLuhan's more utopian outlook, although they started from quite different premises. The emphasis among the Frankfurt group on the media as primary agents for maintaining the dominant monopolies of knowledge and power echoed the profound pessimism of Innis, but from quite another political and cultural vantage point. To varying degrees, several individual thinkers, notably Robert Park, encompassed these tensions within their own work. And the career of Paul Lazarsfeld, key figure in the empirical and behavioral tradition, exemplified the intellectual dialectic, for the refugee who survived by juggling market research contracts also gave T. W. Adorno his first job in America.

What I would like to stress here is the need to recover the historical elements of an as yet uncompleted dialectic in order to further understand the present configuration of American media, to suggest avenues for future research, and to perhaps make sense of the upheaval currently being wrought by new cable, video, and satellite technologies. What follows is a historical sketch of some dialectical tensions in American media as viewed from the three related standpoints of early institutional developments, early popular responses, and the cultural history of media content. Examples are taken mainly from the three media whose histories have already been discussed: the telegraph, motion pictures, and radio.

If the schema presented below seems to have naively favored the utopian side of the dialectic, I can only point to the present dearth of knowledge. We need to redress an imbalance in our historical thinking, to recover a hidden side of media history. At the same time, I have suggested a few nodes on the grimmer side that might prove fertile territory for investigation, areas where the media operate as the excrescence of commercial capitalism.

Finally, I have offered some thoughts on how the historical perspective may help us gain some insight into the latest rash of technological breakthroughs. Here I am less interested in presenting a static, grand theory than in stimulating discussion and action concerning the new fields that are now opening up in three main areas: decentralized distribution networks, greater individual control of hardware, and opportunities for innovative programming.

★

Considered as an institution, each medium that evolved from the work of individual inventors and entrepreneurs was later subsumed into larger corporate or military contexts. The key roles played by small concerns and amateurs in the early history of new communications technologies are too often forgotten. Yet the importance of corporate and military settings for technological progress and of the accompanying support by large capital investments and highly organized research teams clearly intensifies the closer one gets to the present.

Samuel F. B. Morse's perfection of a practical electric telegraph was a lonely and poverty-stricken venture. For six years after the 1838 demonstrations of a workable instrument, Morse failed to obtain any government or corporate subsidy for his work. Congress finally authorized a thirty-thousand dollar appropriation to build the first telegraph line in 1844. However, in refusing Morse's offer to buy him out, Congress thwarted his wish that the government control future telegraph development. The ensuing twenty-five years of wildcat speculation and construction, both fiercely competitive and wasteful, finally ended with the triumph of Western Union, the first of several communications monopolies owned by private enterprise.

In the case of motion pictures, one finds a larger group of individual inventors and small businessmen acting as prime catalysts for technological innovation. The variety of cameras and projectors used in the early years reflected the contributions of numerous inventors from around the world. In the early industry, capital investment as well as creative energy came largely from Jewish petit bourgeois immigrant exhibitors and distributors. They were eager to invest in the new business that was beneath the dignity of traditional sources of capital. With roots deep in the urban thicket of commercial amusements, motion pictures found their first audiences mainly in the ethnic and working-class districts of the large cities.

Each early attempt to standardize or license equipment, films, and distribution was undermined by successive waves of independents. The Motion Picture Patents Company, heavily capitalized and dominated by the Edison interests, looked invincible when formed in 1909, but it lasted only a few years. The Hollywood film colony, later the symbol of authority and rigid control, was originally founded by independents seeking to escape the grip of the patents company. The fluidity of the movie industry congealed after the introduction of sound in the late 1920s. "Talkies" helped solidify the hold of a few major studios as the technological complexity of sound production precluded the sort of independent activity characteristic of the early years.

Individual inventors and amateurs figured prominently in the first years of radio as well. Pioneers such as Marconi, De Forest, and Fessenden laid much of the foundation for wireless technology in small, personal research settings. The technological sophistication required for wireless telephony, as well as the needs of the military in World War I, encouraged more systematic and heavily financed research and development. Still, it is worth remembering that an important part of the strategy of large corporations such as A T & T and GE involved buying out and intimidating individual inventors, the most famous case being the notorious dealings of A T & T with Lee De Forest.

World War I had encouraged a boom in radio research, with close cooperation between A T & T, GE, Westinghouse, and the federal government, and it had led directly to the creation of RCA. But the emergence of broadcasting in 1920 came as a shock. Virtually no one had expected broadcasting, the sending of uncoded messages to a mass audience, to become the main use of wireless technology. By 1926 corporate infighting in the radio world resolved itself, leaving in its wake the basic structure of today's commercial television. A T & T agreed to abandon direct broadcasting and sold its station WEAF to RCA. A T & T then won RCA's assurance that it would drop plans to build an independent long-line system of wires. In addition, RCA, GE, and Westinghouse set up the National Broadcasting Company to exclusively handle broadcasting and contracted to lease the A T & T web of wires. NBC, with this powerful corporate backing, began to offer the first regular national broadcasting over two networks based in New York.

★

The dream of transcendence through machines is an ancient one, and the urge to annihilate space and time found particularly intense expression through new communications media. Overcoming the old constraints of time and space implied a great deal more than mere advances in physics. Generally speaking, popular reactions to dramatic improvements in communication emphasized the possibilities for strengthening a moral community and celebrated the conquering of those vast social and cultural distances that had traditionally kept the large majority of people isolated.

An especially strong utopian cast marked contemporary responses to the telegraph and the wireless. The public greeted the first telegraph lines of the 1840s with a combination of pride, excitement, sheer wonder, and some fear. As telegraph construction proceeded quickly in all directions, doubters, believers, and curious bystanders in dozens of cities and towns flocked to get a firsthand look. In 1844 Alfred Vail, Morse's assistant, reported that at the Baltimore end of their experimental line crowds besieged the office daily for a glimpse of the machine. They promised "they would not say a word or stir and didn't care whether they understood or not, only they wanted to say they had seen it." The first telegraph offices had to take these excited crowds into account. Walling off inquisitive onlookers with glass partitions, an early Pittsburgh office announced: "Ladies and Gentlemen, visiting the room merely as Spectators, are assigned ample space, as the most Perfect Order is desirable for the convenience of the public as well as of the Telegrapher."[1]

Successful completion of the first Atlantic cable in the summer of 1858 inspired wild celebrations around the country. Such intense public feeling about a technological achievement appears rather strange to us now; certainly it is difficult to envision such a reaction today. Bonfires, fireworks, and impromptu parades marked the occasion across the nation. New York City held a huge parade, which was described as the city's largest public celebration ever. Over fifteen thousand people, from working men's clubs, immigrant societies, temperance groups, and the like, marched in a procession that revealed the strength of the telegraph's hold on the public imagination.

A widely evinced sentiment held that "the Telegraph has more than a mechanical meaning; it has an ideal, a religious, and a prospective significance, far-reaching and incalculable in its influences." The subtle spark of electricity, one of the fundamental, if dimly understood, creative forces of the universe, was now at man's disposal. The telegraph applied that "marvellous energy to the transmission of thought from continent to continent with such rapidity as to forestall the flight of Time, and inaugurate new realizations of human powers and possibilities." The divine boon of the telegraph allowed man to become more godlike. "It is the thought that it has metaphysical roots and relations that make it sublime." Such paeans rhetorically united the technological advance in communication with the ancient meaning of that word as common participation or communion. They presumed the success of certain Christian messages; but they also suggested that the creation of a miraculous communications technology was perhaps the most important message of all.[2]

One can discern a direct link between the more spiritually toned early responses and the boom in electronic revivalism today. There seems no doubt in the minds of contemporary evangelists about the answer to Morse's query, "What hath God wrought?" The most effective and avant-garde use of the latest communications technologies is probably being made by the various evangelical preachers who regularly "thank God for television" as they broadcast revivals over vast cable and satellite hookups. As Bishop Fulton J. Sheen, a pioneer in the field, once remarked: "Radio is like the Old Testament, hearing wisdom, without seeing; television is like the New Testament because in it the wisdom becomes flesh and dwells among us."[3]

There were secular prophets as well, equally awed by the transforming potential of instantaneous communication. "I see the electric telegraphs of the earth/I see the filaments of the news of the wars, deaths, losses, gains, passions of my race," sang Walt Whitman in "Salut Au Monde" (1856). We know, of course, that those telegraphs ultimately were appropriated by the corporate power of Western Union and the Associated Press. But perhaps Whitman used "filaments" in a double sense, including its traditional meaning as part of the reproductive organs of a flower. If so, he conjured a potent predictive insight. For the telegraph, which we might take as a historical synecdoche for all the electronic media that followed, did more than carry the news. It helped create novel ways of chronicling, reporting, and dramatizing the "wars, deaths, losses, gains, passions" of the society. Our historical knowledge of these forms and their internal relations—from wire service reports and syndicated columns through tabloids, newsreels, and network news—remains surprisingly skimpy.

A more privatized type of utopian response greeted the first wireless devices of the 1890s and early 1900s. In the writings of scientists, amateur enthusiasts, and trade publications, one finds repeated projections of how wireless technology would soon be tailored to fit the personal needs of operators. Many observers of the rapidly advancing scene believed "we shall talk with our friends at sea or from sea to land, or from New York to Peking almost as freely as we now talk to our neighbors in the next block. An opera performance in London or Berlin will be caught up by this new transmitter set about the stage and thrown into the air for all the world to hear . . . it may be that no farm or fireside will be without one."[4]

Today we think of radio as synonymous with broadcasting, but in the first years after the earliest broadcasts the amateur wireless community scoffed at the idea that radio ought to be dominated by a few big stations. The activity of wireless amateurs from around 1905 through the late 1920s is too often neglected as a factor in the history of radio. The "hams" provided a crucial demand for wireless equipment, supplying the original seed capital and audience for the radio industry. They bought radio equipment and kept up with the latest technical advances before and after the first broadcasting. This group numbered perhaps a quarter of a million around 1920, including some fifteen thousand amateur transmitting stations.

Throughout the 1920s radio mania remained an active, participatory pastime for millions. One had to constantly adjust and rearrange batteries, crystal detectors, and vacuum tubes for the best reception. For numerous radio fans of all classes, the excitement lay precisely in the battle to get clear reception amidst the howling and chatter of the crowded ether. The cult of "DXing," trying to receive the most distant station possible, remained strong for years. In 1924 one newly converted radio fan wrote, not untypically, that he was not especially interested in the various programs. "In radio it is not the substance of communication without wires, but the fact of it that enthralls. It is a sport, in which your wits, learning, and resourcefulness are matched against the endless perversity of the elements. It is not a matter, as you may suppose, of buying a set and tuning in upon what your fancy dictates."[5]

By the end of the 1920s, however, the ascension of corporate-dominated commercial broadcasting radically curtailed this sort of radio activity. Broadcasting, originally conceived as a service by manufacturers for getting people to buy surplus radio equipment, eventually shoved aside the very people who had nurtured it. In its mature state, radio succeeded not in fulfilling the utopian visions first aroused by wireless technology, but rather in incorporating those urges into the service of advertising. First in radio and then in television, commercial broadcasting became the cutting edge of a technologized ideology of consumption. Consumer goods promised to make one happy by returning what had vanished. "Nostalgia," originally a painful melancholy caused by absence from one's home or country, has acquired a primarily temporal sense since the rise of broadcasting. One has nostalgic, bittersweet longings for earlier, "simpler" times, and these times are most frequently signified by a "golden age" of radio, movies, popular music, and so forth. Commercial broadcasting wedded the advertiser's message to older popular cultural forms that were transferred to the new home environment of radio.

Today, the advertising and marketing axis that grew up with radio has made audience demographics the crucial template for the production of most of our culture's symbolic forms of expression. The term *life-style* best captures the essence of the current version of this ideology of consumption. A catchall description for everything from one's clothing, work, or furnishings to preferred leisure pursuits, entertainments, and inebriates, this phrase already seems to have achieved saturation. It reduces all life to a style, equating how one lives with what one consumes. The post–World War II perfection of demographics as a predictive science and as a producer of crucial cultural maps is a story that remains to be told.

★

The cultural history of modern media, that is, the evolution of their content and the relation of that content to the larger popular culture, reveals another set of contradictions at work. To the extent that popular culture may be equated with the popular arts, modern media have operated mainly as business enterprises intent on maximizing profits. Especially within the broadcast media, the authority of advertising has been paramount in the establishment of cultural parameters and in the promotion of the consumption ethic as the supreme virtue. But this hegemony has never been as complete and total as it seemed on the surface. The media have not manufactured content out of thin air. Historically, the raw materials for media fare, as well as its creators, have been drawn from an assortment of cultural milieus.

The cultural histories of American film, radio, and television, particularly in their early years, could arguably be written entirely from the point of view of the contributions of "the others," immigrant, ethnic, and racial minorities in particular. The critical part played by immigrant audiences and Jewish immigrant entrepreneurs in the rise of the movie industry is well known. Slapstick comedy, raucous, vulgar, and universally appealing, was the first style to pack audiences in. It was also the first style to be identified as uniquely American around the world. Only in Hollywood could a Fatty Arbuckle be transformed in three years from a semiskilled plumber's helper into a comedy star making five thousand dollars a week. When the Warner brothers made the great leap into the sound era in 1927, it was not by accident that they chose *The Jazz Singer*, starring Al Jolson, as their vehicle. Its story of how a cantor's son renounces his father's religion for a career as a popular singer encapsulated both the history of the movie industry itself and the rapid secularization of Jewish life in America. The early film industry was energized in large part by a projection of the powerful urge toward collective representation so prominent in Jewish culture. The Jewish moguls reinvented the American dream in the course of creating the Hollywood mythos.

In the case of broadcasting, the exigencies of advertising demanded that programming present an aura of constant newness. Yet the content relied heavily upon traditional forms. Variety shows, hosted by comedians and singers, became the first important style on network radio. Drawing heavily upon the vaudeville format, these shows remained quite popular through World War II; many of the stars continued their success on television. The master of ceremonies served as a focal point for activity and as a means of easy identification with a sponsor's product. Most of the variety stars had long experience in earlier stage entertainment; ethnic and regional

stereotypes, dialect stories, and popular song, all staples of vaudeville and burlesque, easily made the transition to broadcasting. So
too did the pre–Civil War form of minstrelsy. The characters in
radio's first truly national hit show, "Amos n' Andy" (1928), were
direct descendants of blackface minstrel show figures.

These entertainments, and radio in general, seemed to have
played a significant mediating role for certain audiences. There is
intriguing fragmentary evidence suggesting that, in the early years
of radio at least, children of immigrants, particularly in cities, were
more likely to own radios than any other group. The census of 1930
revealed that 57.3 percent of the children in families of foreign or
mixed parentage owned radio sets, as compared with 39.9 percent in
families of native parentage. Among urban families, the figures
were 62.8 percent (highest of any group) and 53.2 percent, respectively. The historical relation between "media mindedness" and
"cultural otherness" is still largely unexplored, beyond a facile notion of "Americanization."[6]

The history of American popular music in this century offers perhaps the clearest example of how media content has been continually
invigorated and revitalized by forms, styles, entertainers, and artists from outside the mainstream. The growth of radio broadcasting
and the recording industry in the 1920s hastened the cross-fertilization of popular (but hitherto localized) musical forms. America's
rich racial and geographical diversity of authentic folk musics—
country, "mountain music," blues, jazz—became commercialized and
available to much broader audiences. The new media allowed audiences and artists exposure to musical forms previously unknown to
them. The post–World War II rise of rock 'n' roll, closely allied to the
more general phenomenon of youth culture, reflected a vital new
amalgam of white country music, black blues, and traditional Tin
Pan Alley show music.

Recent infusions of Third World musics such as reggae, ska, and
salsa point to the growth of an international, multicultural style in
popular music. Beneath all its glitter and flash, the disco boom is
fundamentally based on the popularization of Latin dance rhythms,
spiced with the urban gay sensibility. The power of the recording
and radio industries to standardize and exploit popular music, to
hype stars and trends, ought not to be ignored or minimized. But
denial of the authenticity at the core of much popular music grossly
simplifies the complex tensions existing within our popular culture.

★

Before I discuss several of the latest developments in communications technology, it might prove instructive to cast a fleeting look backward at two early media dreamers, Edward Bellamy and Hugo Gernsback. In 1889 Bellamy, America's preeminent utopian, elaborated an idealized vision of future communications in his short story "With the Eyes Shut." He described the dream of a railroad passenger suddenly transported into a whole new world of media gadgets. Phonographed books and magazines have replaced printed ones in railroad cars. Clocks announce the time with recorded sayings from the great authors. Letters, newspapers, and books are recorded and listened to on phonographic cylinders, instead of being read. With a slide-projecting phonograph, one can even listen to a play while watching the actors. Everybody carries around an indispensable item, a combination tape recorder and phonograph. Bellamy seems most concerned that the sense of hearing threatens to overwhelm that of sight. But what stands out in his fable is the limitless choice of programming available to the individual in a private setting.

Whereas Bellamy's fantasy spun images of inexhaustible "software," Hugo Gernsback, science-fiction writer and wireless enthusiast, was captivated by the radical potential of radio "hardware." In the early 1900s Gernsback tirelessly promoted amateur wireless activity in his own magazines and others. The culmination of this work came in his book *Radio For All* (1922), which projected "the future wonders of Radio" fifty years hence. Gernsback predicted the coming of television, videophones, telex, and remote-controlled aircraft. He managed to think up some devices we seem to have missed: radio-powered roller skates, radio clocks, even a "radio business control" console. As the frontispiece to Gernsback's book shows, he envisioned a future where an individual's radio equipment would be at the very center of business and social life.

Atavistic expressions of the utopian urges given voice by Bellamy and Gernsback appear all around us today. Only now, with the advent of new satellite and video technologies, their fantasies have a firmer material base. Of course, Bellamy's "software socialism" and Gernsback's "hardware socialism" hardly appear to be lurking around the corner; corporate capital has enormous resources invested in the expansion of that material base. The press is filled with stories detailing the maneuvers of RCA, Warner Communications, MCA, SONY, and all the rest in the scramble to get a piece of the new action. No one can deny the central position of big capital in the new advances. But the recent developments may still promise in essence what they appear to deny in substance.

The accelerated evolution of media hardware and software has been fueled largely by the persistence of utopian urges in the population at large. With the impending spread of cheap video hardware to large numbers of people—video cameras, cassette recorders, video disc players, and home computers—the potential exists for individuals and collectives to become producers as well as consumers. The historical gap in broadcasting between the oligopoly of transmission and the democracy of reception may thus be drastically reduced. It is important to see the interaction between the corporate giants and the deep and genuine desire on the part of people to gain more direct control over the means of communication and the content of communications. The recent revival of the cable television industry is a good case in point.

The decentralizing capacity of cable television has long been recognized, if not actually realized. Indeed, by the early 1970s, the "blue-sky" predictions that ended nearly every discussion of cable in the 1960s seemed laughable. The cable industry was in a great depression, with very little wiring of communities taking place. All the talk about public access channels, two-way hookups, video telephones, home computer terminals, and so forth seemed quite hollow because scarcely any cable companies could get financing to wire homes. Even in New York City, potentially the most lucrative market, both cable franchises were losing millions each year. But two new factors added to the scene in the last five years or so have rejuvenated the industry and freed venture capital.

First, the rise of pay cable services such as Home Box Office (HBO) and Showtime revealed an extensive latent demand for alternative programming. These channels charge a premium each month above the basic cable rate. HBO, owned by Time-Life and the dominant force in pay cable, began with a simple formula of old movies and live sports. It is now moving rapidly toward providing more original programming, such as entertainment specials, comedy shows, plays, and even something it dubs "docutainment," which sounds rather like a modern version of the old "March of Time" newsreels.

Second, the success of RCA's and Western Union's communication satellites has created viable distribution networks for the cable companies. Earth station receivers, costing anywhere from two thousand to twenty thousand dollars, allow cable operators to "get on the bird." Programmers are now busily putting together new networks and pay services aimed at reaching the growing cable audience. The availability of new and specialized programming in turn has stimulated a new demand for cable systems in various communities. Presently, about fifteen million American homes are wired for cable; some industry analysts think the figure could be 80 percent of all television homes by 1990.

Insofar as the power of commercial network television is based on its ability to deliver mass audiences to advertisers, its strength may soon be challenged by the decentralizing trend in cable. Several new networks aimed at specialized audiences have been created already: children, Hispanics, senior citizens, sports junkies. Cable and its attendant new video technologies will, at the very least, mean the decline of mass market television, breaking the thirty-year-old grip of the three commercial networks. The potential for eventual direct satellite transmissions to homes, bypassing local stations and cable systems alike, is also very real. The technological stage is now set for the postbroadcasting era.

Many cable programmers hope to profit in much the same way as special interest magazines, by precisely targeting a well-defined fraction of the population that certain advertisers wish to reach exclusively. The concept is known as "narrowcasting." One might legitimately ask what is so promising about these developments; the specter of "demographic" cable programming is rather depressing. For the present, however, one could argue that the revival of the cable industry itself has been a positive development, spurred by the push and pull between people who want alternative programming and programmers who want to see a greater cable market before they invest. There is no doubt that the hardware is now far ahead of the software. The crucial question has become, Can imaginative and innovative programming be created to take advantage of the new technologies?

The key point is that all of the independent program developers, artists, and political activists, who for years have been thwarted by the current system and could never get on the networks, now have a potential way to reach large audiences. A show that reaches twenty million people over network television today is considered a failure; this sort of standard will of necessity change. The new networks of distribution provide possible entry points for independents to reach viewers. Perhaps the most promising new nodes will be local cable and video discs.

Local cable companies all provide a surfeit of channels, including public access and leased channels. For a very small fee, public access channels allow total freedom for live, local programming. Most cable systems also have channels that can be leased by local groups who have lined up sponsors for their program. This whole area is currently in an embryonic state of development, although some communities are farther advanced in exploiting the potential for grass-roots programming.

There are still large unanswered questions about the video disc, which has just begun to be mass marketed. Video discs represent a more passive activity than video cassettes in that one will not be able to make one's own discs; video disc is to video cassette as phonograph records are to tape. The advantage of video disc, however, is said to be its superior quality of picture and sound and its lower cost. The big guns in the field have invested heavily in the home video market of nonbroadcast television. RCA's Selecta-Vision system reportedly represents its largest investment ever in a single product; it has also made a long-term deal with CBS to provide additional disc software. Similarly, N. V. Philips, the Dutch conglomerate, has contracted with MCA to provide software for its Magna-Vision home video center. These kinds of arrangements are likely to increase, but the outlook for software supply, as all concerned agree, leaves more room for independent activity. Local and national networks for video disc rental, sales, and production are already being formed.

Despite all of the high-powered market research and corporate wheeling and dealing, no one is quite certain how the video disc phenomenon will evolve. Incredibly, RCA projects a $7.5 billion video disc market by 1990, but capital could be wrong. Two crucial jokers in the deck are the incompatibility of various disc systems and, more importantly, the increasingly shaky state of the American economy. Will new communications hardware be affordable?

Given the nature of the continuing energy crisis, one could argue that in a broad sense communication must gain primacy over transportation in our society. An awareness of the dialectical tensions within the American media may explain why it is possible to criticize the worst tendencies of modern media—banalization, encouragement of the commodity fetish, the urge toward global hegemony —but at the same time to hold out real hope for future promise. It is less important to curb futurist fantasies than to continually attempt to expose the hidden political and social agenda attending technological progress. The recovery of historical perspective, bringing the contradictions within American media into sharper relief, can perhaps help us to remember the future of modern communication.

Notes

CITATION OF SOURCES

This book was written to appeal to the general reader as well as the historian. Accordingly, the scholarly apparatus has been kept to a minimum, and the documentation is presented as simply as possible. To keep the text uncluttered, the sources for quotations and other items are often summarized in notes covering several paragraphs. Sources in each note are generally given in the order in which the information being documented appears in the text; by matching text and notes, the reader should be able to discern the source for any particular item.

CHAPTER 1

1. Joseph Henry quoted in C. T. McClenachan, *Detailed Report of the Proceedings Had in Commemoration of the Successful Laying of the Atlantic Telegraph Cable* (New York: E. Jones and Co., 1859), p. 227. See also Marshall Lefferts, "The Electric Telegraph; Its Influence and Geographical Distribution," *Bulletin of American Geographical and Statistical Society* 2 (January 1857): 242–64. Some thirty years earlier, the Harvard professor Jacob Bigelow reintroduced the term *technology* into the language, by which he meant to describe "the principles, processes, and nomenclatures of the more conspicuous arts, particularly those which involve application of science, and which may be considered useful, by promoting the benefit of society" (*Elements of Technology* [Boston: Hilliard, Gray, Little, and Wilkins, 1829], p. v).

2. Alexander Jones, *Historical Sketch of the Electric Telegraph* (New York: G. P. Putnam, 1852), pp. 7–12; Carleton Mabee, *Samuel F. B. Morse: The American Leonardo* (New York: Alfred A. Knopf, 1944), pp. 190–92.

3. Samuel F. B. Morse to Sidney Morse, 13 January 1838, in Edward L. Morse, ed., *Samuel F. B. Morse: Letters and Journals*, 2 vols. (Boston: Houghton Mifflin Co., 1914), 2:73. The best account of Morse's struggles in these years is Robert L. Thompson, *Wiring a Continent: The History of The Telegraph Industry in the United States, 1832–1866* (Princeton: Princeton University Press, 1947), pp. 3–34. On the public demonstrations in early 1838, see *New York Journal of Commerce*, 29 January 1838, and Morse, ed., *Letters and Journals*, 2:77–82. The *Congressional Globe*, 21 February 1843, reported on the House debate attending Morse's appropriation; this is reprinted in Morse, ed., *Letters and Journals*, 2:193–95. Figure for telegraph mileage from "Telegraphs," in U.S. Census Office, *Seventh Census, Report of the Superintendent of the Census* (Washington, D.C.: Robert Armstrong, 1853), pp. 106–16.

4. Samuel F. B. Morse to Alfred Vail, 8 May 1844, and Samuel F. B. Morse to Sidney Morse, 31 May 1844, in Morse, *Letters and Journals*, 2:220–21, 224; Alfred Vail to Samuel F. B. Morse, 3 June 1844, quoted in Thompson, *Wiring*, p. 25; Mabee, *American Leonardo*, pp. 276–79.

5. *Rochester Daily American*, 20 May 1846; *Philadelphia North American*, 15 January 1846. For a detailed description of the operations of the original experimental line, including illustrations and relevant reports of Congress, see Alfred Vail, *The American Electro Magnetic Telegraph* (Philadelphia: Lea and Blanchard, 1845).

6. *Cincinnati Daily Commercial*, 6 August 1847; *Zanesville Courier*, 17 July 1847. These and other contemporary press accounts may be found in the Henry O'Rielly Collection, First Series, vol. 1, and Journalistic Series, vols. 1–2, New York Historical Society, New York, NY. O'Rielly was the most important of the early telegraph entre-

preneurs. On the telegraph in frontier districts, see also W. L. Stackhouse, "Telegraphic Communication in Michigan," *Michigan History Magazine* 24 (Winter 1940): 75–90; Ben Hur Wilson, "Telegraph Pioneering," *The Palimpsest* 6 (November 1925): 373–93; Ellis B. Usher, "The Telegraph in Wisconsin," *Proceedings of the State Historical Society of Wisconsin of 1913* (1914), pp. 91–109.

7. Philip Dorf, *The Builder: A Biography of Ezra Cornell* (New York: Macmillan, 1953), pp. 69–70.

8. William Bender Wilson, "The Telegraph in Peace and War," in *From the Hudson to the Ohio* (Philadelphia: Kensington Press, 1902), pp. 36–37. See also W. J. Johnston, *Telegraphic Tales and Telegraphic History* (New York: W. J. Johnston, 1880).

9. Daniel Davis, *Book of the Telegraph* (Boston: D. Davis, 1851), p. 3; E. Laurence, "The Progress of Electricity," *Harper's New Monthly* 39 (September 1869): 548; Charles Briggs and Augustus Maverick, *The Story of the Telegraph and a History of the Great Atlantic Cable* (New York: Rudd and Carleton, 1858), p. 13; Jones, *Historical Sketch*, p. vi.

10. Ezra S. Gannett, *Discourse on the Atlantic Telegraph* (Boston: Crosby, Nichols, and Co., 1858), p. 7; Laurence, "Progress of Electricity," p. 548; Jones, *Historical Sketch*, p. v; Lefferts, "Electric Telegraph," p. 264.

11. Taliaferro P. Shaffner, "The Ancient and Modern Telegraph," *Shaffner's Telegraph Companion* 1 (February 1854):85. See also Taliaferro P. Shaffner, *The Telegraph Manual* (New York: Pudney and Russell, 1859).

12. H. L. Wayland, "Results of the Increased Facility and Celerity of Inter-Communication," *New Englander* 16 (November 1858): 800; Briggs and Maverick, *Story of the Telegraph*, pp. 21–22. On the close affinity between the revivalistic mentality of this period and the celebration of technological advance, see Perry Miller, *The Life of the Mind in America* (New York: Harcourt, Brace, and World, 1965), pp. 299–313.

13. Briggs and Maverick, *Story of the Telegraph*, p. 13; *New York Times*, 9 August 1858.

14. See "Communication," *Oxford English Dictionary*, s.v.; "Communication," in Raymond Williams, *Keywords: A Vocabulary of Culture and Society* (New York: Oxford University Press, 1976), pp. 62–63. For an insightful discussion of the difference between the "ritual" and "transmission" meanings of communication, see James W. Carey, "A Cultural Approach to Communication," unpublished essay, 1973. Also see Carey's essay, "Mass Communication Research and Cultural Studies: An American View," in James Curran et al., eds., *Mass Communication and Society* (Beverly Hills: Sage Publications, 1977), pp. 409–25.

15. Henry D. Thoreau, *Walden*, Riverside Editions (Boston: Houghton Mifflin Co., 1957), p. 36.

16. Samuel F. B. Morse to House Committee on Commerce, 15 February 1838, in U. S. House, Committee on Commerce, *Electro-Magnetic Telegraphs*, 25th Cong., 2d sess., 1838, H. Rept. 753, app. C, p. 2; "The Nerve of the Continent," *Philadelphia North American*, 15 January 1846; William F. Channing, "On the Municipal Telegraph," *American Journal of Science and Arts*, 2d ser. 63 (May 1852): 58–59. See also George Prescott, *History, Theory and Practice of the Electric Telegraph* (Boston: Ticknor and Fields, 1860), pp. 435–38.

17. U.S. House, Committee of Ways and Means, *Magnetic Telegraph from Baltimore to New York*, 28th Cong., 2d sess., 1845, H. Rept. 187, p. 7; Laurence Turnbull, *Electro-Magnetic Telegraph, with an Historical Account of its Rise, Progress and Present Condition* (Philadelphia: A. Hart, 1853), p. 148; Donald Mann, "Telegraphing of Election Returns," *American Telegraph Magazine* 1 (November 1852): 74, 76; Davis, *Book of the Telegraph*, p. 44.

18. *New Orleans Price Current*, 1 September 1848. For further comments on the

telegraph and commerce, see, for example, McClenachan, *Detailed Report*, p. 7; Turnbull, *Telegraph*, pp. 77–78. On the various problems plaguing early telegraph lines, see Thompson, *Wiring*, pp. 217–26; and Wilson, "Telegraph."

19. Associated Press report, *New York Times*, 6 August 1858; Gannett, *Discourse*, p. 3. See also Joseph A. Copp, *The Atlantic Telegraph: A Discourse* (Boston: T. R. Marvin and Sons, 1858). For other reports on demonstrations around the nation, see *New York Times*, 5–20 August 1858.

20. *New York Times*, 9 August, 1–2 September 1858. See also McClenachan, *Detailed Report*; and Briggs and Maverick, *Story of the Telegraph*, pp. 245–50.

21. Frank L. Mott, *American Journalism* (New York: Macmillan Co., 1941), p. 48; Edwin Emery, *The Press and America* (Englewood Cliffs: Prentice-Hall, 1972), p. 193; Alfred M. Lee, *The Daily Newspaper in America* (New York: Macmillan Co., 1947), pp. 37–57.

22. Emery, *Press*, pp. 165–75; Mott, *American Journalism*, pp. 48–49, 243–44, 384–85. On the importance of the penny press, see also Walter L. Hawley, "Development of the American Newspaper," *Popular Science Monthly* 56 (December 1899): 186–204.

23. On the crucial significance of the telegraph for news gathering, see Victor Rosewater, *History of Cooperative Newsgathering in the United States* (New York: D. Appleton and Co., 1930), pp. 12–34; Emery, *Press*, pp. 196–98; Frederic Hudson, *Journalism in the United States from 1690 to 1872* (New York: Harper and Brothers, 1873), pp. 596–600; W. F. S. Shanks, "How We Get Our News," *Harper's Magazine* 34 (May 1867): 511–22. Michael Schudson, *Discovering the News: A Social History of American Newspapers* (New York: Basic Books, 1978), pp. 12–35, offers a useful discussion of the interaction between technological change and business enterprise, with particular reference to the penny press.

24. Swain: Thompson, *Wiring*, pp. 43, 48; James D. Reid, *The Telegraph in America* (New York: Derby Brothers, 1879), pp. 130–41; Rosewater, *Cooperative Newsgathering*, pp. 40–41; Bennett: Hudson, *Journalism*, p. 480; Calder M. Pickett, "Six New York Newspapers and their Response to Technology in the Nineteenth Century" (Ph.D. dissertation, University of Minnesota, 1959), pp. 174–78.

25. Emery, *Press*, pp. 199–201; Rosewater, *Cooperative Newsgathering*, pp. 45–47; Hudson, *Journalism*, p. 600. See also William H. Smith, "The Press as a News Gatherer," *Century Magazine* 42 (August 1891): 524–36. Smith, general manager of the Associated Press, argued that the 1830s and 1840s were a key transition period in American journalism when the emergence of "the demonstrable value of news" took place.

26. Rosewater, *Cooperative Newsgathering*, pp. 47–48; Bennett quoted in Isaac C. Pray, *Memoirs of James G. Bennett and His Times* (New York, Stringer and Townsend, 1855), pp. 363–64.

27. Richard Schwarzlose, "Harbor News Association: The Formal Origins of the AP," *Journalism Quarterly* 45 (Summer 1968): 253–60; Lee, *Daily Newspaper in America*, pp. 495–516; Smith, "The Press as a News Gatherer," p. 524. Rosewater, *Cooperative Newsgathering*, pp. 64–70, has examples and descriptions of earlier attempts.

28. Thompson, *Wiring*, pp. 220–24; Rosewater, *Cooperative Newsgathering*, pp. 52–56. For examples of rules of the telegraph companies regarding the press, see Thompson, *Wiring*, pp. 47, 221; for regulations of early news gathering agencies, see Schwarzlose, "Harbor News Association."

29. Jones, *Historical Sketch*, pp. 123, 136. See also Lee, *Daily Newspaper*, pp. 494–96. Jones includes examples of commercial and economic ciphers of the day.

30. Hawley, "Development of the American Newspaper," p. 186. Figures for newspapers are from Lee, *Daily Newspaper*, p. 718.

31. Pickett, "Six New York Newspapers and Their Response to Technology in the

Nineteenth Century"; Simon N. D. North, *History and Present Condition of the Newspaper and Periodical Press of the United States* (Washington, D.C.: Census Office, 1884), p. 110.

32. "The Intellectual Effects of Electricity," *The Spectator* 63 (9 November 1889): 631–32.

33. W. J. Stillman, "Journalism and Literature," *Atlantic Monthly* 68 (November 1891): 694. See also, for example, Henry R. Elliott, "The Ratio of News," *Forum* 5 (March 1888): 99–107; Noah Brooks, "The Newspaper of the Future," *Forum* 9 (July 1890): 569–78.

34. Conde B. Pallen, "Newspaperism," *Lippincott's Monthly* 38 (November, 1866): 476. See also D. O. Kellogg, "The Coming Newspaper," *The American* 20 (9 August 1890): 328–30.

35. George M. Beard, *American Nervousness* (New York: G. P. Putnam's Sons, 1881), pp. vi, 99, 134.

36. U.S. House, *Report of the Postmaster General*, 29th Cong., 2d sess., 1846, H. Doc. 4, p. 689; Samuel F. B. Morse to House Committee on Commerce, 15 February 1838, in U.S. House, Committee on Commerce, *Electro-Magnetic Telegraphs*, 25th Cong., 2d sess., 1838, H. Rept. 753, app. C, pp. 8–9. The most persuasive early argument for a government telegraph run by the post office can be found in U.S. House, Committee of Ways and Means, *Magnetic Telegraph from Baltimore to New York*, 28th Cong., 2d sess., 1845, H. Rept. 187. It is not clear how much the telegraph patent rights would have cost the government in 1845, as Congress never even permitted negotiation with Morse and his partners. For a review of the fragmentary evidence on this question, see Thompson, *Wiring*, p. 34.

37. The best detailed accounts of Western Union growth are in Thompson, *Wiring*, pp. 259–99, 406–40, and Reid, *Telegraph in America*, pp. 455–76. Also useful are Alvin F. Harlow, *Old Wires and New Waves: The History of the Telegraph, Telephone and Wireless* (New York: D. Appleton-Century Co., 1936), pp. 250–59; and James M. Herring and Gerald C. Cross, *Telecommunications: Economics and Regulation* (New York: McGraw-Hill Book Co., 1936), pp. 1–18. On the importance of railroad contracts, see Thompson, *Wiring*, pp. 290, 443–44; and Harlow, *Old Wires and New Waves*, pp. 213–14. On the relationship between Western Union and the telephone industry, see N. R. Danielian, *A. T. & T: The Story of Industrial Conquest* (New York: Vanguard Press, 1939), pp. 41–75.

38. These two tables are compiled from the following sources: U.S. Bureau of the Census, *Tenth Census of the United States, 1880*, vol. 4., *Report on the Agencies of Transportation in the United States*, "Report on the Statistics of Telegraphs and Telephones in the United States"; John Richards, *A Talk on Telegraphic Topics* (Chicago: n.p., 1882), p. 18; Nathaniel P. Hill, "Postal Telegraph," in *Speeches and Papers on the Silver, Postal Telegraph and Other Economic Questions* (Colorado Springs: Gazette Printing Co., 1890), p. 221.

39. Testimony of Daniel H. Craig, in U.S. Senate, Education and Labor Committee, *Report upon the Relations between Labor and Capital*, 4 vols. (Washington, D.C.: Government Printing Office, 1885), 2:1268; Peter Knights, "Conflict between the New York Associated Press and the Western Associated Press, 1866–1867" (Master's thesis, University of Wisconsin, 1965), p. 11; Reid, *Telegraph in America*, pp. 410–11.

40. Rosewater, *Cooperative Newsgathering*, pp. 86–98; Hudson, *Journalism*, pp. 613–15.

41. Knights, "Conflict," pp. 9–10, 20–64; Rosewater, *Cooperative Newsgathering*, pp. 100–107, 111–37. For examples of agreement between Western Union and the press associations, see U.S. Senate, Committee on Post Office and Railroads, *Testimony, Statements, etc. Taken by the Senate Committee on Post Office and Railroads*, 48th Cong., 1st sess., 1884, S. Rept. 577, pt. 2, pp. 317–22.

42. U.S. House, Committee on Appropriations, *To Connect the Telegraph with the*

Postal Service, 42d Cong., 3d sess., 1872, H. Rept. 6, p. 7

43. U.S. Senate, Committee on Post Offices and Post Roads, *Postal Telegraph*, 43d Cong., 1st sess., 1874, S. Rept. 242, pp. 1, 3. See also U.S. Senate, Committee on Post Offices and Post Roads, *Telegraph Lines as Post Roads*, 43d Cong., 2d sess., 1875, S. Rept. 624, pp. 3–4.

44. Testimony of Henry George, *Report upon the Relations between Labor and Capital*, 1:481–83; Henry George, Jr., *Life of Henry George* (New York: Doubleday and McClure, 1900), pp. 182–87. See also Testimony of Walter P. Phillips, secretary and general manager of the United Press, and Testimony of Lloyd Brezee of the *Detroit Evening Journal, Testimony on Post Office and Railroads*, pp. 287–314.

45. Testimony of James W. Simonton, U.S. Senate, Committee on Railroads, *Competing Telegraph Lines*, 45th Cong., 3d sess., 1879, S. Rept. 805, pp. 38, 51; Testimony of William H. Smith, *Testimony on Post Office and Railroads*, pp. 292, 300.

46. Testimony of William Orton, U.S. House, Select Committee on the Postal Telegraph, *Postal Telegraph in the United States*, 41st Cong., 2d sess., 1870, H. Rept. 114, p. 99.

47. A complete list of the various bills and reports can be found in Frank Parsons, *The Telegraph Monopoly* (Philadelphia: C. F. Taylor, 1899), pp. 17–18. Another useful summary of telegraph reform measures is in Hill, "Postal Telegraph," pp. 198–235.

48. Charles A. Sumner, *The Postal Telegraph* (San Francisco: Bacon and Co., 1879), p. 9.

49. U.S. House, *Report of the Postmaster General*, 51st Cong., 2d sess., 1890, H. Exec. Doc. 1, pt. 4, p. 8. This report includes a list of groups favoring telegraph reform, as well as a detailed argument for the telegraph as a natural extension of the post office. See also Parsons, *Telegraph Monopoly*, pp. 12–14.

50. Sumner, *The Postal Telegraph*, p. 6. On the Western Union lobbying effort, particularly the franking privileges supplied to officials, see William Orton's own description of its political importance in Hill, "Postal Telegraph," p. 224.

CHAPTER 2

1. Edward B. Tylor, *Primitive Culture: Researches into the Development of Mythology, Philosophy, Religion, Art, and Custom*, 2 vols. (New York: Henry Holt and Co., 1877), 1:1. For a succinct summary of the evolution of the term *culture* in Western thought, see *Encyclopedia of Philosophy*, 1967 ed., s.v. "Culture and Civilization," by Raymond Williams. The most comprehensive treatment of the word is that by A. L. Kroeber and Clyde Kluckhohn in *Culture: A Critical Review of Concepts and Definitions* (Cambridge, Mass.: Peabody Museum, 1952), which focuses on the "culture concept" as it has been used by anthropologists.

2. Matthew Arnold, *Culture and Anarchy*, 1882 ed., edited, with introduction and notes by Ian Gregor (Indianapolis: Dobbs-Merrill, 1071), p. 56; John Addington Symonds, "Culture: Its Meaning and Uses," *New Review* 7 (July 1892): 107–8.

3. Arnold, *Culture and Anarchy*, pp. 36–37; Symonds, "Culture," p. 106.

4. Matthew Arnold, *Civilization in the United States: First and Last Impressions of America* (Boston: Cupples and Hurd, 1888), p. 189.

5. Thomas Wentworth Higginson, "A Plea for Culture," *Atlantic Monthly* 19 (January 1867): 30.

6. A. A. Stevens, "The Way to Larger Culture," *Harper's Monthly* 107 (June 1903): 47; William T. Brewster, "Some Recent Guides to Culture," *Forum* 38 (January 1907): 381; Henry Hartshorne, "American Culture," *Lippincott's Magazine* 1 (June 1868): 647; "Concerning Culture," *Outlook* 48 (9 December 1893): 1073.

7. Symonds, "Culture," p. 105.

8. Arnold, *Culture and Anarchy*, pp. 56, 37, 42. See Raymond Williams, *Culture*

and Society, 1780–1850 (New York: Harper and Row, 1958), pp. 110–129, for a critical yet sympathetic treatment of Arnold's political ideas in the context of British thought.

9. Charles D. Warner, "What is Your Culture to Me?," *Scribner's Monthly* 4 (August 1872): 475, 473, 478; F. W. Gunsaulus, "The Ideal of Culture," *The Chautauguan* 16 (October 1892): 63.

10. Arnold, *Culture and Anarchy*, p. 56; Alfred Berlyn, "Culture for the Million," *Living Age* 279 (13 December 1913): 701–2. See also John Morley, "On Popular Culture: An Address," *Eclectic Magazine* 88 (February 1877): 129–40.

11. Ralph Waldo Emerson, "Introductory," first in a series of lectures on human culture delivered in 1837–38, in S. E. Whicher, R. E. Spiller, and W. E. Williams, eds., *The Early Lectures of Ralph Waldo Emerson*, vol. 2, *1836–1838* (Cambridge: Harvard University Press, Belknap Press, 1964), pp. 221, 216. Or, as Emerson wrote in "The American Scholar": "I ask not for the great, the remote, the romantic. . . . I embrace the common, I explore and sit at the feet of the familiar, the low. Give me insight into today, and you may have the antique and future worlds."

12. Van Wyck Brooks, "The Culture of Industrialism" (1918), in *Three Essays on America* (New York: E. P. Dutton and Co., 1934), pp. 129, 135; Randolph Bourne, "Our Cultural Humility," *Atlantic Monthly* 114 (October 1914): 505, 506.

13. Walt Whitman, "Democracy," *Galaxy* 4 (December 1867): 930–31.

14. Whitman, "Democracy," pp. 930, 931, and *Democratic Vistas* (London: Walter Scott, 1888), p. 43.

15. The best account of the prehistory of the motion picture is in Kenneth MacGowan, *Behind the Screen: The History and Techniques of the Motion Picture* (New York: Delacorte Press, 1965), pp. 25–84. Also useful are Kurt W. Marek, *Archaeology of the Cinema* (London: Thames and Hudson, 1965); and Frederick A. Talbot, *Moving Pictures: How They are Made and Worked* (Philadelphia: J. B. Lippincott, 1912), pp. 1–29. On the specific contributions of Marey, Muybridge, and others, see Robert Sklar, *Movie-Made America* (New York: Random House, 1975), pp. 5–9; MacGowan, *Behind the Screen*, pp. 45–64.

16. Gordon Hendricks, *The Edison Motion Picture Myth* (Berkeley: University of California Press, 1961), p. 142. The Edison quotation is taken from his preface to W. K. L. Dickson and Antonia Dickson, *History of the Kinetograph, Kinetoscope, and Kinetophonograph* (New York: n.p., 1895), the Dicksons' own history of the inventions.

17. On the success and wide geographical dispersion of kinetoscopes, see Gordon Hendricks, *The Kinetoscope* (New York: Beginnings of the American Film, 1966), pp. 64–69. These parlors often contained phonographs and other machine novelties. On the kinetoscope at the Chicago fair, see Robert Grau, *The Theater of Science: A Volume of Progress and Achievement in the Motion Picture Industry* (New York: Broadway Publishing Co., 1914), pp. 3–4; and Hendricks, *Kinetoscope*, pp. 40–45.

18. For descriptions of these early films and how they were made, see Dickson and Dickson, *History*, pp. 23–40; Hendricks, *Kinetoscope*, pp. 21–28, 70–97; Joseph H. North, *The Early Development of the Motion Picture, 1887–1900* (New York: Arno Press, 1973), pp. 1–26.

19. Gordon Hendricks, *Beginnings of the Biograph* (New York: Beginnings of the American Film, 1964); MacGowan, *Behind the Screen*, pp. 75–84; North, *Early Development*, pp. 23–33; Terry Ramsaye, "The Motion Picture," *Annals of the American Academy of Political and Social Science* 128 (November 1926): 1–19.

20. Norman C. Raff and Frank R. Gammon, two of Edison's business partners, to Thomas Armat, 5 March 1896, in Terry Ramsaye, *A Million and One Nights: A History of the Motion Picture* (New York: Simon and Schuster, 1926), p. 224.

21. FILMS IN VAUDEVILLE: "Edison Vitascope Cheered," *New York Times*, 24 April 1896; Grau, *Theater of Science*, pp. 11–12; Benjamin B. Hampton, *History of the American Film Industry* (1931; reprint ed., New York: Dover Publications, 1971), pp.

12–14. ITINERANT EXHIBITORS: Grau, *Theater of Science*, pp. 28–33; North, *Early Development*, pp. 55–56; George Pratt, "'No Magic, No Mystery, No Sleight of Hand,'" *Image* 8 (December 1959): 192–211. PENNY ARCADES: Lewis Jacobs, *The Rise of the American Film* (New York: Harcourt, Brace and Co., 1939), pp. 5–8; Grau, *Theater of Science*, pp. 11–16; Hampton, *History*, pp. 12–14.

22. Jacobs, *Rise*, pp. 52–66, 81–85; Hampton, *History*, pp. 64–82; Ramsaye, *Million and One Nights*, pp. 59–72. An important review of the activities of the Motion Picture Patents Company is Ralph Cassady, Jr., "Monopoly in Motion Picture Production and Distribution: 1908–1915," *Southern California Law Review* 32 (Summer 1959): 325–90.

23. The rise of the independents and their contributions to both film industry and film art is a whole story in itself. See Jacobs, *Rise*, pp. 51–94; Hampton, *History*, pp. 83–145; Anthony Slide, *Early American Cinema* (New York: A. S. Barnes, 1970), pp. 102–35.

24. Tally's advertisement reproduced in MacGowan, *Behind the Screen*, p. 128; Hampton, *History*, pp. 44–46; Jacobs, *Rise*, pp. 52–63.

25. I have compiled these figures from several sources, using the more conservative estimates where there is conflict. 1907: Joseph M. Patterson, "The Nickelodeon," *Saturday Evening Post* 180 (23 November 1907): 10; "The Nickelodeon," *Moving Picture World* 1 (4 May 1907): 140. 1911: Patents Company figures are in Cassady, "Monopoly in Motion Picture Production and Distribution," p. 363 (a little over half of these were licensed by the trust, paying the weekly two-dollar fee); William Inglis, "Morals and Moving Pictures," *Harper's Weekly* 54 (30 July 1910): 12–13. 1914: Frederic C. Howe, "What to do With the Motion Picture Show," *Outlook* 107 (20 June 1914): 412–16. Howe, chairman of the National Board of Censorship of Moving Pictures, estimated a daily attendance of between seven and twelve million; W. P. Lawson, "The Miracle of the Movie," *Harper's Weekly* 60 (2 January 1915): 7–9.

26. Statistics gathered from the following sources: U.S. Department of Commerce, *Thirty-eighth Statistical Abstract of the United States* (Washington, D.C.: Government Printing Office, 1915). NEW YORK: Michael M. Davis, *The Exploitation of Pleasure: A Study of Commercial Recreation in New York* (New York: Russell Sage Foundation, 1911). Davis's careful study of the attendance at New York City theaters estimated 900,000 for Manhattan movie houses alone. Three years later the National Board of Censorship placed the New York daily attendance between 850,000 and 900,000, so the 1.5 million weekly figure for 1911 is probably low. CLEVELAND: Robert O. Bartholomew, *Report of Censorship of Motion Pictures* (Cleveland: n.p., 1913). DETROIT: Rowland Haynes, "Detroit Recreation Survey" (1912), cited in Richard H. Edwards, *Popular Amusements* (New York: Association Press, 1915), pp. 50–51. SAN FRANCISCO: "Public Recreation," *Transactions of the Commonwealth Club of California* (1913), cited in Edwards, *Popular Amusements*, pp. 16, 51. MILWAUKEE: Rowland Haynes, "Recreation Survey, Milwaukee, Wisconsin," *Playground* 6 (May 1912): 38–66. KANSAS CITY: Rowland Haynes and Fred F. McClure, *Second Annual Report of the Recreation Department of the Board of Public Welfare* (Kansas City: n.p., 1912). INDIANAPOLIS: F. R. North, "Indianapolis Recreation Survey" (1914), cited in Edwards, *Popular Amusements*, p. 33. TOLEDO: J. J. Phelan, *Motion Pictures as a Phase of Commercialized Amusements in Toledo, Ohio* (Toledo: Little Book Press, 1919).

27. Howard R. Knight, *Play and Recreation in a Town of 6000: A Recreation Survey of Ipswich, Mass.* (New York: Russell Sage Foundation, 1914); Lee F. Hanmer and Clarence A. Perry, *Recreation in Springfield, Illinois* (New York: Russell Sage Foundation, 1914). The Iowa study was done by Irving King and is cited in Hanmer and Perry, *Recreation in Springfield*.

28. Edward A. Ross, Introduction to Richard H. Edwards, *Popular Amusements* (New York: Associated Press, 1915), p. 5; Edwards, *Popular Amusements*, pp. 20–21, 133; Francis R. North, *A Recreation Survey of the City of Providence* (Providence: Providence Playground Association, 1912), p. 58; Belle L. Israels, "Recreation in Rural

Communities," *Proceedings of the International Conference of Charities and Correction* (Fort Wayne: n.p., 1911), p. 105; Frederic C. Howe, "Leisure," *Survey* 31 (3 January 1914): 415–16; Davis, *Exploitation of Pleasure*, p. 4.

29. Raymond Fosdick, *A Report on the Condition of Moving Picture Shows in New York* (New York: n.p., 1911), p. 11. See also Charles de Young Elkus, "Report on Motion Pictures," *Transactions of the Commonwealth Club of California* 8 (1914): 251–72, a report on fifty-eight motion picture houses in San Francisco.

30. Dr. George M. Gould in the *Journal of the American Medical Association*, quoted in "Health," *Survey* 29 (15 February 1913): 677; John Collier, *The Problem of Motion Pictures*, (New York: National Board of Censorship, 1910), p. 5; Jane Addams, *The Spirit of Youth and the City Streets* (New York: Macmillan Co., 1910), p. 86; John Collier, "Light on Moving Pictures," *Survey* 25 (1 October 1910): 801. See also Vice Commission of Chicago, *The Social Evil in Chicago* (Chicago: Gunthrop Warner, 1911), p. 247, for claims that "children have been influenced for evil by the conditions surrounding some of these shows."

31. Davis, *Exploitation of Pleasure*, p. 54; Haynes and McClure, *Recreation Survey of Kansas City*, p. 78, quotes examples of the handbills. For further descriptions of what went on inside the nickelodeons, as well as the reasons for their rapid spread across the country, see the trade papers, for example: "Trade Notes," *Moving Picture World* 1 (30 March 1907): 57–58; Melville C. Rice, "The Penny Arcade as a Side Show," *The Nickelodeon* 1 (January 1909): 23; "Vaudeville in Picture Theaters," *The Nickelodeon* 1 (March 1909): 85–86. See also Edward Wagenknecht, *Movies in the Age of Innocence* (Norman: University of Oklahoma Press, 1962), Introduction.

32. Simon N. Patten, *Product and Climax* (New York: B. W. Huebsch, 1909), pp. 18–19.

33. Ibid., p. 28.

34. Collier, *The Problem of Motion Pictures*, p. 5; Grau, *Theater of Science*, pp. 19–20; Marcus Loew, "The Motion Picture and Vaudeville," in Joseph P. Kennedy, ed., *The Story of the Films* (Chicago: A. W. Shaw, 1927), pp. 285–300; William T. Foster, *Vaudeville and Motion Picture Shows: A Study of Theaters in Portland, Oregon* (Portland: Reed College, 1914), pp. 12–13; "Moving Pictures in Indianapolis," *Survey* 24 (23 July 1910): 614; Bartholomew, *Report of Censorship of Motion Pictures*, p. 14.

35. "Vaudeville or Not?" *The Nickelodeon* 1 (November 1909): 134. For an example of provaudevillian sentiment in the trade, see "The Elevation of Vaudeville," *Moving Picture World* 1 (18 May 1907): 164. See also Boyd Fisher, "The Regulation of Motion Picture Theaters," *American City* 7 (September 1912): 520–22; John Collier, " 'Movies' and the Law," *Survey* 27 (20 January 1912): 1628–29.

36. "Say Picture Shows Corrupt Children," *New York Times*, 24 December 1908; "Picture Shows All Put Out of Business," *New York Times*, 25 December 1908; "Picture Show Men Organize to Fight," *New York Times*, 26 December 1908; "Mayor Makes War on Sunday Vaudeville," *New York Times*, 29 December 1908; Sonya Levien, "New York's Motion Picture Law," *American City* 9 (October 1913): 319–21. See also Sklar, *Movie-Made America*, pp. 30–31.

37. " 'Movie' Manners and Morals," *Outlook* 113 (26 July 1916): 695; Patterson, "The Nickelodeon," p. 11; Ramsaye, "The Motion Picture." Good descriptions of the working class audience at the movies can be found in Barton W. Currie, "The Nickel Madness," *Harper's Weekly* 51 (24 August 1907): 1246–47; Mary Heaton Vorse, "Some Picture Show Audiences," *Outlook* 97 (24 June 1911): 442–47; Lucy F. Pierce, "The Nickelodeon," *The World Today* 15 (October 1908): 1052–57.

38. Davis, *Exploitation of Pleasure*, table 8, p. 30; a table note explains: "The social groups considered were three—working class, business or clerical class, and leisure class. Costume and demeanor enabled the observer, after a little experience, to place his people quite readily." Charles Stelzle, "How One Thousand Working Men Spent Their Spare Time," *Outlook* 106 (4 April 1914): 722–66; this article summarizes the

results of a Ph.D. dissertation done at Columbia University by George E. Bevans.

39. Elizabeth B. Butler, *Women and the Trades: Pittsburgh, 1907–1908* (New York: Charities Publication Committee of the Russell Sage Foundation, 1909), p. 333.

40. Ibid.

41. Margaret F. Byington, *Homestead: The Households of a Mill Town* (New York: Charities Publication Committee of the Russell Sage Foundation, 1910), p. 111.

42. Russell Merritt, "Nickelodeon Theaters 1905–1914; Building an Audience for the Movies," in Tino Balio, ed., *The American Film Industry* (Madison: University of Wisconsin Press, 1976), p. 65.

43. Charles F. Morris, "A Beautiful Picture Theater," *The Nickelodeon* 1 (March 1909): 65–67. On the desirability of finer theaters and their requirements for better pictures, see "The Modern Motion Picture Theater," *Motion Picture News* 8 (6 December 1913).

44. "A Newsboy's Point of View," included in Herbert A. Jump, *The Religious Possibilities of the Motion Picture* (New Britain Conn.: n.p., 1910?). This item can be found in the National Board of Review of Motion Pictures Collection, 1911–26, NC 17, 225, Lincoln Center Theater Library, New York; Merritt, "Nickelodeon Theaters," pp. 64–65. For examples of those who were more sanguine about movies as a positive agent for assimilation, see Knight, "Americanization of the Immigrant Through Recreation," in *Play and Recreation in a Town of 6000*, pp. 60–65; Constance D. Leupp, "The Motion Picture as a Social Worker," *Survey* 24 (27 August 1910): 739–41; "The Moving Pictures and the National Character," *Review of Reviews* 42 (September 1910): 315–20.

45. "Censors Inspect Nickel Theaters," *Chicago Tribune*, 1 May 1907; Jane Addams, *Twenty Years at Hull House* (New York: Macmillan, 1910), p. 386.

46. "Social Workers to Censor Shows," *Chicago Tribune*, 3 May 1907.

47. Addams, *The Spirit of Youth*, pp. 86–87, 75–76, 103. For views late in life, see Jane Addams, *The Second Twenty Years at Hull House* (New York: Macmillan Co., 1930), especially the chapter on "The Play Instinct and the Arts."

48. *Report of the National Board of Censorship of Motion Pictures* (New York: National Board of Censorship, 1913), p. 6; *The Standards of the National Board of Censorship* (New York: National Board of Censorship, 1914?).

49. *Report of the National Board*, pp. 3–4; *Standards of the National Board*, pp. 3–5; W. P. Lawson, *The Movies: Their Importance and Supervision* (New York: National Board of Censorship, 1915), p. 6. For descriptions of the daily work of the National Board of Censorship, see Charles W. Tevis, "Censoring the Five Cent Drama," *The World Today* 19 (October 1910): 1132–39, Orrin G. Cocks, "Applying Standards to Motion Picture Films," *Survey* 32 (27 June 1914): 337–38.

50. Foster, *Vaudeville and Motion Picture Shows in Portland, Oregon*, p. 12; Pennsylvania State Board of Censorship, *Rules and Standards* (Harrisburg: J. L. L. Kuhn, 1918), pp. 15–17. See also Elkus, "Report on Motion Pictures," on the continuing need for local censorship.

51. See A. Nicholas Vardac, *Stage to Screen: Theatrical Method from Garrick to Griffith* (Cambridge: Harvard University Press, 1949); John R. Fell, "Dissolves by Gaslight: Antecedents to the Motion Picture in Nineteenth-Century Melodrama," *Film Quarterly* 23 (Spring 1970): 22–34. For contemporary discussions on this relationship, see Robert Grau, "The Motion Picture Show and the Living Drama," *Review of Reviews* 45 (March 1912): 329–36; Bennet Musson and Robert Grau, "Fortunes in Films: Moving Pictures in the Making," *McClure's* 40 (December 1912): 193–202.

52. Brander Matthews, "Are the Movies a Menace to the Drama?" *North American Review* 205 (March 1917): 451, 454.

53. Walter P. Eaton, "The Canned Drama," *American Magazine* 68 (September 1909): 495, 500.

54. Walter P. Eaton, "The Menace of the Movies," *American Magazine* 76 (September 1909): 55–60, and "A New Epoch in the Movies," *American Magazine* 78 (October 1914): 44.

55. Walter P. Eaton, "Class Consciousness and the 'Movies,'" *Atlantic Monthly* 115 (January 1915): 55.

56. Robert Coady, "Censoring the Motion Picture," *Soil* 1 (December 1916): 38. See also Clayton Hamilton, "The Art of the Moving Picture Play," *The Bookman* 32 (January 1911): 512–16; "A Democratic Art," *The Nation* 97 (28 August 1913): 193. Myron D. Lounsbury, "'Flashes of Lightning': The Moving Picture in the Progressive Era," *Journal of Popular Culture* 3 (Spring 1970): 769–97, contains a useful analysis of two of the earliest regular film critics, Louis Reeves Harrison and Frank Woods.

57. Hugo Muensterberg, *The Photoplay: A Psychological Study* (New York: D. Appleton and Co., 1916), pp. 52, 71, 88, 106–7, 173, 228, 230.

58. Vachel Lindsay, *The Art of the Moving Picture* (New York: Macmillan Co., 1915), pp. 65–66, 206, 224, 7.

CHAPTER 3

1. For general reviews of telegraphy by conduction and induction, see J. J. Fahie, *A History of Wireless Telegraphy, 1838–1899* (New York: Dodd, Mead and Co., 1899), pp. 1–78; Silvanus P. Thompson, "Telegraphy Across Space," *Journal of the Society of the Arts* 46 (1 April 1898): 453–60, and "Telegraphy Without Wires," *Saturday Review* 83 (26 June 1897): 708–9; G. G. Blake, *History of Radio Telegraphy and Telephony* (London: Radio Press, 1926), pp. 5–11, 32–48. On Edison's motograph, see Thomas A. Edison, "The Air Telegraph," *North American Review* 142 (March 1886): 285–91. On Preece, see W. H. Preece, "Aetheric Telegraphy," *Journal of the Society of the Arts* 47 (5 May 1899): 519–25, and "Wireless Telephony," *The Independent* 52 (4 October 1900): 2368–69.

2. John Trowbridge, "Telegraphing Through the Air Without Wires," *The Chautauquan* 15 (April 1892): 54, 57. For a similarly pessimistic view, see Thompson, "Telegraphy Across Space."

3. The standard work on the development of early wireless technology is now Hugh G. J. Aitken, *Syntony and Spark: The Origins of Radio* (New York: John Wiley and Sons, 1976), a book which came to my attention only after this chapter had been completed. Aitken's careful, closely reasoned study focuses on the contributions of Hertz, Lodge, and Marconi, and the concept of "syntony" as it related to their efforts. Good summaries of the contributions of Maxwell and Hertz can also be found in William Maver, "Wireless Telegraphy: Its Past and Present Status and Its Prospects," *Annual Report of the Smithsonian Institution* (1902), pp. 261–74; Oliver Lodge, *The Work of Hertz and Some of His Successors* (London: Electrician Printing and Publishing Co., 1894); W. Rupert MacLaurin, *Invention and Innovation in the Radio Industry* (New York: Macmillan Co., 1949), pp. 12–20; Blake, *History of Radio Telegraphy*, pp. 49–56; Fahie, *History of Wireless Telegraphy*, pp. 177–89.

4. On the work of Branly, Lodge, and Popov, see Oliver Lodge, *Past Years: An Autobiography* (London: Hodder and Stoughton, 1931), pp. 225–36; Lodge, *The Work of Hertz and Some of His Successors*, pp. 22–26; Maver, "Wireless Telegraphy" pp. 261–74; MacLaurin, *Invention and Innovation*, pp. 19–21; Blake, *History of Radio Telegraphy*, pp. 62–64.

5. William Crookes, "Some Possibilities of Electricity," *Fortnightly Review* 51 (February 1892): 174–75.

6. On the early work of Marconi, see Orrin E. Dunlap, *Marconi: The Man and His Wireless* (New York: Macmillan Co., 1937), pp. 33–59; Richard Kerr, *Wireless Telegraphy* (London: Seeley and Co., 1898), pp. 61–80; Gleason L. Archer, *History of Radio to 1926* (New York: American Historical Society, 1938), pp. 55–59; MacLaurin,

Invention and Innovation, pp. 31–55; Guglielmo Marconi, "Origin and Development of Wireless and Telegraphy," *North American Review* 168 (May 1899): 625–29, and "The Practicability of Wireless Telegraphy," *Fortnightly Review* 77 (June 1902): 931–41; Cleveland Moffett, "Marconi's Wireless Telegraph," *McClure's* 13 (June 1899): 99–112; Ernesto Mancini, "Telegraphy Without Wires," *The Chautauquan* 26 (February 1898): 511–15.

7. J. Ambrose Fleming, "Scientific History and Future Uses of Wireless Telegraphy," *North American Review* 168 (May 1899): 640; Agnes M. Clerke, "Ethereal Telegraphy," *Living Age* 219 (3 December 1898): 619–28; W. A. Shenstone, "Some Recent Theories of the Ether," *Living Age* 246 (9 September 1905): 724–34. See also Kenneth F. Shaffner, *Nineteenth Century Aether Theories* (New York: Pergamon Press, 1972), especially pp. 3–19, 76–98; *Encyclopedia of Philosophy*, 1967 ed., s.v., "Ether," by Mary Hesse.

8. Oliver Lodge, *Modern Views of Electricity*, 3d ed., rev. (London: Macmillan and Co., 1907), pp. 370, 341.

9. William H. Preece quoted in Clerke, "Ethereal Telegraphy," p. 627; Lodge, *Modern Views of Electricity*, p. 461; Amos E. Dolbear, "The Ether and its Newly Discovered Properties," *Arena* 6 (June 1892): 1–7; William Ayrton quoted during a discussion after a paper given by Marconi at the Royal Society, in Guglielmo Marconi, "Syntonic Wireless Telegraphy," *Journal of the Society of the Arts* 49 (17 May 1901): 516–17. On the connections suggested between wireless and telepathy, see also John Trowbridge, "Wireless Telegraphy," *Popular Science Monthly* 56 (November 1899): pp. 59–73, and Crookes, "Some Possibilities of Electricity," pp. 173–81.

10. Lodge, *Modern Views of Electricity*, p. 462.

11. On Marconi's successful transatlantic signaling and its impact on both scientists and the general public, see Ray Stannard Baker, "Marconi's Achievement," *McClure's* 18 (February 1902): 291–99; Carl Snyder, "Wireless Telegraphy and Signor Marconi's Triumph," *Review of Reviews* 25 (February 1902): 173–6; "American Wireless Telegraphy," *Harper's Weekly* 47 (21 February 1903): 298. On the growth of the Marconi organization, see Aitken, *Syntony and Spark*, pp. 232–44. Also see Guglielmo Marconi, "Recent Advances in Wireless Telegraphy," *Annual Report of the Smithsonian Institution* (1906), pp. 131–45; "The American Marconi Organization," *The Marconigraph* 1 (December 1912): 109–19; Erik Barnouw, *A History of Broadcasting in the United States*, 3 vols. (New York: Oxford University Press, 1966–70), 1:15–18. On the principle of "selling communication," the Marconi organization maintained an adamant position, not unlike that of A T & T: "Wireless telegraphy owes its present commercial utility solely to one thing: the basic axiom laid down by Marconi, that apparatus should not be sold and the owner left to work out his own salvation" (*The Ownership of Wireless Equipment* [New York: Marconi Wireless Telegraph Co., 1914], p. 4).

12. On the establishment of the first American wireless companies, and the early work of Fessenden and De Forest, see Archer, *History of Radio*, pp. 60–76; R. A. Fessenden, "A Brief History of Wireless Telegraphy," *Scientific American* 67 (Supplement, 9 January 1909): 18–19, 44–45, 60–61; "A Decade of Wireless Telegraphy," *Scientific American* 94 (16 June 1906): 490–1; William Maver, "Progress in Wireless Telegraphy," *Annual Report of the Smithsonian Institution* (1904), pp. 275–80; Lawrence Perry, "Commercial Wireless Telegraphy," *The World's Work* 5 (March 1905): 3194–201; MacLaurin, *Invention and Innovation*, pp. 59–87.

13. On the problem of tuning, see "Commercial Value of Wireless," *Scientific American* 80 (17 June 1899): 388; Marconi, "Syntonic Wireless Telegraphy," pp. 506–17; Blake, *History of Radio Telegraphy*, pp. 99–106. Aitken, *Syntony and Spark*, pp. 31–47, offers the most comprehensive treatment of the concept of syntony.

For Marconi's views on military uses, see H. J. W. Dam, "Telegraphing Without Wires: A Possibility of Electrical Science," *McClure's* 8 (March 1897): 383–92; Marconi, "Origin and Development of Wireless Telegraphy." For other views on military uses, see, for example, Kerr, *Wireless Telegraphy*, pp. 93–99; H. M. Hozier, "Wireless Telegraphy," *Nineteenth Century* 60 (July 1906): 49–56; "Wireless Telegraphy in the Next War," *Harper's Weekly* 47 (21 March 1903): 454; John Trowbridge, "The First Steps in Wireless Telegraphy," *The Chautauquan* 29 (July 1899): 375–78.

14. Ray Stannard Baker, "Marconi's Achievement," *McClure's* 18 (February 1902): 298; the remarks of Ayrton are in Marconi, "Syntonic Wireless Telegraphy," pp. 516–17. See also Perry, "Commercial Wireless Telegraphy" for similar projections.

15. Robert A. Morton, "The Amateur Wireless Operator," *Outlook* 94 (15 January 1910): 131–35; "The Good of Amateur Wireless," *Scientific American* 116 (17 March 1917): 276; John W. Purssell, "In Defense of the Amateur Wireless Operator," *Scientific American* 106 (8 June 1912): 515; Robert A. Morton, "Regulation of Radiotelegraphy," *Scientific American* 73 (Supplement, 23 March 1912): 180–81; Paul Schubert, *The Electric Word: The Rise of Radio* (New York: Macmillan Co., 1928), pp. 194–97; Archer, *History of Radio*, pp. 91–106; Barnouw, *History of Broadcasting*, 1:28–38.

16. L. S. Howeth, *History of Communications Electronics in the United States Navy* (Washington, D.C.: Government Printing Office, 1963), pp. 67–83; Barnouw, *History of Broadcasting*, 1:31–33, 291–99; Archer, *History of Radio*, pp. 104–6.

17. On the principles of wireless telephony, see R. A. Fessenden, "Wireless Telephony," *Scientific American* 67 (Supplement, 13 March 1909): 172–74, 180–82, 196–98; William C. Ballard, *Elements of Radio Telephony* (New York: McGraw-Hill Book Co., 1922), pp. 1–5; Alfred N. Goldsmith, "Radio Telephony," *Wireless Age* 4 (January 1917): 248–55. On the contributions of Fessenden and De Forest, see also Lee De Forest, "The Audion—A New Receiver for Wireless Telegraphy," *Scientific American* 64 (Supplement, 30 November 1907): 348–50, 354–56; Herbert T. Wade, "Wireless Telephony by the De Forest System," *Review of Reviews* 35 (June 1907): 681–85; "Communicating Over Great Distances: The Invention of the Telegraph, Telephone, and Wireless Telegraphy," *Scientific American* 112 (5 June 1915): p. 351; MacLaurin, *Invention and Innovation*, pp. 59–87; Archer, *History of Radio*, pp. 69–94.

18. Frank Jewett, 1932, quoted in N. R. Danielian, *A T & T: The Story of Industrial Conquest* (New York: Vanguard Press, 1939), p. 196. On how A T & T and General Electric aggressively pursued patents in wireless research to protect their investments, both through their own research labs and by buying out independent inventors, see David F. Noble, *America By Design: Science, Technology, and the Rise of Corporate Capitalism* (New York: Alfred A. Knopf, 1977), pp. 91–101.

19. On the position of A T & T, GE, and American Marconi: Horace Coon, *American Telephone and Telegraph* (New York and Toronto: Longmans, Green, and Co., 1939), pp. 197–98; Danielian, *A T & T*, pp. 107–19; MacLaurin, *Invention and Innovation*, pp. 88–99; Archer, *History of Radio*, pp. 106–21. On the A T & T-Navy long distance tests: Howeth, *History of Communications Electronics*, pp. 221–35; "The Wireless Telephone Tests," *Wireless Age* 3 (November 1915): 111–16. On wireless and the U.S. government during the war: U.S. Federal Trade Commission Report, *Radio Industry* (Washington, D.C.: Government Printing Offiice, 1923), pp. 9–18; N. H. Slaughter, "Wireless Telephony," *Annual Report of the Smithsonian Institution* (1919), pp. 177–92; Howeth, *History of Communications Electronics*, pp. 215–312; Archer, *History of Radio*, pp. 122–55.

20. On the Wilson administration and the wireless: Howeth, *History of Communications Electronics*, pp. 313–18, 353–55; Archer, *History of Radio*, pp. 148–50, 164–65; Statement of Josephus Daniels, U.S. House, Committee on the Merchant Marine and Fisheries, *Government Control of Radio Communication*, 65th Cong., 3d sess., 13–14 December 1918, pt. 1. On the consensus, see, for example, Frank B. Jewett, "Wireless Telephony," *Review of Reviews* 59 (May 1919): 500–503; W. C. White (GE Research Laboratory), "Radiotelephony," *Scientific American* 80 (Supplement, 4 September 1915): 146–47; E. H. Colpitts (Western Electric research engineer), "The Future of Radio Telephony," *Scientific American* 113 (4 December 1915): p. 485.

The great exception to the consensus on postwar radio was David Sarnoff, future head of RCA. In the fall of 1916 he composed the famous "music box" memo for his superiors at American Marconi; in it he proposed "a plan of development which would make radio a 'household utility' in the same sense as the piano or the phonograph. The idea is to bring music into the home by wireless." Sarnoff projected sales of one million sets at $75 each, for a gross of $75 million. But the cold reception given his plan showed just how out of touch he was with the conventional wisdom of his day. See Carl Dreher, *Sarnoff: An American Success* (New York: Quadrangle Books, 1977), pp. 39–42, and Eugene Lyons, *David Sarnoff* (New York: Harper and Row, 1966), pp. 70–73. Dreher debunks some of the still persisting legends that have grown up around Sarnoff, but there is still a need for a comprehensive, scholarly biography.

21. Harry P. Davis, "The Early History of Broadcasting in the United States," in Anton De Haas, ed., *The Radio Industry: The Story of its Development* (Chicago: A. W. Shaw, 1928), pp. 194–96. On KDKA and Westinghouse, see Harry P. Davis, "American Beginnings," in Martin Codel, ed., *Radio and its Future* (New York: Harper and Brothers, 1930), pp. 3–11; Barnouw, *History of Broadcasting*, 1:64–74; Archer, *History of Radio*, pp. 200–210. Westinghouse also obtained the valuable Armstrong-Pupin patents (including the "feed-back device" that greatly improved the effectiveness of De Forest's audion) from the International Radio Telegraph Co., a successor to Fessenden's original National Electric Signalling Co.

22. On early "radio mania" and the first broadcasters: Hugo Gernsback, *Radio For All* (Philadelphia: J. B. Lippincott Co., 1922), pp. 165–70; Alfred N. Goldsmith and Austin C. Lescarboura, *This Thing Called Broadcasting* (New York: Henry Holt and Co., 1930), pp. 22–56; Schubert, *The Electric Word*, pp. 212–49; "Who Will Ultimately Do the Broadcasting?" *Radio Broadcast* 2 (1 April 1923): 524–25; Barnouw, *History of Broadcasting*, 1: 91–105; Dudley Siddall, "Who Owns Our Broadcasting Stations?" *Radio Broadcast* 4 (February 1925): 726–30. On the Washington radio conferences, see Edward F. Sarno, "The National Radio Conferences," *Journal of Broadcasting* 13 (Spring 1969): 189–202.

23. On the nature of early programming: WHA Program Logs, 1922–26, in John S. Penn Papers; Wendell Hall Papers; William H. Easton, "What the Radio Audience Tells Us," and S. M. Kintner, "Radio Communication," in the M. C. Batsel Papers; all in the Mass Communication Research Center, State Historical Society of Wisconsin, Madison, Wis. See also L. H. Rosenberg, "A New Era in Wireless," *Scientific American* 124 (4 June 1921): 449; "The Long Arm of the Radio is Reaching Everywhere," *Current Opinion* 72 (May 1922): 684–87; Ben Gross, *I Looked and I Listened: Informal Recollections of Radio and TV* (New York: Random House, 1954), pp. 82–98.

24. Pierre Boucheron, "News and Music from the Air," *Scientific American* 125A (December 1921): 104. On the attitudes of amateurs toward the new radio fans and broadcasting see, for example, Hugo Gernsback, "The Broadcast Listener," *Radio News* 4 (June 1923): 1, and other issues of the magazine. Good examples of those who forecasted a minor role for broadcasting in radio's future: Raymond F. Yates, "The Long Arm of Radio," *Current History* 15 (March 1922): 980–85; Hugo Gernsback, "Radio Achievements in Recent Years," *Current History* 18 (April 1923): 113–20, "The Long Arm of Radio is Reaching Everywhere," pp. 684–87. The original and most famous wireless amateur, Marconi, remained relatively unimpressed with broadcasting's possibilities. He doubted that it would ever be as important as wire communication, the press, or the stage. He continued to focus on the problem of communication over long distance, the initial inspiration of his work. See Stanley Frost, "Marconi and His Views of Wireless Progress," *Review of Reviews* 66 (August 1922): 166–70.

25. Robert S. Lynd and Helen M. Lynd, *Middletown: A Study in Modern American Culture* (New York: Harcourt, Brace, and Co., 1929), p. 269; Howard V. O'Brien, "It's Great to Be a Radio Maniac," *Collier's Weekly* 74 (13 September 1924): 15–16. For other descriptions of early radio listening and "DXing," see Orange E. McMeans, "The Great Audience Invisible," *Scribner's Magazine* 73 (March 1923): 410–16; Bruce Bli-

ven, "The Legion Family and the Radio," *Century* 108 (October 1924): 811–18; Alida Chanler, "Unexplored Harmonies," *Atlantic* 127 (March 1921): 363–66; Goldsmith and Lescarboura, *This Thing Called Broadcasting*, pp. 309–11; Schubert, *Electric Word*, pp. 212–30.

26. J. Hannaford Elton, "Tomorrow in Radio," *Illustrated World* 37 (June 1922): 502; Edwin E. Slosson, "Voices in the Air," *New York Independent* 108 (18 April 1922): 386. See also Waldemar Kaempffert, "Radio Broadcasting," *Review of Reviews* 65 (April 1922): 395–401; Stanley Frost, "Radio: Our Next Great Step Forward," *Collier's Weekly* 69 (18 April 1922): 3; French Strother, "The Unfolding Marvels of Wireless," *World's Work* 43 (April 1922): 647–61.

27. David Sarnoff, Speech to the Chicago Chamber of Commerce, April 1924, quoted in Samuel L. Rothafel and Raymond F. Yates, *Broadcasting: Its New Day* (New York: Century, 1925), p. 181; A. H. Griswold, Speech at Bell System Radio Conference, February 1923, quoted in Danielian, *A T & T*, pp. 123–24. On varieties of government control: Raymond F. Yates, "What Will Happen to Broadcasting," *Outlook* 136 (19 April 1924): 604–6; Grover A. Whalen, "Radio Control," *Nation* 119 (23 July 1924): 90–91 (Whalen helped launch WNYC, New York's municipal station); Bruce Bliven, "How Radio is Remaking Our World," *Century* 108 (June 1924): 147–54. On limited federal involvement: Hudson Maxim, "Radio—The Fulcrum," *Nation* 119 (23 July 1924): 91. On a common industry fund: "About the Radio Round Table" (results of a panel discussion among top industry leaders), *Scientific American* 127 (December 1922): 378–79; "Radio Currents: An Editorial Interpretation," *Radio Broadcast* 1 (May 1922): 1–4. Griswold's position reflected a strong view held for years at A T & T to the effect that "so far nothing in the way of actual public communication has been done in wireless telephony except through the instrumentalities of the Company." This was historically false, but the arrogant tone is noteworthy. See Theodore N. Vail, *The A T & T Co. and Its Relations with and Obligations toward Wireless Communication* (New York: n.p., 1915), p. 3.

28. See William P. Banning, *Commercial Broadcasting Pioneer: The WEAF Experiment, 1922–1926* (Cambridge: Harvard University Press, 1946); Coon, *American Telephone and Telegraph*, pp. 205–13.

29. Herbert Hoover, Speech to First Washington Radio Conference, 27 February 1922, in Herbert Hoover, "Reminiscences," Radio Unit of the Oral History Project, 1950, Columbia University, New York, NY; Herbert Hoover, 1924 interview with the *New York World*, quoted in Rothafel and Yates, *Broadcasting*, p. 60. See also Hoover's statement before the House Committee on Merchant Marine and Fisheries (1924), which was considering a radio bill; his address to the National Electric Light Association, Atlantic City, (21 May 1924); "Report of the Department of Commerce Conference on Radio Telephony" (April 1922); all in Herbert C. Hoover Papers, 1921–32 (Pertaining to Early Radio Development), Mass Communication Research Center, State Historical Society of Wisconsin, Madison, Wis. Hoover's *Memoirs*, vol. 2, *The Cabinet and the Presidency* (New York: Macmillan Co., 1952), is a less reliable source here because several of his original speeches and pronouncements are altered in the book. See also Barnouw, *History of Broadcasting*, 1:177–79. For examples of early antiadvertising views, see Joseph H. Jackson, "Should Radio Be Used for Advertising?" *Radio Broadcast* 2 (November 1922): 72–76; Austin C. Lescarboura, "Radio For Everybody," *Scientific American* 126 (March 1922): 166; Bliven, "How Radio is Remaking Our World"; Kaempffert, "Radio Broadcasting."

30. Edgar H. Felix, *Using Radio In Sales Promotion* (New York: McGraw-Hill Book Co., 1927), pp. 1, 6; Harry P. Davis, Foreword to Frank P. Arnold, *Broadcast Advertising: The Fourth Dimension* (New York: John Wiley and Sons, 1931), p. xv; Arnold, *Broadcast Advertising*, pp. 41–42; Frank Presbrey, *The History and Development of Advertising* (New York: Doubleday and Co., 1929), p. 581. See also Kenneth Goode, *Manual of Modern Advertising* (New York: Greenberg Publishers, 1932), pp. 307–23; Earl Reeves, "The New Business of Broadcasting," *Review of Reviews* 72 (November 1925): 529–32.

For a provocative discussion of the "political ideology of consumption" as it developed in the 1920s among business interests, see Stuart Ewen, *Captains of Consciousness: Advertising and the Social Roots of the Consumer Culture* (New York: McGraw-Hill Book Co., 1976), pp. 51–109. Ewen, it should be noted, does not deal at all with radio advertising.

31. For the full story of the various internal disputes, arbitrations, and final agreements among the patent allies, see Gleason L. Archer, *Big Business and Radio* (New York: American Historical Co., 1939), and Barnouw, *History of Broadcasting*, 1:180–88. See also Kurt Borchardt, *Structure and Performance of the U.S. Communications Industry* (Boston: Graduate School of Administration, Harvard University, 1970), chap. 3.

32. On the events leading to the 1927 radio act and the early work of the FRC, see Marvin R. Bensman, "The Zenith-WJAZ Case and the Chaos of 1926–27," *Journal of Broadcasting* 14 (Fall 1970): 423–40; "The Problem of Radio Reallocation," *Congressional Digest* 7 (October 1928): 255–86; Sarno, "The National Radio Conferences"; Barnouw, *History of Broadcasting*, 1:195–201, 209–19.

33. Leslie J. Page, Jr., "The Nature of the Broadcast Receiver and its Market in the United States from 1922 to 1927," *Journal of Broadcasting* 4 (Spring 1960): 174–82; John W. Spalding, "1928: Radio Becomes a Mass Advertising Medium," *Journal of Broadcasting* 8 (Winter 1963–64): 31–44.

34. Figures compiled from: *Broadcasting Yearbook*, February 1940, pp. 11–14; U.S. Bureau of the Census, *Fifteenth Census of the United States, 1930, Population*, vol. 6, *Families* (Washington, D.C.: Department of Commerce, 1933), p. 33; Herman S. Hettinger, *A Decade of Radio Advertising* (Chicago: University of Chicago Press, 1933), pp. 107–12; Siddall, "Who Owns Our Radio Broadcasting Stations?".

35. On the early history of CBS, see Robert Metz, *CBS: Reflections in a Bloodshot Eye* (New York: Playboy Press, 1975), pp. 1–36; Erik Barnouw, *History of Broadcasting*, 2:57–58.

36. Figures on advertising from *Broadcasting Yearbook*, pp. 11–14; figures on network wattage from Ruth Brindze, "Who Owns the Air?" *Nation* 144 (17 April 1937): 430–32. On the rise of the ad agencies, see Arnold, *Broadcast Advertising*, pp. 120–26; Barnouw, *History of Broadcasting*, 2:8–18. On the weakness of the FRC, an astute contemporary analysis is E. Pendleton Herring, "Politics and Radio Regulation," *Harvard Business Review* 13 (January 1935): 167–78.

37. Roy S. Durstine, "We're On the Air," *Scribner's Magazine* 83 (May 1928): 630–31; Arnold, *Broadcast Advertising*, p. 50.

38. Merrill Denison, "Why Isn't Radio Better?" *Harper's* 168 (April 1934): 580; Mitchell Dawson, "Censorship on the Air," *American Mercury* 31 (March 1934): 262; James Rorty, "The Impending Radio War," *Harper's* 163 (November 1931): 714.

39. H. V. Kaltenborn, "On the Air," *Century* 112 (October 1926): 673, 675–6; William Green, *Report of the Chairman, Committee on Labor, NBC Advisory Council Reports* 7 (1931): 49. For extended discussions of censorship, with scores of examples, see Harrison B. Summers, ed., *Radio Censorship* (New York: H. W. Wilson, 1939); Ruth Brindze, *Not to Be Broadcast: The Truth About Radio* (New York: Vanguard Press, 1933), pp. 172–95; Deems Taylor, "Radio: A Brief for the Defense," *Harper's* 166 (April 1933): 554–63.

40. See Tracy F. Tyler, ed., *Radio as a Cultural Agency* (Washington, D.C.: National Committee on Education by Radio, 1934); Rorty, "The Impending Radio War," pp. 714–26.

41. Table 4 is based on two tables prepared by Lawrence L. Lichty and C. H. Sterling from Harrison B. Summers, *A Thirty Year History of Programs on National Radio Networks in the United States, 1926–1956* (Columbus: Ohio State University, 1958). For the discussion that follows, sources include the tape recordings of the following shows in the Radio Laboratory, Department of Communication Arts, University of Wisconsin, and in other libraries, as well as Frank Buxton and Bill Owen, *The Big Broadcast, 1920–1950* (New York: Viking Press, 1972). VARIETY AND COMEDY: Fred

Allen Show (1940), Ed Wynn Show (1935), Arthur Godfrey Show (1939), Amos n' Andy (1932), Charlie McCarthy Show (1936), Breakfast Club (1939), The Aldrich Family (1939); SERIALS: Ma Perkins (1933), Clara Lou and Em (1932); THRILLER: Inner Sanctum (1940), Suspense (1943); ADVENTURE: Lone Ranger (1933), Smilin' Jack (1939), Hop Harrigan (1942), Tom Mix (1933); NEWS: March of Time (1931, including first show), Edward R. Murrow, from London (1940).

42. See Charles J. Correll and Freeman F. Gosden, *All About Amos & Andy* (New York: Rand McNally, 1929). For more on the minstrel show tradition in American entertainment, see Robert C. Toll, *Blacking Up: The Minstrel Show in Nineteenth Century America* (New York: Oxford University Press, 1974), especially pp. 51–56.

43. Herta Herzog, "On Borrowed Experience: An Analysis of Listening to Daytime Sketches," *Studies in Philosophy and Social Science* 9 (1941): 91. On the historical context of the soap opera, see Raymond W. Stedman, *The Serials: Suspense and Drama by Installment* (Norman: University of Oklahoma Press, 1971), pp. 225–81.

44. Archibald MacLeish, Foreword to *The Fall of the City* (New York: Farrar and Rinehart, 1937), p. x. Several good collections of the radio drama representative of this period are: Norman Corwin, *Thirteen by Corwin* (New York: Henry Holt, 1942); Douglas Coulter, ed., *Columbia Workshop Plays: Fourteen Radio Dramas* (New York: McGraw-Hill Book Co., 1939); Arch Oboler, *Fourteen Radio Plays* (New York: Random House, 1940), including Oboler's perceptive essay "The Art of Radio Writing," pp. xv–xxix. On the short-lived flowering of radio drama, see also Barnouw, *History of Broadcasting*, 2:65–76, 88–90.

45. In Llewellyn White, *The American Radio: A Report on the Broadcasting Industry in the U.S. from the Commission on Freedom of the Press* (Chicago: University of Chicago Press, 1947), p. 47.

46. This account based on: Karl Bickel, *New Empires: The Newspaper and the Radio* (Philadelphia: J. B. Lippincott Co., 1930); Clippings Scrapbooks, 1926–35, in the Martin Codel Collection, Mass Communication Research Center, State Historical Society of Wisconsin, Madison, Wis.; Alfred M. Lee, *The Daily Newspaper in America* (New York: Macmillan Co., 1947), pp. 559–64; George E. Lott, Jr., "The Press Radio War of the 1930's," *Journal of Broadcasting* 14 (Summer 1970): 275–86; an unpublished paper by Daniel Czitrom, "Press-Radio Conflict in America, 1920–1940: The Rise of Audible Journalism."

47. These examples in Dowling Leatherwood, *Journalism On The Air* (Minneapolis: Burgess Publishing Co., 1939), pp. 52–53.

48. H. V. Kaltenborn, *I Broadcast the Crisis* (New York: Random House, 1938); and Kaltenborn, "Reminiscences," Radio Unit of the Oral History Project, 1950, Columbia University, New York, NY; Robert R. Smith, "The Origin of Radio Network News Commentary," *Journal of Broadcasting* 9 (Spring 1965): 113–22.

CHAPTER 4

1. Charles H. Cooley, Journal, vol. 15, 1902, Charles Horton Cooley Papers, Michigan Historical Collections, Bentley Historical Library, Ann Arbor, Michigan (hereafter cited as CHC Papers).

2. Cooley, Journal, vol. 10, 21 July 1895; vol. 22, 15 June 1923; vol. 12, 2 May 1897, CHC Papers.

3. Cooley, Journal, vol. 6, 24 May 1890 and 9 July 1890, CHC Papers. See also the standard biography, Edward C. Jandy, *Charles Horton Cooley: His Life and His Social Thought* (New York: Dryden Press, 1942), especially pp. 1–80.

4. Charles H. Cooley, "Reflections Upon the Sociology of Herbert Spencer," *American Journal of Sociology* 26 (September 1920): 129; Herbert Spencer, *The Principles of Sociology* (1876), in J. D. Y. Peel, ed., *Herbert Spencer on Social Evolution: Selected Writings* (Chicago: University of Chicago Press, 1972), pp. 136, 124; Cooley, "Reflec-

tions," p. 138. For a more comprehensive treatment of Cooley's critique of Spencer, see Marshall J. Cohen, "Self and Society: Charles Horton Cooley and the Idea of Social Self in American Thought" (Ph.D. dissertation, Harvard University, 1967), especially pp. 17–95.

5. Concerning Dewey's influence on Cooley, see Cooley, Journal, vol. 11, 28 February 1897, CHC Papers; Charles H. Cooley, "The Development of Sociology at Michigan" (1928), in Robert C. Angell, ed., *Charles H. Cooley, Sociological Theory and Social Research* (New York: Henry Holt and Co., 1930), pp. 5–6. The CHC Papers contain Cooley's set of notes for Dewey's course in "Anthropological Ethics" (1894). John Dewey, *Outlines of a Critical Theory of Ethics* (1891), in John Dewey, *The Early Works, 1882–1898*, 5 vols. (Carbondale: Southern Illinois University Press, 1971), 3:239–388 (hereafter cited as *Early Works*). See also George Dykhuizen, "John Dewey and the University of Michigan," *Journal of the History of Ideas* 23 (October–December 1962): 513–44.

6. Charles H. Cooley, "The Theory of Transportation" (1894), in Angell, *Sociological Theory and Social Research*, pp. 40–41; Cooley, "Development of Sociology, " p. 7. Cooley goes on to describe his teaching on communication and transportation, noting that "communication was thus my first real conquest and the thesis a forecast of the organic view of society I have been working out ever since."

7. Charles H. Cooley, "The Process of Social Change," *Political Science Quarterly* 12 (March 1897): 73–74, 77, 81.

8. Cooley, Journal, vol. 11, 18 July 1896, CHC Papers. Charles H. Cooley, *Social Process* (New York: Charles Scribner's Sons, 1918), p. 28.

9. The works he refers to are William James, *The Principles of Psychology*, 2 vols. (New York: Henry Holt and Co., 1890), especially vol. 1, chap 10, "The Consciousness of Self"; and James Mark Baldwin, *Social and Ethical Interpretations in Mental Development* (New York: Macmillan Co., 1897). See Charles H. Cooley, *Human Nature and the Social Order*, rev. ed. (New York: Charles Scribner's Sons, 1922), p. 125, for Cooley's acknowledgment.

10. Cooley, *Human Nature*, pp. 119–21, 183–84. Compare these remarks with those of James: "A man's social self is the recognition which he gets from his mates. . . . Properly speaking, a man has as many social selves as there are individuals who recognize him and carry an image of him in their mind" (James, *Principles of Psychology*, 1:293–94).

11. Charles H. Cooley, *Social Organization: A Study of the Larger Mind* (New York: Charles Scribner's Sons, 1909), p. 23; see especially pp. 32–50.

12. Cooley, *Social Organization*, pp. 61, 80–81. See also Cooley, *Human Nature*, pp. 75, 145–47. For another treatment of Cooley on modern communication, see Jean B. Quandt, *From the Small Town to the Great Community: The Social Thought of Progressive Intellectuals* (New Brunswick: Rutgers University Press, 1970), chap. 4, "Charles Horton Cooley and the Communications Revolution."

13. Cooley, *Social Organization*, pp. 54, 97.

14. Cooley, Journal, vol. 12, 7 May, 16 July, 24 July, and 31 July 1898; vol. 11, 28 February 1897, vol. 13, 2 August 1898; vol. 14, 13 September 1901, CHC Papers.

15. Cooley, *Human Nature*, p. 145. See also Cooley, *Social Organization*, pp. 98–103, and "Notes on Communication," Box 3, CHC Papers.

16. Quotations are from Charles H. Cooley, *Life and the Student* (New York: Alfred A. Knopf, 1927), p. 134; Cooley, *Social Organization*, pp. 170–71.

17. Cooley, *Social Process*, pp. 415, 412; Charles H. Cooley, "A Primary Culture for Democracy," *American Sociological Society Publications* 13 (1918): 4, 7; Cooley, Journal, vol. 23, 24 October 1926, CHC Papers.

18. Cooley, *Social Process*, pp. 406–7; Ralph Waldo Emerson, "The American Scholar," in Stephen E. Whicher, ed., *Selections from Ralph Waldo Emerson*, Riverside Edition (Boston: Houghton Mifflin Co., 1960), p. 70. For a good critique of Cooley's theory of society, written just after his death, see George H. Mead, "Cooley's Con-

tribution to American Social Thought," *American Journal of Sociology* 35 (March 1930): 693–706.

19. The best sources for Dewey's early life are George Dykhuizen, *The Life and Mind of John Dewey* (Carbondale: Southern Illinois University Press, 1973), and Jane Dewey, ed., "Biography of John Dewey," in Paul A. Schilpp, ed., *The Philosophy of John Dewey* (Evanston: Northwestern University, 1939), pp. 3–45. I have also relied on the excellent interpretive work by Neil Coughlan, *Young John Dewey: An Essay in American Intellectual History* (Chicago: University of Chicago Press, 1975).

20. John Dewey, "From Absolutism to Experimentalism," in George P. Adams and William P. Montague, eds., *Contemporary American Philosophy: Personal Statements*, 2 vols. (New York: Macmillan Co., 1930), 2:19. On Dewey at Hopkins, see Coughlan, *Young John Dewey*, pp. 37–53.

21. John Dewey, *The Study of Ethics: A Syllabus* (1894), in *Early Works*, 4:262, 264; John Dewey, "Moral Theory and Moral Practice" (1891), in *Early Works*, 3:95. On the influence of James and evolutionary biology, see Dewey, "From Absolutism to Experimentalism." On this period, see also Burleigh Taylor Wilkins, "James, Dewey, and Hegelian Idealism," *Journal of the History of Ideas* 17 (June 1956): 332–46, and Dykhuizen, "John Dewey and the University of Michigan."

22. Franklin Ford, *Draft of Action* (Ann Arbor: n.p., 1892?), p. 58.

23. Robert Park in Paul J. Baker, ed., "The Life Histories of W. I. Thomas and Robert E. Park," *American Journal of Sociology* 79 (September 1973): 254–55.

24. Ford, *Draft of Action*, pp. 8, 9.

25. Ibid., pp. 5, 27.

26. John Dewey to William James, 3 June 1891, in Ralph Barton Perry, ed., *The Thought and Character of William James*, 2 vols. (Boston: Little, Brown and Co., 1935), 2:518–19. Another source on the Ford-Dewey relationship is the work of Ford's brother, Corydon, an even more bizarre character than Franklin. See Corydon Ford, *The Child of Democracy: Being the Adventures of the Embryo State, 1856–1894* (Ann Arbor: J. V. Sheehan Co., 1894), pp. 173–75. Lewis S. Feuer, "John Dewey and the Back to the People Movement in American Thought," *Journal of the History of Ideas* 20 (October–December 1959): 545–68, also discusses the alliance. But Feuer's article is flawed by a rather simplistic description of Dewey as a "socialistic mystic" in this period of his life.

27. Dewey, *Outlines of a Critical Theory of Ethics* (1891), in *Early Works*, 3:320. In the preface to this work, Dewey acknowledged a debt to Ford for his "treatment of the social bearings of science and art."

28. *Michigan Daily*, 16 March 1892, quoted in Willinda Savage, "John Dewey and 'Thought News' at the University of Michigan," *Michigan Quarterly Review* 56 (Spring 1950): 204–5. Though brief, the Savage article is the best narrative account of the "Thought News" episode. See also Coughlan, *Young John Dewey*, pp. 93–106.

29. *Michigan Daily*, 8 April 1892, quoted in Coughlan, *Young John Dewey*, p. 103.

30. *Detroit Tribune*, 11 April 1892, quoted in Savage, "John Dewey and 'Thought News,'" p. 207.

31. *Detroit Tribune*, 13 April 1892, quoted in Savage, "John Dewey and 'Thought News,'" p. 207. Coughlan interprets the "Thought News" adventure as a response by Dewey to the "provincial isolation that marked much of American intellectual life until the 1890's," an attempt to somehow link the scattered intelligentsia of America. See Coughlan, *Young John Dewey*, pp. 108–12.

32. Dewey to Willinda Savage, 30 May 1949, quoted in Savage, "John Dewey and 'Thought News,'" p. 209. A more acerbic view, blaming Dewey for backing out, can be found in Ford, *Child of Democracy*, p. 175.

33. John Dewey, *Democracy and Education* (New York: Macmillan Co., 1915), p. 4.

34. John Dewey, *Experience and Nature* (1929; reprint, New York: Dover Publications, 1958), pp. 165, 166.

35. Ibid., pp. 204–5.

36. John Dewey, *Art As Experience* (New York: Minton, Balch, and Co., 1934), pp. 105, 244, 5–6. See also pp. 103–5.

37. Walter Lippmann, *Public Opinion* (1922; reprint ed., Glencoe: Free Press, 1965), pp. 19, 249, 234, 235–36.

38. John Dewey, "Public Opinion," *New Republic* 30 (3 May 1922): 288; "Practical Democracy," *New Republic* 45 (2 December 1925): 54. Concerning the influence of Dewey's philosophy upon the very experts celebrated by Lippmann, see Sidney Kaplan, "Social Engineers as Saviors: Effects of World War I on Some American Liberals," *Journal of the History of Ideas* 17 (June 1956): 347–69.

39. John Dewey, *The Public and Its Problems* (1927; reprint ed., Chicago: Swallow Press, 1954), pp. 126, 142, 184. References to Cooley's primary groups can be found on pp. 97, 211.

40. For example, consider the box Dewey got himself into when he considered the relation of social science to social planning: "The building up of social science, that is, of a body of knowledge in which facts are ascertained in their significant relations, is dependent upon putting social planning into effect. . . . I am not arguing here for the desirability of social planning and control. That is another question. Those who are satisfied with the present conditions and are hopeful of turning them to account for personal profit and power will answer it in the negative. What I am saying is that if we want something to which the name 'social science' may be given, there is only one way to go about it, namely by entering upon the path of social planning and control." "Social Science and Social Control," *New Republic* 67 (29 July 1931): 276–77.

41. Compare Dewey's two articles, "Our Un-Free Press," *Common Sense* 4 (November 1935): 6–7, and "Radio's Influence on the Mind," *School and Society* 40 (15 December 1934): 805.

42. Baker, "The Life Histories of W. I. Thomas and Robert E. Park," pp. 251–60.

43. Robert Park, "Autobiographical Note," in *The Collected Papers of Robert Park*, 3 vols. (Glencoe: Free Press, 1950), 1:v–ix (hereafter cited as *Park Papers*); Ellsworth Faris, "Robert E. Park," *American Sociological Review* 9 (June 1944): 321–25; Fred H. Matthews, *Quest For An American Sociology: Robert E. Park and the Chicago School* (Montreal: McGill-Queens University Press, 1977), pp. 10–30.

44. Baker, "The Life Histories of W. I. Thomas and Robert E. Park," p. 254; Matthews, *Quest*, pp. 31–35.

45. Robert Park, *The Crowd and the Public* (originally *Masse und Publikum*, 1904), trans. from German by Charlotte Elsner, edited and with an introduction by Henry Elsner, Jr. (Chicago: University of Chicago Press, 1972), pp. 79–80, 46. For a review of the tradition within which Park wrote his thesis, see Matthews, *Quest*, pp. 30–50.

46. Robert Park and E. W. Burgess, *Introduction to the Science of Sociology* (Chicago: University of Chicago Press, 1921), pp. 42, 505–11, 735.

47. See for example, Robert Park, "The City: Suggestions for the Investigation of Human Behavior in the Urban Environment," *American Journal of Sociology* 20 (March 1916): 577–612; Robert Park, E. W. Burgess, and R. D. McKenzie, *The City* (Chicago: University of Chicago Press, 1925); Robert Park, "The Urban Community as a Spatial and a Moral Order," *Publications of the American Sociological Society* 20 (1925): 1–14; Robert Park, "Human Ecology," *American Journal of Sociology* 42 (July 1936): 1–15. See also Matthews, *Quest*, pp. 121–25.

48. Robert Park, "The Yellow Press," *Sociology and Social Research* 12 (September–October 1927): 1–12; Robert Park, "News and the Human Interest Story" (1940), in *Park Papers*, 3:112. See also Robert Park, "Natural History of the Newspaper," *American Journal of Sociology* 29 (November 1923): 80–98; Robert Park, "American Newspaper Literature," *American Journal of Sociology* 32 (March 1927): 806–13.

49. Robert Park, *The Immigrant Press and Its Control* (New York: Harper and Brothers, 1922), p. 468. See also Robert Park, "Foreign Language Press and Social Progress," *Proceedings of the National Conference of Social Work* (1920): 493–500;

Robert Park, "Immigrant Community and Immigrant Press," *American Review* (March–April 1925): 143–52.

50. Robert Park, "News As a Form of Knowledge," *American Journal of Sociology* 45 (March 1940): 686.

51. Robert Park, "News and the Power of the Press," *American Journal of Sociology* 47 (July 1941): 2; Robert Park, "Morale and the News," *American Journal of Sociology* 47 (November 1941): 372.

52. Robert Park, "Reflections on Communication and Culture," *American Journal of Sociology* 44 (September 1938): 197.

53. Robert Park, "Community Organization and the Romantic Temper," *Social Forces* 3 (May 1925): 675.

54. Cooley, *Social Organization*, p. 4.

CHAPTER 5

1. Harold Lasswell, *Propaganda Technique in the World War* (New York: Alfred A. Knopf, 1927), pp. 2, 9. Other important early propaganda studies include: F. E. Lumley, *The Propaganda Menace* (New York: Century, 1933); O. W. Riegel, *Mobilizing for Chaos: The Story of the New Propaganda* (New Haven: Yale University Press, 1934); Leonard W. Doob, *Propaganda: Its Psychology and Technique* (New York: Henry Holt and Co., 1935); W. H. Irwin, *Propaganda and the News* (New York: McGraw-Hill Book Co., 1936). For examples of widely read postwar exposés on propaganda during the war, see George Creel, *How We Advertised America* (New York: Harper and Brothers, 1920), and Heber Blankenhorn, *Adventures in Propaganda* (Boston: Houghton Mifflin, 1919).

2. Walter Lippmann, *Public Opinion* (1922; reprint ed., Glencoe: Free Press, 1965), pp. 19, 18. See also Walter Lippmann, *Liberty and the News* (New York: Harcourt, Brace, and Howe, 1920), and *The Phantom Public* (New York: Harcourt, Brace and Co., 1925).

3. "Editorial Foreword," *Public Opinion Quarterly* 1 (January 1937): 3. See also William Albig, *Public Opinion* (New York: McGraw-Hill Book Co., 1939) for a useful contemporary survey of the new field.

4. W. W. Charters, *Motion Pictures and Youth: A Summary* (New York: Macmillan Co., 1934), pp. 5, 16; Blumer is quoted on p. 39. A listing of the twelve individual studies can be found at the beginning of the Charters book. Garth Jowett, *Film: The Democratic Art* (Boston: Little, Brown, and Co., 1976), pp. 220–29, tells the fascinating story of how the Payne Fund studies were distorted in various presentations to the public, and how they were used to attack the movie industry.

5. A brief account of the development of market research can be found in Daniel Boorstin, *The Americans: The Democratic Experience* (New York: Random House, 1973), pp. 148–56. On the adaptation of marketing research in early radio, see Herman S. Hettinger, *A Decade of Radio Advertising* (Chicago: University of Chicago Press, 1933); Frederick H. Lumley, *Measurement in Radio* (Columbus: Ohio State University, 1934); Edgar H. Felix, *Using Radio in Sales Promotion* (New York: McGraw-Hill Book Co., 1927).

6. Malcolm Willey and Stuart Rice, "The Agencies of Communication," in President's Research Committee on Social Trends, *Recent Social Trends* (New York: McGraw-Hill Book Co., 1933), p. 203.

7. Paul F. Lazarsfeld, "An Episode in the History of Social Research: A Memoir," in Donald Fleming and Bernard Bailyn, eds., *The Intellectual Migration: Europe and America, 1930–1960* (Cambridge: Harvard University Press, 1969), pp. 270–337 (hereafter cited as "A Memoir"). See also Laura Fermi, *Illustrious Immigrants: The Intellectual Migration* (Chicago: University of Chicago Press, 1968), pp. 336–43.

8. On the development of and different emphases within European "action" re-

search, see Paul F. Lazarsfeld, "Historical Notes on the Empirical Study of Action" (1958), in Paul F. Lazarsfeld, *Qualitative Analysis: Historical and Critical Essays* (Boston: Allyn and Bacon, 1972), pp. 53–105.

9. Paul F. Lazarsfeld and Arthur W. Kornhauser, *The Techniques of Market Research from the Standpoint of a Psychologist* (New York: American Management Association, 1935), pp. 24, 4; Paul F. Lazarsfeld, "The Psychological Aspect of Market Research," *Harvard Business Review* 13 (October 1934): 54–71. Lazarsfeld also wrote several chapters on psychology and marketing for one of the earliest and most widely used texts in the field, American Marketing Society, *The Technique of Marketing Research* (New York: McGraw-Hill Book Co., 1937), chaps. 3, 4, 15, 16.

10. Lazarsfeld, "A Memoir," p. 270, and a quotation from a 1937 letter to Hadley Cantril, p. 306. See also Lazarsfeld's presidential address to the American Sociological Association in 1962, "The Sociology of Empirical Social Research," in Lazarsfeld, *Qualitative Analysis*, pp. 321–40, for his discussion of what he viewed as the crucial links between the institute structure and empirical social research.

11. Hadley Cantril and Gordon Allport, *The Psychology of Radio* (New York: Harper and Brothers, 1935). Laboratory experiments directed by Cantril and Allport centered on such questions as judging personality by voice, comparing male to female announcers, and the relative effectiveness of radio, lectures, and print as learning tools. Yet these experiments dealt exclusively with simple spoken materials, not music, drama, interviews, variety programs, or political speeches. In short, the bulk of radio fare was ignored since "such broadcasts have too complex a structure for experimentation."

12. Paul F. Lazarsfeld, "Radio Research and Applied Psychology," Special Issue of the *Journal of Applied Psychology*, edited by Paul F. Lazarsfeld, 23 (February 1939): 1, 6.

13. Paul F. Lazarsfeld, "Radio Research and Applied Psychology," Special Issue of the *Journal of Applied Psychology*, edited by Paul F. Lazarsfeld, 24 (December 1940): 661, 663–64. This issue's studies were grouped under five headings: "Commercial Effects of Radio," "Educational and Other Effects of Radio," "Program Research," "General Research Techniques," and "Measurement Problems."

14. Paul F. Lazarsfeld, *Radio and the Printed Page* (New York: Duell, Sloan, and Pearce, 1940), p. 332.

15. "Research in Mass Communication" (1940), on microfilm in the Mass Communication Research Center, State Historical Society of Wisconsin, Madison, Wis. Signers were Lyman Bryson, Lloyd A. Free, Geoffrey Gorer, Harold Lasswell, Paul F Lazarsfeld, Robert Lynd, John Marshall, Charles A. Siepmann, Donald Slesinger, and Douglas Waples.

16. "Research in Mass Communication," pp. 5, 19, 37. For an elaboration of the "four questions" model, see Harold Lasswell, "The Structure and Function of Communication in Society," in Lyman D. Bryson, ed., *The Communication of Ideas* (New York: Harper and Brothers, 1948), pp. 37–51.

17. See, for example, Ernst Kris and Howard White, "The German Radio Home News in Wartime"; Hans Speier and Margaret Otis, "German Propaganda to France During the Battle of France"; and Hans Herma, "Some Principles of German Propaganda and Their Application to Radio," all in Paul F. Lazarsfeld and Frank N. Stanton, eds., *Radio Research, 1942–1943* (New York: Duell, Sloan, and Pearce, 1944), pp. 178–261. Robert J. E. Silvey, "Radio Audience Research in Great Britain," and Charles Siepmann, "American Radio in Wartime: An Interim Survey of the OWI Radio Bureau," can also be found in this volume, pp. 111–177. On daytime serials and the war effort, see Herta Herzog, "What Do We Really Know About Daytime Serial Listeners?" and Rudolph Arnheim, "The World of the Daytime Serial," both in Lazarsfeld and Stanton, *Radio Research, 1942–1943*, pp. 3–85. A useful summary of the propaganda studies made at the Bureau of Applied Social Research during the war is Robert K. Merton and Paul F. Lazarsfeld, "Studies in Radio and Film Prop-

aganda," in Robert K. Merton, *Social Theory and Social Structure* (Glencoe: Free Press, 1957), pp. 563–82.

18. On continuing audience research, see, for example, Paul F. Lazarsfeld and Harry Field, *The People Look at Radio* (Chapel Hill: University of North Carolina Press, 1946), based on a 1945 national survey of 2,500 Americans. For early examples of the "uses and gratifications" approach, see Herzog, "What Do We Really Know About Daytime Serial Listeners?"; Bernard Berelson, "What 'Missing the Newspaper' Means," in Paul F. Lazarsfeld and Frank N. Stanton, eds., *Communications Research, 1948–1949* (New York: Harper and Brothers, 1949), pp. 111–29; Helen J. Kaufman, "The Appeal of Specific Daytime Serials," in Lazarsfeld and Stanton, *Radio Research, 1942–1943*, pp. 86–107. A condensation of the 1944 NBC-BASR study is in Paul F. Lazarsfeld and Helen Dinerman, "Research for Action," in Lazarsfeld and Stanton, *Communications Research*, pp. 73–108.

19. Carl I. Hovland, Arthur A. Lumsdaine, and Fred D. Sheffield, *Experiments on Mass Communication* (Princeton: Princeton University Press, 1949), pp. 247, 254–55. This was volume 3 of *Studies in Social Psychology in World War II*.

20. Carl I. Hovland, Irving L. Janis, and Harold H. Kelley, *Communication and Persuasion: Psychological Studies of Opinion Change* (New Haven: Yale University Press, 1953), p. v; see especially pp. 1–17. The chapters in this classic work, each covering several studies, are organized around such issues as "Credibility of the Communicator," "Fear-Arousing Appeals," "Personality and Susceptibility to Persuasion," and "Retention of Opinion Change." For a historical appraisal of the experimental tradition, see Arthur A. Lumsdaine, "On Mass Communication Experiments and the Like," in Daniel Lerner and Lyle M. Nelson, eds., *Communication Research: A Half-Century Appraisal* (Honolulu: University Press of Hawaii, 1977), pp. 37–69.

21. Paul F. Lazarsfeld, Bernard Berelson, and Hazel Gaudet, *The People's Choice: How the Voter Makes Up His Mind in a Presidential Campaign* (New York: Duell, Sloan, and Pearce, 1944), p. 151; see especially chap. 16, "The Nature of Personal Influence." An example of the type of study inspired by this work is Robert K. Merton, "Patterns of Influence: A Study of Interpersonal Influence and of Communications Behavior in a Local Community," in Lazarsfeld and Stanton, *Communications Research*, pp. 180–219. Merton locates and contrasts "locals" and "cosmopolitans" in community affairs. For a summary review of the latter literature on the "two-step flow" concept, see Elihu Katz, "The Two-Step Flow of Communication: An Up-to-Date Report on a Hypothesis," *Public Opinion Quarterly* 21 (Spring 1957): 61–78.

22. Elihu Katz and Paul F. Lazarsfeld, *Personal Influence: The Part Played by People in the Flow of Mass Communication* (Glencoe: Free Press, 1955), pp. 32–33, 133.

23. For a review of the rediscovery of the primary group concept in the social sciences, see Edward A. Shils, "The Study of the Primary Group," in Daniel Lerner and Harold Lasswell, eds., *The Policy Sciences* (Stanford: Stanford University Press, 1951), pp. 44–69.

24. Eliot Friedson, "Communications Research and the Concept of the Mass," *American Sociological Review* 18 (March 1953): 316. See also Elihu Katz, "Communications Research and the Image of Society: Convergence of Two Traditions," *American Journal of Sociology* 65 (March 1960): 435–40, and his "The Two-Step Flow of Communication."

25. Leon Bramson, *The Political Context of Sociology* (Princeton: Princeton University Press, 1961), pp. 118, 121, 152–53; for Bramson's argument that mass society theorists purport to present that theory scientifically, see pp. 116–17. See also Edward A. Shils, "Daydreams and Nightmares: Reflections on the Criticism of Mass Culture," *Sewanee Review* 65 (Autumn 1957): 587 608; Daniel Bell, *The End of Ideology* (New York: Collier Books, 1961), chap. 1. Obviously, some of the writers mentioned by Bramson did use the term "mass society." But the usage of that phrase

by, say, C. Wright Mills in his chapter on "The Mass Society" in *The Power Elite* (New York: Oxford University Press, 1956) differs markedly from its use by, say, the Frankfurt group. For one thing, Mills used the terms *mass* and *public* as ideal types and tendencies in American political life.

26. Bramson, *The Political Context of Sociology*, p. 96, and especially chap. 5, "The American Critique of the Theory of Mass Society: Research in Mass Communication," pp. 96–118; Raymond Bauer and Alice Bauer, "America, Mass Society, and Mass Media," *Journal of Social Issues* 16, no. 3 (1960): 22, 29. In a similar vein, see John W. Riley and Matilda W. Riley, "Mass Communication and the Social System," in Robert K. Merton, Leonard Broom, and Laurence Cottrell, eds., *Sociology Today* (New York: Basic Books, 1959), pp. 537–78. See also Talcott Parsons and Winston White, "The Mass Media and the Structure of American Society," *Journal of Social Issues* 16, no. 3 (1960): 67–77. They conclude that the fundamental fallacy of mass culture theorists is the assumption that this is an "atomized society," with the relations between one individual and another getting increasingly amorphous. In reality, Parsons and White hold, America is a "pluralist society" with great structural differentiation.

27. Joseph T. Klapper, *The Effects of Mass Communication* (Glencoe: Free Press, 1960), pp. 8, 5. Klapper divided his review of the research literature into two parts: part 1, The Effects of Persuasive Communication; part 2, The Effects of Specific Types of Media Material. An earlier version of this book was published by the Bureau of Applied Social Research in 1949.

28. Klapper, *Effects*, p. 257, and see as well pp. 249–57; Bauer and Bauer, "America, Mass Society, and Mass Media," p. 25. For another example of the call to raise scientific standards of research, see Melvin L. De Fleur, *Theories of Mass Communication*, 2d ed. (New York: David McKay Co., 1970), pp. 151–54.

29. For examples of these: GENERAL REVIEW: Steven H. Chaffee, "Mass Media Effects: New Research Perspectives," in Lerner and Nelson, eds., *Communication Research*, pp. 210–41; SOCIALIZATION: Jack M. McLeod and Garrett J. O'Keefe, Jr., "The Socialization Perspective and Communications Behavior," in F. Gerald Kline and Phillip J. Tichenor, eds., *Current Perspectives in Mass Communications Research* (Beverly Hills: Sage Publications, 1972), pp. 121–68; FUNCTIONAL ANALYSIS: Charles R. Wright, "Functional Analysis and Mass Communication," *Public Opinion Quarterly* 24 (Winter 1960): 605–20; and Joseph T. Klapper, "Mass Communications Research: An Old Road Resurveyed," *Public Opinion Quarterly* 27 (Winter 1963): 515–27; MASS MEDIA AS SOCIAL SYSTEMS: De Fleur, "Mass Media as Social Systems," the concluding chapter in his *Theories of Mass Communication*, pp. 155–72, especially p. 166; USES AND GRATIFICATIONS: W. Phillips Davison, "On the Effects of Communication," *Public Opinion Quarterly* 24 (Fall 1960): 344–60.

30. See the latest and most exhaustive review of the literature, George Comstock et al., *Television and Human Behavior* (New York: Columbia University Press, 1978).

31. Siegfried Kracauer, *From Caligari to Hitler: A Psychological History of German Film* (Princeton: Princeton University Press, 1947), pp. 5, 6, 8. His "Propaganda and the Nazi War Film" (1942) is reprinted in this volume as a supplement.

32. Barbara Deming, *Running Away From Myself: A Dream Portrait of America Drawn from the Films of the Forties* (New York: Grossman Publishers, 1969), pp. 1, 6, 201. This book is based on Deming's 1950 manuscript, "A Long Way from Home: Some Film Nightmares of the Forties," for which she could not find a publisher at the time. However, parts of the earlier version were published in contemporary film journals.

33. Martha Wolfenstein and Nathan Leites, *Movies: A Psychological Study* (Glencoe: Free Press, 1950), pp. 13, 300. See especially "Note on Data and Interpretation," pp. 303–7, which discusses the application of psychoanalytic techniques to explain "the emotional significance of recurrent themes." Another work that deserves mention with this group is Hortense Powdermaker, *Hollywood: The Dream Factory* (Boston: Little, Brown, and Co., 1950). Powdermaker, a cultural anthropologist, spent a

year in Hollywood studying it just as she would a South Sea island aboriginal society. Her aim was to "understand and interpret Hollywood, its relationship to the dreams it manufactures, and to our society" (p. 11). "Hollywood," she argued, "is engaged in the mass production of pre-fabricated daydreams. It tries to adapt the American dream, that all men are created equal, to the view that all men's dreams should be made equal" (p. 39).

34. Robert S. Lynd, *Knowledge For What?: The Place of Social Science in American Culture* (Princeton: Princeton University Press, 1939), p. 120.

35. C. Wright Mills, "Abstracted Empiricism," in *The Sociological Imagination* (New York: Oxford University Press, 1959), pp. 67, 71–72. See also Mills's essays, "Two Styles of Social Science Research" (1953) and "IBM Plus Reality Plus Humanism = Sociology" (1954), both in Irving Louis Horowitz, ed., *Power, Politics, and People: The Collected Essays of C. Wright Mills* (New York: Oxford University Press, 1963), pp. 553–76. For a critique of "scientism" in communications research, see also Dallas W. Smythe, "Some Observations on Communications Theory," *Audio-Visual Communication Review* 2 (Winter 1954): 24–37. Smythe's analysis paralleled Mills's in his questioning of the "assumption that the only evidence worthy of credence must come from the laboratory blessed with statistical measures of variance" (p. 28). Smythe attacked what he saw as the dominant stance of communications researchers: "they will accept as 'knowledge' only what has been demonstrated through 'controlled experiments'" (p. 26).

36. The best introduction to critical theory in English is the selected essays of Max Horkheimer, *Critical Theory*, trans. Matthew J. O'Connell et al. (New York: Herder and Herder, 1972), especially "Traditional and Critical Theory," pp. 188–243, and "The Latest Attack on Metaphysics," pp. 132–87. The standard intellectual history of the Frankfurt School is Martin Jay, *The Dialectical Imagination: A History of the Frankfurt School and the Institute of Social Research, 1923–1950* (Boston: Little, Brown, and Co., 1973). Also valuable is Jay's article, "The Frankfurt School in Exile," *Perspectives in American History* 6 (1972): 339–85.

37. Leo Lowenthal, "Historical Perspectives of Popular Culture" (1950), in Bernard Rosenberg and David M. White, eds., *Mass Culture: The Popular Arts in America* (Glencoe: Free Press, 1957), pp. 52, 56. See also Lowenthal's Introduction to his *Literature, Popular Culture, and Society* (Englewood Cliffs: Prentice-Hall, 1961). Lowenthal also produced one of the best examples of research into mass communication that combined a critical perspective with empirical methods, "Biographies in Popular Magazines," in Lazarsfeld and Stanton, *Radio Research, 1942–1943*, pp. 507–48; here he noted the general shift from "idols of production" to "idols of consumption" between 1900 and 1940.

38. T. W. Adorno, "Scientific Experiences of a European Scholar in America," in Bailyn and Fleming, eds., *Intellectual Migration*, pp. 343, 347. See also Adorno's articles, "The Radio Symphony," in Paul F. Lazarsfeld and Frank N. Stanton, eds., *Radio Research, 1941* (New York: Duell, Sloan, and Pearce, 1941), pp. 110–39, and "On Popular Music," *Studies in Philosophy and Social Science* 9, no. 1 (1941): 17–48.

39. Max Horkheimer and T. W. Adorno, "The Culture Industry: Enlightenment as Mass Deception" (1944), in *Dialectic of Enlightenment*, trans. John Cumming (New York: Herder and Herder, 1972), pp. 120–67; Max Horkheimer, "Art and Mass Culture," *Studies in Philosophy and Social Science* 9, no. 1 (1941): 290–304. Concerning the Frankfurt influence on David Riesman and Dwight Macdonald and the mass culture debate, see Jay, "Frankfurt School in Exile," pp. 365–75, although his argument here is not entirely convincing. Rosenberg and White's *Mass Culture* contains the widest spectrum of contributions to that debate, including works by Riesman and Macdonald.

40. Paul F. Lazarsfeld, "Remarks on Administrative and Critical Communications Research" (1941), in Lazarsfeld, *Qualitative Analysis*, p. 160.

CHAPTER 6

1. Biographical information was taken from Donald Creighton, *Harold Adams Innis: Portrait of a Scholar* (Toronto: University of Toronto Press, 1957), chaps. 1–2; and Robin Neill, *A New Theory of Value: The Canadian Economics of H. A. Innis* (Toronto: University of Toronto Press, 1972), chap 1.

2. Harold Innis, "Autobiography" (unpublished), p. 8, cited in Neill, *New Theory of Value*, p. 12.

3. Thorstein Veblen, *The Instinct of Workmanship and the State of the Industrial Arts* (New York: Macmillan Co., 1914), especially "The Machine Industry," pp. 299–351. Veblen considered this his most important work. See also his essay, "Why is Economics Not an Evolutionary Science?" (1898), reprinted in Thorstein Veblen, *The Place of Science in Modern Civilization and Other Essays* (New York: Macmillan Co., 1919). I am indebted in this discussion to Michael E. Starr, particularly for two chapter drafts from his uncompleted dissertation, "The Political Economy of American Institutionalism": "Veblen: Death Penalty for a Nation" and "The Overdeveloped Society." See also David Seckler, *Thorstein Veblen and the Institutionalists: A Study in the Social Philosophy of Economics* (Boulder: Colorado Associated University Press, 1975), especially pp. 52–67.

4. Harold Innis, "A Bibliography of Thorstein Veblen," *Southwestern Political and Social Science Quarterly* 10, no. 1 (1929): 67, 68.

5. Harold Innis, *The Fur Trade in Canada: An Introduction to Canadian Economic History* (rev. ed., Toronto: University of Toronto Press, 1956), pp. 15–16.

6. Ibid., p. 385. See the masterful conclusion to *Fur Trade in Canada*, pp. 383–401, as well as the conclusion to *The Cod Fisheries: The History of an International Economy* (New Haven: Yale University Press, 1940), pp. 484–508. See also Harold Innis, "Transportation as a Factor in Canadian Economic History," *Papers and Proceedings of the Annual Meeting of the Canadian Political Science Association* 3 (May 1931): 166–84, and "Significant Factors in Canadian Economic Development," *Canadian Historical Review* 18 (December 1933): 374–84. For recent assessments of the staples thesis, see Melville H. Watkins, "A Staple Theory of Economic Growth," *Canadian Journal of Economics and Political Science* 19 (May 1963): 141–58; Kenneth Buckley, "The Role of Staples Industries in Canada's Economic Development," *Journal of Economic History* 18 (December 1958): 439–50; W. A. Mackintosh, "Innis on Canadian Economic Development," *Journal of Political Economy* 61 (June 1953): 185–94; W. T. Easterbrook, "Trends in Canadian Economic Thought," *South Atlantic Quarterly* 58 (Winter 1959): pp. 91–107.

7. Harold Innis, "Penetrative Powers of the Price System," *Canadian Journal of Economic and Political Science* 4 (August 1938): 299–319; Harold Innis, "Economic Nationalism," *Papers and Proceedings of the Annual Meeting of the Canadian Political Science Association* 6 (1934): 17–31. See also W. T. Easterbrook, "Innis and Economics," *Canadian Journal of Economics and Political Science* 19 (August 1953): 291–303; Neill, *New Theory of Value*, pp. 50–61.

8. Harold Innis, review of *The Newsprint Industry* by J. A. Guthrie, *The Background and Economics of American Papermaking* by L. T. Stevenson, *Canada Gets the News* by C. M. McNaught, *AP: The Story of the News* by O. Gramling, and *News and the Human Interest Story* by H. M. Hughes, in *Canadian Journal of Economics and Political Science* 7 (November 1941): 583. Starting in 1940, Innis began contributing numerous reviews such as this to the journals.

9. Harold Innis, "The Newspaper in Economic Development," *Journal of Economic History* 2 (Supplement, December 1942): 1–33.

10. This seems to be the position of Neill's book, *New Theory of Value*, which reduces Innis's entire output to a one-dimensional working out of various intramural disputes in Canadian economics.

11. See Daniel Drache, "Harold Innis: A Canadian Nationalist," *Journal of Canadian Studies* 4 (May 1969): 7–12.

12. Harold Innis, *Empire and Communications* (1950; reprint ed. Toronto: University of Toronto Press, 1972), p. 7.

13. On the cultural implications of time and space biases, I am indebted to James W. Carey's excellent essay, "Harold Adams Innis and Marshall McLuhan" (1965), reprinted in Raymond B. Rosenthal, ed., *McLuhan: Pro and Con* (New York: Funk and Wagnalls, 1968), pp. 270–308.

14. Innis, *Empire and Communications*, p. 57; Harold Innis, *The Bias of Communication* (1951; reprint ed.; Toronto: University of Toronto Press, 1971), p. 191.

15. Innis, *Empire and Communications*, p. 115.

16. Harold Innis, "A History of Communications," chaps. 5–6 of an incomplete and unrevised manuscript, microfilmed for private circulation, University of Toronto, Toronto, n.d.; Innis, *Empire and Communications*, pp. 116–48.

17. Innis, *Changing Concepts of Time* (Toronto: University of Toronto Press, 1952), pp. 15, 16, 108.

18. Innis, *Empire and Communications*, p. 170; Innis, *Bias of Communication*, p. 189.

19. *Royal Commission on Broadcasting Report*, 2 vols. (Ottawa: E. Cloutier, 1957) 2:69–70. The dangers of American communications media also dominated the conclusions expressed in the *Royal Commission on National Development in the Arts, Letters, and Sciences*, 2 vols. (Ottawa: E. Cloutier, 1951); see especially 1:11–65, as well as two articles in the second volume: B. K. Sandwell's "Present Day Influences on Canadian Society," 2:1–11; and Wilfred Eggleston's "The Press of Canada," 2:41–53.

20. Innis, *Changing Concepts of Time*, pp. 127, 128. See especially the two essays, "Military Implications of the American Constitution," pp. 21–45, and "Roman Law and the British Empire," pp. 47–76.

21. Henry Adams, "A Letter to American Teachers of History" (1910), in his *Degradation of Democratic Dogma* (New York: Macmillan Co., 1919), p. 212.

22. Innis, *Bias of Communication*, p. 86. See also Harold Innis, "Industrialism and Cultural Values," *American Economic Review* 41 (Papers and Proceedings, May 1951): 201–9. Innis had written in a similar vein in his article, "On the Economic Significance of Culture," *Journal of Economic History* 4 (Supplement, December 1944): 80–97: "Concentration on the price system, driven by mathematics, involves neglect of the technological conditions under which prices operate. The rise of liquidity preference as a concept in the study of economic history emphasizes short run points of view acceptable to the price system rather than long run points of view which necessitate perspective. An equilibrium of approaches to the study of economic phenomena becomes exceedingly difficult to achieve with the insistence on short run interests and the obsession with the present" (p. 83).

23. Robert Park, "Physics and Society," *Canadian Journal of Economics and Political Science* 6 (May 1940): 147. See also Harold Innis, "Political Economy in the Modern State," "A Plea for the University Tradition," and "The University in Modern Crisis," in his *Political Economy in the Modern State* (Toronto: University of Toronto Press, 1946); Innis, "Adult Education and Universities," app. 2 in his *Bias of Communication*, pp. 203–14.

24. Innis, "Industrialism and Cultural Values," pp. 209, 202. See also Innis's last address before his death, unfortunately titled "The Decline in the Efficiency of Instruments Essential in Equilibrium" (unfinished presidential address), *American Economic Review* 43 (March 1953): 16–25, with additional comments by his son, D. Q. Innis.

25. The most important of these are: Donald F. Theall, *The Medium is the Rear View Mirror: Understanding McLuhan* (Montreal: McGill-Queens University Press, 1971). Theall, who wrote his doctoral dissertation under McLuhan at Toronto, offers a critique of McLuhan from an essentially literary perspective. Jonathan Miller's *Mar-*

shall McLuhan (New York: Viking Press, 1971) is part of the Modern Masters Series edited by Frank Kermode. It is short but extremely useful, especially for the discussions of McLuhan's ideas on language and television. John Fekete's "McLuhanacy: Counterrevolution in Cultural Theory," *Telos*, no. 15 (Spring 1973): 75–123, is a full-scale attack on McLuhan from a neo-Marxist perspective. Fekete makes several important arguments, particularly on the affinity between McLuhan and Thomism, but his piece is marred by the often impenetrable post-Frankfurt critical theory style of writing that characterizes *Telos*. Although they somewhat overlap, there are two important collections of short essays on McLuhan's work: Rosenthal, *McLuhan: Pro and Con*, and Gerald E. Stearn, ed., *McLuhan: Hot and Cool* (New York: Dial Press, 1967), which also contains a rebuttal by McLuhan to his critics.

26. Biographical information is taken from Rosenthal, *McLuhan: Pro and Con*, pp. 15–22; and from the "Introduction" in Stearn, *McLuhan: Hot and Cool*, p. xv–xviii.

27. Marshall McLuhan, "G. K. Chesterton: A Practical Mystic," *Dalhousie Review* 15 (1936): 457. See also F. R. Leavis, *For Continuity* (Cambridge: Minority Press, 1933); Miller, *Marshall McLuhan*, pp. 9–32.

28. See McLuhan's three essays, "Edgar Poe's Tradition" (1944), "The Southern Quality" (1947), and "An Ancient Quarrel in Modern America" (1946), which are reprinted in Eugene McNamara, ed., *The Interior Landscape: The Literary Criticism of Marshall McLuhan, 1943–1962* (New York: McGraw-Hill Book Co., 1969).

29. John Crowe Ransom, "Reconstructed But Unregenerate," in *I'll Take My Stand* (New York: Harper and Brothers, 1930), p. 3. Other essays in the volume are relevant to understanding the early McLuhan's position, especially those by Donald Davidson, "A Mirror For Artists"; John Gould Fletcher, "Education, Past and Present"; and Lyle H. Lanier, "A Critique of the Philosophy of Progress."

30. Marshall McLuhan, *The Mechanical Bride: Folklore of Industrial Man* (1951; reprint, Boston: Beacon Press, 1967), p. v.

31. Ibid., pp. 21, 113, 50.

32. Ibid., pp. 98–100, 42, 128.

33. See, for example, McLuhan, "An Ancient Quarrel in Modern America."

34. McLuhan, *Mechanical Bride*, pp. 72, 45.

35. Marshall McLuhan, "Effects of the Improvement of Communications Media," *Journal of Economic History* 20 (December 1960): 568; Theall, *The Medium is the Rear View Mirror*, pp. 80–81.

36. Marshall McLuhan, *The Gutenberg Galaxy* (Toronto: University of Toronto Press, 1962), pp. 63–65.

37. Marshall McLuhan, "The Later Innis," *Queen's Quarterly* 60 (Autumn 1953): 389, 392. See also McLuhan's introductions to the reissues of Innis's *The Bias of Communication* (1971), pp. vii–xvi, and *Empire and Communications* (1972), pp. v–xii.

38. McLuhan, "The Later Innis," pp. 385–94; McLuhan, Introduction to Innis, *The Bias of Communication*, pp. vii–xvi; Marshall McLuhan, "Innis and Communication," *Explorations*, no. 3 (August 1954): 96–104.

39. See the opening statement in *Explorations*, no. 1 (December 1953); Introduction to Marshall McLuhan and Edmund Carpenter, eds., *Explorations in Communication* (Boston: Beacon Press, 1960), an anthology collection of articles from the journal.

40. Dorothy Lee's "Lineal and Nonlineal Codification of Reality" and Siegfried Giedion's "Space Conceptions in Prehistoric Art" are reprinted in McLuhan and Carpenter, *Explorations in Communication*. For Carpenter's work on the Eskimos, see "Eskimo Space Concepts," *Explorations*, no. 5 (June 1955): 131–45, and *Explorations*, no. 9 (last issue, 1959), which was entirely devoted to Eskimo culture. See also Dorothy Lee, "Linguistic Reflections of Winti Thought," and Jacqueline Tynwhit, "The Magic Eye" (on ancient Indian architecture), also reprinted in *Explorations in Communication*.

41. Marshall McLuhan and Edmund Carpenter, "Acoustic Space," reprinted in

Explorations in Communication, pp. 65–70. See also Edmund Carpenter, *Oh, What A Blow That Phantom Gave Me* (New York: Holt, Rinehart, and Winston, 1973), Carpenter's critical reflections on his involvement with bringing modern media to aborigines in New Guinea.

42. Marshall McLuhan, "Five Sovereign Fingers Taxed the Breath" (1955), in McLuhan and Carpenter, *Explorations in Communication*, p. 208. See also Marshall McLuhan, "Notes on the Media as Art Forms," *Explorations*, no. 1 (December 1953): 6–13.

43. This distinction between Innis and McLuhan is the central thesis of Carey, "Harold Adams Innis and Marshall McLuhan."

44. McLuhan, *The Gutenberg Galaxy*, p. 33. For a critique of this position see Miller, *Marshall McLuhan*, pp. 84–110.

45. McLuhan, *The Gutenberg Galaxy*, p. 65.

46. Ibid., pp. 153, 176.

47. Ibid., pp. 165, 330.

48. U.S. House, Committee on Commerce, *Electro-Magnetic Telegraphs*, 25th Cong., 2d sess., 1838, H. Rept. 753, app. C., p. 9; Marshall McLuhan, *Understanding Media: The Extensions of Man* (New York: New American Library, 1965), p. 136.

49. McLuhan, *Understanding Media*, p. 32.

50. Ibid., pp. 51, 54, 55.

51. Ibid., p. 56.

52. Marshall McLuhan, "Interview," *Playboy* 16 (March 1969): 158.

53. McLuhan, *Understanding Media*, p. 41; McLuhan, "Interview," p. 74.

54. McLuhan, *Understanding Media*, pp. 272–73; see the "Television" chapter, pp. 268–94. For a useful technical critique of McLuhan on television, see Miller, *Marshall McLuhan*, pp. 112–19. On McLuhan's neo-Thomism, see Fekete, "McLuhancy: Counterrevolution in Cultural Theory."

55. McLuhan, "Effects of the Improvement of Communications Media," p. 575; McLuhan, *Understanding Media*, pp. 221, and see also 304–6.

56. S. R. Green, chief executive officer, Lintas International, in Barry Day, *The Message of Marshall McLuhan* (London: Lintas, 1967), p. 15. See the bibliography of the Day volume for samples of the scores of articles on McLuhan in advertising and business trade journals in the 1960s.

57. I cannot possibly offer a treatment of these fields here, but I can at least note the importance, for my own thinking, of the work of Claude Levi-Strauss, Noam Chomsky, and Roland Barthes. For a short but useful review of these and other thinkers in the structuralist tradition, as they relate to the study of modern media, see Varda Langholz Leymore, *Hidden Myth: Structure and Symbolism in Advertising* (London: William Heinemann, 1975), pp. 1–17.

EPILOGUE

1. Alfred Vail to Samuel F. B. Morse, 3 June 1844, quoted in Robert L. Thompson, *Wiring a Continent: The History of the Telegraph Industry in the United States, 1832–1866* (Princeton: Princeton University Press, 1947), p. 25; regulations posted in Pittsburgh office of the Atlantic and Ohio Telegraph Company, in the Henry O'Rielly Collection, First Series, vol. 1, New York Historical Society, New York, NY.

2. Charles Briggs and Augustus Maverick, *The Story of the Telegraph and the History of the Great Atlantic Cable* (New York: Rudd and Carleton, 1858), pp. 21, 14; *New York Times*, 9 August 1858.

3. Bishop Sheen quoted in Michael E. Starr, "Prime Time Jesus," *Cultural Correspondence*, no. 4 (Spring 1977): 21.

4. Carl Snyder, "The World's New Marvels: The Wireless Telephone," *Collier's Weekly* 52 (25 October 1913): 23.

5. Howard V. O'Brien, "It's Great to Be A Radio Maniac," *Collier's Weekly* 74 (13 September 1924): 16.

6. U.S. Bureau of the Census, *Fifteenth Census of the United States, 1930*, Population, vol. 6, *Families*, p. 33.

Bibliography

ARCHIVES AND MANUSCRIPT COLLECTIONS

Ann Arbor, Michigan
  Bentley Historical Library, Michigan Historical Collections
    Charles Horton Cooley Papers
Madison, Wisconsin
  State Historical Society of Wisconsin, Mass Communication Research Center
    M. C. Batsel Papers
    Charles E. Butterfield Papers
    Martin Codel Collection
    Robert W. Desmond Collection
    Wendell Hall Papers
    William S. Hedges Papers
    Herbert C. Hoover Papers, 1921–32 (Pertaining to Early Radio Development)
    John S. Penn Papers
New York, New York
  Columbia University
    Radio Unit of the Oral History Project
  Lincoln Center Theater Library
    National Board of Review of Motion Pictures Collection, 1911–26
  New York Historical Society
    Henry O'Rielly Collection

U.S. GOVERNMENT DOCUMENTS

U.S. Bureau of the Census. *Tenth Census of the United States, 1880*. Vol. 4, *Report on the Agencies of Transportation in the United States*. Washington, D.C.: Census Office, 1883.
———. *Fifteenth Census of the United States, 1930. Population*. Vol. 6, *Families*. Washington, D.C.: Department of Commerce, 1933.
U.S. Census Office. *Seventh Census*. "Telegraphs," in *Report of the Superintendent of the Census*, pp. 106–16. Washington, D.C.: Robert Armstrong, 1853.
U.S. Department of Commerce. *Thirty-eighth Statistical Abstract of the United States*. Washington, D.C.: Government Printing Office, 1915.
U.S. Federal Trade Commission Report. *Radio Industry*. Washington, D.C.: Government Printing Office, 1923.
U.S. House. Committee on Appropriations. *To Connect the Telegraph with the Postal Service*. 42d Cong., 3d sess., 1872, H. Rept. 6.
———. Committee on Commerce. *Electro-Magnetic Telegraphs*. 25th Cong., 2d sess., 1838, H. Rept. 753.
———. Committee on Education. *Motion Picture Commission: Hearings*. 2 pts. 63d Cong., 2d sess., 1914. Washington, D.C.: Government Printing Office, 1914.
———. Committee on Education. *Federal Motion Picture Commission*. 63d Cong., 3d sess., 1915, H. Rept. 1411.
———. Committee on the Merchant Marine and Fisheries. *Government Control of Radio Communication: Hearings*. 2 pts. 65th Cong., 3d sess., 1918.
———. Committee of Ways and Means. *Magnetic Telegraph from Baltimore to New York*. 28th Cong., 2d sess., 1845, H. Rept. 187.

———. *Report of the Postmaster General*. 29th Cong., 2d sess., 1846, H. Doc. 4.

———. *Report of the Postmaster General*. 51st Cong., 2d sess., 1890, H. Exec. Doc. 1.

———. Select Committee on the Postal Telegraph in the United States. *Postal Telegraph in the United States*. 41st Cong., 2d sess., 1870, H. Rept. 114.

U.S. Senate. Committee on Post Offices and Post Roads. *Postal Telegraph*. 43d Cong., 1st sess., 1874, S. Rept. 242.

———. Committee on Post Offices and Post Roads. *Telegraph Lines as Post Roads*. 43d Cong., 2d sess., 1875, S. Rept. 624.

———. Committee on Post Office and Railroads. *Testimony, Statements, etc. Taken by the Senate Committee on Post Office and Railroads*. 48th Cong., 1st sess., 1884, S. Rept. 577.

———. Committee on Railroads. *Competing Telegraph Lines*. 45th Cong., 3d sess., 1879, S. Rept. 805.

———. Education and Labor Committee. *Report upon the Relations between Labor and Capital*. 4 vols. Washington, D.C.: Government Printing Office, 1885.

NEWSPAPERS AND PERIODICALS

American Telegraph Magazine. 1852–53.
Chicago Tribune. 1907.
Explorations, nos. 1–9. 1953–59.
The Marconigraph. 1911–13.
Moving Picture News. 1909–15.
Moving Picture World. 1907–15.
New Orleans Price Current. 1848.
New York Times. 1858, 1909.
The Nickelodeon. 1909–11.
Philadelphia North American. 1846.
Public Opinion Quarterly. 1937.
Radio Broadcast. 1922–24.
Radio News. 1919–25.
Rochester Daily American. 1846.
Shaffner's Telegraph Companion. 1854–55.
Wireless Age. 1913–25.

BOOKS, ARTICLES, AND THESES

"About the Radio Round Table." *Scientific American* 127 (December 1922): 378–79.

Adams, Henry. *The Degradation of Democratic Dogma*. New York: Macmillan Co., 1919.

Addams, Jane. *The Second Twenty Years at Hull House*. New York: Macmillan Co., 1930.

———. *The Spirit of Youth and the City Streets*. New York: Macmillan Co., 1910.

———. *Twenty Years at Hull House*. New York: Macmillan Co., 1910.

Adorno, T. W. "On Popular Music." *Studies in Philosophy and Social Science* 9, no. 1 (1941): 17–48.

———. "The Radio Symphony." In *Radio Research*, edited by Paul F. Lazarsfeld and Frank N. Stanton, pp. 110–39. New York: Duell, Sloan, and Pearce, 1941.

———. "Scientific Experiences of a European Scholar in America." In *The Intellectual Migration: Europe and America, 1920–1960*, edited by Donald Fleming and Bernard Bailyn, pp. 338–70. Cambridge: Harvard University Press, 1969.

Aitken, Hugh G. J. *Syntony and Spark: The Origins of Radio*. New York: John Wiley and Sons, 1976.

Albig, William. *Public Opinion*. New York: McGraw-Hill Book Co., 1939.

"The American Marconi Organization." *The Marconigraph* (December 1912): 109–19.

American Marketing Society. *The Technique of Marketing Research*. New York: McGraw-Hill Book Co., 1937.

Angell, Robert C., ed. *Charles H. Cooley: Sociological Theory and Social Research*. New York: Henry Holt and Co., 1930.

Archer, Gleason L. *Big Business and Radio*. New York: American Historical Co., 1939.

———. *History of Radio to 1926*. New York: American Historical Society, 1938.

Arnold, Frank P. *Broadcast Advertising: The Fourth Dimension*. New York: John Wiley and Sons, 1931.

Arnold, Matthew, *Civilization in the United States: First and Last Impressions of America*. Boston: Cupples and Hurd, 1888.

———. *Culture and Anarchy*. Edited by Ian Gregor. Indianapolis: Bobbs-Merrill Co., 1971.

Baker, Paul J., ed. "The Life Histories of W. I. Thomas and Robert E. Park." *American Journal of Sociology* 79 (September 1973): 243–60.

Baker, Ray Stannard. "Marconi's Achievement." *McClure's* 18 (February 1902): 291–99.

Baldwin, James Mark. *Social and Ethical Interpretations in Mental Development*. New York: Macmillan Co., 1897.

Ballard, William C. *Elements of Radio Telephony*. New York: McGraw-Hill Book Co., 1922.

Banning, William P. *Commercial Broadcasting Pioneer: The WEAF Experiment, 1922–1926*. Cambridge: Harvard University Press, 1946.

Barnouw, Erik. *A History of Broadcasting in the United States*. 3 vols. Vol. 1, *A Tower in Babel*. Vol. 2, *The Golden Web*. Vol. 3, *The Image Empire*. New York: Oxford University Press, 1966–70.

Bartholomew, Robert O. *Report of Censorship of Motion Pictures*. Cleveland: n.p., 1913.

Bauer, Raymond, and Bauer, Alice. "America, Mass Society, and Mass Media." *Journal of Social Issues* 16, no. 3 (1960): 3–66.

Beard, George M. *American Nervousness*. New York: G. P. Putnam's Sons, 1881.

Bell, Daniel. *The End of Ideology*. New York. Collier Books, 1961.

Bensman, Marvin R. "The Zenith-WJAZ Case and the Chaos of 1926–27." *Journal of Broadcasting* 14 (Fall 1970): 423–40.

Berlyn, Alfred. "Culture for the Million." *Living Age* 279 (13 December 1913): 701–2.

Bickel, Karl. *New Empires: The Newspaper and the Radio*. Philadelphia: J. B. Lippincott Co., 1930.

Bigelow, Jacob. *Elements of Technology*. Boston: Hilliard, Gray, Little, and Wilkins, 1829.

Blake, G. G. *History of Radio Telegraphy and Telephony*. London: Radio Press, 1926.

Blankenhorn, Heber. *Adventures in Propaganda*. Boston: Houghton Mifflin Co., 1919.

Bliven, Bruce. "How Radio is Remaking Our World." *Century Magazine* 108 (June 1924): 147–54.

———. "The Legion Family and the Radio." *Century Magazine* 108 (October 1924): 811–18.

Boorstin, Daniel. *The Americans: The Democratic Experience*. New York: Random House, 1973.

Borchardt, Kurt. *Structure and Performance of the U.S. Communications Industry*. Boston: Graduate School of Administration, Harvard University, 1970.

Boucheron, Pierre. "News and Music From the Air." *Scientific American* 125A (December 1921): 104–5.

Bourne, Randolph. "Our Cultural Humility." *Atlantic Monthly* 114 (October 1914): 503–7.

Bramson, Leon. *The Political Context of Sociology*. Princeton: Princeton University Press, 1961.

Brewster, William T. "Some Recent Guides to Culture." *Forum* 38 (January 1907): 381–93.

Briggs, Charles, and Maverick, Augustus. *The Story of the Telegraph and the History of the Great Atlantic Cable*. New York: Rudd and Carleton, 1858.

Brindze, Ruth. *Not to Be Broadcast: The Truth about Radio*. New York: Vanguard Press, 1933.

———. "Who Owns the Air?" *Nation* 144 (17 April 1937): 430–32.

Broadcasting Yearbook. 1 February 1940.

Brooks, Noah. "The Newspaper of the Future." *Forum* 9 (July 1890): 569–78.

Brooks, Van Wyck. *Three Essays on America*. New York: E. P. Dutton and Co., 1934.

Buckley, Kenneth. "The Role of Staples Industries in Canada's Economic Development." *Journal of Economic History* 18 (December 1958): 439–50.

Butler, Elizabeth B. *Women and the Trades: Pittsburgh, 1907–1908*. New York: Charities Publication Committee of the Russell Sage Foundation, 1909.

Buxton, Frank, and Owen, Bill. *The Big Broadcast, 1920–1950*. New York: Viking Press, 1972.

Byington, Margaret F. *Homestead: The Households of a Mill Town*. New York: Charities Publication Committee of the Russell Sage Foundation, 1910.

Cantril, Hadley, and Allport, Gordon. *The Psychology of Radio*. New York: Harper and Brothers, 1935.

Carpenter, Edmund. *Oh, What A Blow That Phantom Gave Me*. New York: Holt, Rinehart, and Winston, 1973.

Carey, James W. "Communication and Culture." *Communication Research* 2 (April 1975): 176–91.

———. "A Cultural Approach to Communication." Unpublished essay, 1973.

———. "Harold Adams Innis and Marshall McLuhan." In *McLuhan: Pro and Con*, edited by Raymond B. Rosenthal, pp. 270–308. New York: Funk and Wagnalls, 1968.

———. "Mass Communication Research and Cultural Studies: An American View." In *Mass Communication and Society*, edited by James Curran et al., pp. 409–25. Beverly Hills: Sage Publications, 1977.

Cassady, Ralph, Jr. "Monopoly in Motion Picture Production and Distribution: 1908–1915." *Southern California Law Review* 32 (Summer 1959): 325–90.

Chanler, Alida. "Unexplored Harmonies." *Atlantic* 127 (March 1921): 363–66.

Channing, William F. "On the Municipal Electric Telegraph." *American Journal of Science and Arts*, 2d ser. 63 (May 1852): 58–83.

Charters, W. W. *Motion Pictures and Youth: A Summary*. New York: Macmillan Co., 1934.

Clerke, Agnes M. "Ethereal Telegraphy." *Living Age* 219 (3 December 1898): 619–28.

Coady, Robert. "Censoring the Motion Picture." *Soil* 1 (December 1916): 37–38.

Cocks, Orrin G. "Applying Standards to Motion Picture Films." *Survey* 32 (27 June 1914): 337–38.

Codel, Martin, ed. *Radio and its Future*. New York: Harper and Brothers, 1930.

Cohen, Marshall J. "Self and Society: Charles Horton Cooley and the Idea of Social Self in American Thought." Ph.D. dissertation, Harvard University, 1967.

Collier, John. "Light on Moving Pictures." *Survey* 25 (1 October 1910): 80.

———. "'Movies' and the Law." *Survey* 27 (20 January 1912): 1628–29.

———. *The Problem of Motion Pictures*. New York: National Board of Censorship, 1910.

Colpitts, E. H. "The Future of Radio Telephony." *Scientific American* 113 (4 December 1915): 485.

"Communicating Over Great Distances: The Invention of the Telegraph, Telephone, and Wireless Telegraphy." *Scientific American* 112 (5 June 1915): 531.

Comstock, George, et al. *Television and Human Behavior*. New York: Columbia
University Press, 1978.
"Concerning Culture." *Outlook* 48 (9 December 1893): 1072–73.
Cooley, Charles H. *Human Nature and the Social Order*. Rev. ed. New York: Charles
Scribner's Sons, 1922.
———. *Life and the Student*. New York: Alfred A. Knopf, 1927.
———. "A Primary Culture for Democracy." *American Sociological Society Publica-
tions* 13 (1918): 1–10.
———. "The Process of Social Change." *Political Science Quarterly* 12 (March 1897):
63–81.
———. "Reflections Upon the Sociology of Herbert Spencer." *American Journal of
Sociology* 26 (September 1920): 129–45.
———. *Social Organization: A Study of the Larger Mind*. New York: Charles
Scribner's Sons, 1909.
———. *Social Process*. New York: Charles Scribner's Sons, 1918.
Coon, Horace. *American Telephone and Telegraph*. New York and Toronto: Longmans,
Green, and Co., 1939.
Copp, Joseph A. *The Atlantic Telegraph: A Discourse*. Boston: T. R. Marvin and Sons,
1858.
Correll, Charles J., and Gosden, Freeman F. *All About Amos & Andy*. New York:
Rand McNally and Co., 1929.
Corwin, Norman. *Thirteen by Corwin*. New York: Henry Holt and Co., 1942.
Coughlan, Neil. *Young John Dewey: An Essay in American Intellectual History*.
Chicago: University of Chicago Press, 1975.
Coulter, Douglas, ed. *Columbia Workshop Plays: Fourteen Radio Dramas*. New York:
McGraw-Hill Book Co., 1939.
Creel, George. *How We Advertised America*. New York: Harper and Brothers, 1920.
Creighton, Donald. *Harold Adams Innis: Portrait of a Scholar*. Toronto: University of
Toronto Press, 1957.
Crookes, William. "Some Possibilities of Electricity." *Fortnightly Review* 51 (Feb-
ruary 1892): 173–81.
Currie, Barton W. "The Nickel Madness." *Harper's Weekly* 51 (24 August 1907):
1246–47.
Dam, H. J. W. "Telegraphing Without Wires: A Possibility of Electrical Science."
McClure's 8 (March 1897): 383–92.
Danielian, N. R. *A. T. & T.: The Story of Industrial Conquest*. New York: Vanguard
Press, 1939.
Davis, Daniel. *Book of the Telegraph*. Boston: D. Davis, 1851.
Davis, Harry P. "The Early History of Broadcasting in the United States." In *The
Radio Industry: The Story of its Development*, edited by Anton De Haas, pp.
189–225. Chicago: A. W. Shaw, 1928.
Davis, Michael M. *The Exploitation of Pleasure: A Study of Commercial Recreation in
New York*. New York: Russell Sage Foundation, 1911.
Davison, W. Phillips. "On the Effects of Communication." *Public Opinion Quarterly* 24
(Fall 1960): 344–60.
Dawson, Mitchell. "Censorship on the Air." *American Mercury* 31 (March 1934):
257–68.
Day, Barry. *The Message of Marshall McLuhan*. London: Lintas, 1967.
"The Decay of Vaudeville." *American Magazine* 69 (April 1910): 840–48.
De Fleur, Melvin L. *Theories of Mass Communication*. 2d ed. New York: David
McKay Co., 1970.
De Forest, Lee. "The Audion—A New Receiver for Wireless Telegraphy." *Scientific
American* 64 (Supplement, 20 November 1907): 348–56.
Deming, Barbara. *Running Away From Myself: A Dream Portrait of America Drawn
from the Films of the Forties*. New York: Grossman Publishers, 1969.

Denison, Merrill. "Why Isn't Radio Better?" *Harper's* 168 (April 1934): 576–86.
Dewey, Jane, ed. "Biography of John Dewey." In *The Philosophy of John Dewey*, edited by Paul A. Schilpp, pp. 3–45. Evanston: Northwestern University Press, 1939.
Dewey, John. *Art As Experience*. New York: Minton, Balch, and Co., 1934.
———. *Democracy and Education*. New York: Macmillan Co., 1915.
———. *The Early Works of John Dewey, 1882–1898*. 5 vols. Carbondale: Southern Illinois University Press, 1971.
———. *Experience and Nature*. 1929. Reprint ed. New York: Dover Publications, 1958.
———. "From Absolutism to Experimentalism." In *Contemporary American Philosophy: Personal Statements*, edited by George P. Adams and William P. Montague, 2 vols., 2:13–27. New York: Macmillan Co., 1930.
———. "Our Un-Free Press." *Common Sense* 4 (November 1935): 6–7.
———. "Practical Democracy." *New Republic* 45 (2 December 1925): 52–54.
———. *The Public and Its Problems*. 1927. Reprint. Chicago: Swallow Press, 1954.
———. "Public Opinion." *New Republic* 30 (3 May 1922): 286–88.
———. "Radio's Influence on the Mind." *School and Society* 40 (15 December 1934): 805.
———. "Social Science and Social Control." *New Republic* 67 (29 July 1931): 276–77.
Dickson, W. K. L., and Dickson, Antonia. *History of the Kinetograph, Kinetoscope, and Kinetophonograph*. New York: n.p., 1895.
"Documents Relating to Discussions on the Study of Mass Communication." Microfilm. Madison: State Historical Society of Wisconsin, Mass Communication Research Center, 1940.
Dolbear, Amos E. "The Ether and its Newly Discovered Properties." *Arena* 6 (June 1892): 1–7.
Doob, Leonard W. *Propaganda: Its Psychology and Technique*. New York: Henry Holt and Co., 1935.
Dorf, Philip. *The Builder: A Biography of Ezra Cornell*. New York: Macmillan Co., 1953.
Drache, Daniel. "Harold Innis: A Canadian Nationalist." *Journal of Canadian Studies* 4 (May 1969): 7–12.
Dreher, Carl. *Sarnoff: An American Success*. New York: Quadrangle Books, 1977.
Dunlap, Orrin E. *Marconi: The Man and His Wireless*. New York: Macmillan Co., 1937.
Durstine, Roy S. "We're On the Air." *Scribner's Magazine* 83 (May 1928): 623–31.
Dykhuizen, George. "John Dewey and the University of Michigan." *Journal of the History of Ideas* 23 (October–December 1962): 513–44.
———. *The Life and Mind of John Dewey*. Carbondale: Southern Illinois University Press, 1973.
Easterbrook, W. T. "Innis and Economics." *Canadian Journal of Economics and Political Science* 19 (August 1953): 291–303.
———. "Trends in Canadian Economic Thought." *South Atlantic Quarterly* 58 (Winter 1959): 91–107.
Eaton, Walter P. "The Canned Drama." *American Magazine* 68 (September 1909): 493–500.
———. "Class Consciousness and the 'Movies.'" *Atlantic* 115 (January 1915): 48–56.
———. "The Menace of the Movies." *American Magazine* 76 (September 1913): 55–60.
———. "A New Epoch in the Movies." *American Magazine* 78 (October 1914): 44.
Edison, Thomas A. "The Air Telegraph." *North American Review* 142 (March 1886): 285–91.
Edwards, Richard H. *Popular Amusements*. New York: Association Press, 1915.
Eisenstein, Elizabeth L. *The Printing Press as an Agent of Change: Communications*

and Cultural Transformations in Early-Modern Europe. 2 vols. Cambridge: Cambridge University Press, 1979.

"The Elevation of Vaudeville." *Moving Picture World* 1 (18 May 1907): 164.

Elkus, Charles de Young. "Report on Motion Pictures." *Transactions of the Commonwealth Club of California* 8 (1914): 251–72.

Elliott, Henry R. "The Ratio of News." *Forum* 5 (March 1888): 99–107.

Elton, J. Hannaford. "Tomorrow in Radio." *Illustrated World* 37 (June 1922): 499–505.

Emery, Edwin. *The Press and America.* Englewood Cliffs: Prentice-Hall, 1972.

Enzensberger, Hans Magnus. *The Consciousness Industry.* New York: Seabury Press, 1974.

Ewen, Stuart. *Captains of Consciousness: Advertising and the Social Roots of Consumer Culture.* McGraw-Hill Book Co., 1976.

Fahie, J. J. *A History of Wireless Telegraphy, 1838–1899.* New York: Dodd, Mead and Co., 1899.

Faris, Ellsworth. "Robert E. Park." *American Sociological Review* 9 (June 1944): 321–25.

Fekete, John. "McLuhanacy: Counterrevolution in Cultural Theory." *Telos*, no. 15 (Spring 1973), pp. 75–123.

Felix, Edgar H. *Using Radio in Sales Promotion.* New York: McGraw-Hill Book Co., 1927.

Fell, John R. "Dissolves by Gaslight: Antecedents to the Motion Picture in Nineteenth Century Melodrama." *Film Quarterly* 23 (Spring 1970): 22–34.

Fermi, Laura. *Illustrious Immigrants: The Intellectual Migration.* Chicago: University of Chicago Press, 1968.

Fessenden, R. A. "A Brief History of Wireless Telegraphy." *Scientific American* 67 (Supplement, 9 January 1909): 18.

———. "Wireless Telephony." *Scientific American* 67 (Supplement, 13 March 1909): 172.

Feuer, Lewis S. "John Dewey and the Back to the People Movement in American Thought." *Journal of the History of Ideas* 20 (October–December 1959): 545–68.

Fisher, Boyd. "The Regulation of Motion Picture Theaters." *American City* 7 (September 1912): 520–22.

Fleming, J. Ambrose. "Scientific History and Future Uses of Wireless Telegraphy." *North American Review* 168 (May 1899): 630–40.

Ford, Corydon. *The Child of Democracy: Being the Adventures of the Embryo State, 1856–1894.* Ann Arbor: J. V. Sheehan Co., 1894.

Ford, Franklin. *Draft of Action.* Ann Arbor: n.p., 1892?.

Ford, James L. "The Fad of Imitation Culture." *Munsey's Magazine* 24 (October 1900): 153–57.

Fosdick, Raymond. *A Report on the Condition of Moving Picture Shows in New York.* New York: n.p., 1911.

Foster, William T. *Vaudeville and Motion Picture Shows: A Study of Theaters in Portland, Oregon.* Portland: Reed College, 1914.

Friedson, Eliot. "Communications Research and the Concept of the Mass." *American Sociological Review* 18 (March 1953): 313–17.

Frost, Stanley. "Marconi and His Views of Wireless Progress." *Review of Reviews* 66 (August 1922): 166–70.

———. "Radio: Our Next Great Step Forward." *Collier's Weekly* 69 (18 April 1922): 3.

Gannett, Ezra S. *Discourse on the Atlantic Telegraph.* Boston: Crosby, Nichols, and Co., 1858.

Gans, Herbert J. *Popular Culture and High Culture: An Analysis and Evaluation of Taste.* New York: Basic Books, 1974.

Geertz, Clifford. *The Interpretation of Cultures.* New York: Basic Books, 1973.

George, Henry, Jr. *Life of Henry George.* New York: Doubleday and McClure, 1900.

Gernsback, Hugo. "The Broadcast Listener." *Radio News* 4 (June 1923): 1.
_____. "Radio Achievements in Recent Years." *Current History* 18 (April 1923): 113–20.
_____. *Radio for All*. Philadelphia: J. B. Lippincott Co., 1922.
Goldsmith, Alfred N. "Radio Telephony." *Wireless Age* 4 (January 1917): 248–55.
Goldsmith, Alfred N., and Lescarboura, Austin C. *This Thing Called Broadcasting*. New York: Henry Holt and Co., 1934.
Goode, Kenneth. *Manual of Modern Advertising*. New York: Greenberg Publishers, 1932.
Grau, Robert. "The Motion Picture Show and the Living Drama." *Review of Reviews* 45 (March 1912): 329–36.
_____. *The Theater of Science: A Volume of Progress and Achievement in the Motion Picture Industry*. New York: Broadway Publishing Co., 1914.
Green, William. "Report of the Chairman, Committee on Labor." *National Broadcasting Company Advisory Council Reports* 7 (1931): 49–52.
Gross, Ben. *I Looked and I Listened: Informal Recollections of Radio and TV*. New York: Random House, 1954.
Gunsaulus, F. W. "The Ideal of Culture." *The Chautauquan* 16 (October 1892): 59–64.
Hamilton, Clayton. "The Art of the Moving Picture Play." *The Bookman* 32 (January 1911): 512–16.
Hampton, Benjamin B. *History of the American Film Industry*. 1931. Reprint. New York: Dover Publications, 1971.
Hanmer, Lee F., and Perry, Clarence A. *Recreation in Springfield, Illinois*. New York: Department of Recreation, Russell Sage Foundation, 1914.
Harlow, Alvin F. *Old Wires and New Waves: The History of the Telegraph, Telephone, and Wireless*. New York: D. Appleton-Century Co., 1936.
Hartshorne, Henry. "American Culture." *Lippincott's Magazine* 1 (June 1868): 645–47.
Hawley, Walter L. "Development of the American Newspaper." *Popular Science Monthly* 56 (December 1899): 186–204.
Haynes, Rowland. "Recreation Survey, Milwaukee, Wisconsin." *Playground* 6 (May 1912): 38–66.
Haynes, Rowland, and McClure, Fred F. *Second Annual Report of the Recreation Department of the Board of Public Welfare*. Kansas City: n.p., 1912.
Hendricks, Gordon. *Beginnings of the Biograph*. New York: Beginnings of the American Film, 1964.
_____. *The Edison Motion Picture Myth*. Berkeley: University of California Press, 1961.
_____. *The Kinetoscope*. New York: Beginnings of the American Film, 1966.
Herring, E. Pendleton. "Politics and Radio Regulation." *Harvard Business Review* 13 (January 1935): 167–78.
Herring, James M., and Cross, Gerald C. *Telecommunications: Economics and Regulation*. New York: McGraw-Hill Book Co., 1936.
Herzog, Herta. "On Borrowed Experience: An Analysis of Listening to Daytime Sketches." *Studies in Philosophy and Social Science* 9, no. 1 (1914): 65–95.
Hesse, Mary. "Ether." In *Encyclopedia of Philosophy*, 1967 ed., s.v., pp. 66–69.
Hettinger, Herman S. *A Decade of Radio Advertising*. Chicago: University of Chicago Press, 1933.
Higginson, Thomas Wentworth. "A Plea for Culture." *Atlantic Monthly* 19 (January 1867): 29–37.
Hill, Nathaniel P. *Speeches and Papers on the Silver, Postal Telegraph, and Other Economic Questions*. Colorado Springs: Gazette Printing Co., 1890.
Hoover, Herbert. *Memoirs*. Vol. 2, *The Cabinet and the Presidency*. New York: Macmillan Co., 1952.

_____. "Reminiscences." Radio Unit of the Oral History Project, 1950. Columbia University, New York, NY.

Horkheimer, Max. "Art and Mass Culture." *Studies in Philosophy and Social Science* 9, no. 1 (1941): 290–304.

_____. *Critical Theory*. Translated from German by Matthew J. O'Connell et al. New York: Herder and Herder, 1972.

Horkheimer, Max, and Adorno, T. W. *Dialectic of Enlightenment*. Translated by John Cumming. New York: Herder and Herder, 1972.

Horowitz, Irving Louis, ed. *Power, Politics, and People: The Collected Essays of C. Wright Mills*. New York: Oxford University Press, 1963.

Hovland, Carl I.; Janis, Irving L.; and Kelley, Harold H. *Communication and Persuasion: Psychological Studies of Opinion Change*. New Haven: Yale University Press, 1953.

Hovland, Carl I.; Lumsdaine, Arthur A.; and Sheffield, Fred D. *Experiments on Mass Communication*. Princeton: Princeton University Press, 1949.

Howe, Frederic C. "Leisure." *Survey* 31 (3 January 1914): 415–16.

_____. "What to do With the Motion Picture Show." *Outlook* 107 (20 June 1914): 412–16.

Howeth, L. S. *History of Communications Electronics in the United States Navy*. Washington, D.C.: Government Printing Office, 1963.

Hozier, H. M. "Wireless Telegraphy." *Nineteenth Century* 60 (July 1906): 49–56.

Hubbard, Gardiner G. "The Proposed Changes in the Telegraph System." *North American Review* 117 (July 1873): 80–107.

I'll Take My Stand: The South and the Agrarian Tradition by Twelve Southerners. New York: Harper and Brothers, 1930.

"Influence of the Telegraph Upon Literature." *Democratic Review* 22 (May 1848): 409–13.

Inglis, William. "Morals and Moving Pictures." *Harper's Weekly* 54 (30 July 1910): 12–13.

Innis, Harold. "A Bibliography of Thorstein Veblen." *Southwestern Political and Social Science Quarterly* 10, no. 1 (1929): 56–68.

_____. *The Bias of Communication*. 1951. Reprint. Toronto: University of Toronto Press, 1971.

_____. *Changing Concepts of Time*. Toronto: University of Toronto Press, 1952.

_____. *The Cod Fisheries: The History of an International Economy*. New Haven: Yale University Press, 1940.

_____. "The Decline in the Efficiency of Instruments Essential in Equilibrium." *American Economic Review* 43 (March 1953): 16–25.

_____. "Economic Nationalism." *Papers and Proceedings of the Annual Meeting of the Canadian Political Science Association* 6 (1934): 17–31.

_____. *Empire and Communications*. 1950. Reprint. Toronto: University of Toronto Press, 1972.

_____. *Essays in Canadian Economic History*. Toronto: University of Toronto Press, 1956.

_____. *The Fur Trade in Canada: An Introduction to Canadian Economic History*. Rev. ed. Toronto: University of Toronto Press, 1956.

_____. "A History of Communications." Incomplete and unrevised manuscript. Microfilmed for private circulation. Toronto: University of Toronto, n.d.

_____. "Industrialism and Cultural Values." *American Economic Review* (Papers and Proceedings) 41 (May 1951): 201–9.

_____. "The Newspaper in Economic Development." *Journal of Economic History* 2 (Supplement, December 1942): 1–33.

_____. "On the Economic Significance of Culture." *Journal of Economic History* 4 (Supplement, December 1944): 80–97.

_____. "Penetrative Powers of the Price System." *Canadian Journal of Economic and Political Science* 4 (August 1938): 299–319.

_____. *Political Economy in the Modern State*. Toronto: University of Toronto Press, 1946.

_____. "Significant Factors in Canadian Economic Development." *Canadian Historical Review* 18 (December 1933): 374–84.

_____. "Transportation as a Factor in Canadian Economic History." In *Papers and Proceedings of the Annual Meeting of the Canadian Political Science Association* 3 (May 1931): 166–84.

"The Intellectual Effects of Electricity." *The Spectator* 63 (9 November 1889): 631–32.

Irwin, W. H. *Propaganda and the News*. New York: McGraw-Hill Book Co., 1936.

Israels, Belle L. "Recreation in Rural Communities." In *Proceedings of the National Conference of Charities and Correction*, pp. 103–7. Fort Wayne, Ind.: n.p., 1911.

Jackson, Joseph H. "Should Radio Be Used for Advertising?" *Radio Broadcast* 2 (November 1922): 72–76.

Jacobs, Lewis. *The Rise of the American Film*. New York: Harcourt, Brace and Co., 1939.

James, William. *The Principles of Psychology*. 2 vols. New York: Henry Holt and Co., 1890.

Jandy, Edward C. *Charles Horton Cooley: His Life and His Social Thought*. New York: Dryden Press, 1942.

Jay, Martin. *The Dialectical Imagination: A History of the Frankfurt School and the Institute of Social Research, 1920–1950*. Boston: Little, Brown and Co., 1973.

_____. "The Frankfurt School in Exile." *Perspectives in American History* 6 (1972): 339–85.

Jewett, Frank B. "Wireless Telephony." *Review of Reviews* 59 (May 1919): 500–503.

Jones, Alexander. *Historical Sketch of the Electric Telegraph*. New York: G. P. Putnam, 1852.

Jowett, Garth. *Film: The Democratic Art*. Boston: Little, Brown, and Co., 1976.

Jump, Herbert A. *The Religious Possibilities of the Motion Picture*. New Britain, Ct.: n.p., 1910?.

Kaempffert, Waldemar. "Radio Broadcasting." *Review of Reviews* 65 (April 1922): 395–401.

Kaltenborn, H. V. *I Broadcast the Crisis*. New York: Random House, 1938.

_____. "On the Air." *Century Magazine* 112 (October 1926): 666–76.

_____. "Reminiscences." Radio Unit of the Oral History Project, 1950. Columbia University, New York, NY.

Kaplan, Sidney. "Social Engineers as Saviors: Effects of World War I on Some American Liberals." *Journal of the History of Ideas* 17 (June 1956): 347–69.

Katz, Elihu. "Communications Research and the Image of Society: Convergence of Two Traditions." *American Journal of Sociology* 65 (March 1960): 435–40.

_____. "The Two-Step Flow of Communication: An Up-to-Date Report on a Hypothesis." *Public Opinion Quarterly* 21 (Spring 1957): 61–78.

Katz, Elihu, and Lazarsfeld, Paul F. *Personal Influence: The Part Played by People in the Flow of Mass Communication*. Glencoe: Free Press, 1955.

Kellogg, D. O. "The Coming Newspaper." *The American* 20 (9 August 1890): 328–30.

Kerr, Richard. *Wireless Telegraphy*. London: Seeley and Co., 1898.

Klapper, Joseph T. *The Effects of Mass Communication*. Glencoe: Free Press, 1960.

_____. "Mass Communications Research: An Old Road Resurveyed." *Public Opinion Quarterly* 27 (Winter 1963): 515–27.

Kline, F. Gerald, and Tichenor, Phillip J., eds. *Current Perspectives in Mass Communications Research*. Beverly Hills: Sage Publications, 1972.

Kluckholn, Clyde, and Kroeber, A. L. *Culture: A Critical Review of Concepts and Definitions*. Cambridge, Mass.: Peabody Museum, 1952.

Knight, Howard R. *Play and Recreation in a Town of 6000: A Recreation Survey of Ipswich, Mass*. New York: Russell Sage Foundation, 1914.

Knights, Peter. "Conflict Between the New York Associated Press and the Western Associated Press, 1866–1867." Master's thesis, University of Wisconsin, 1965.

Kracauer, Siegfried. *From Caligari to Hitler: A Psychological History of German Film*. Princeton: Princeton University Press, 1947.

Langholz-Leymore, Varda. *Hidden Myth: Structure and Symbolism in Advertising*. London: William Heinemann, 1975.

Larned, J. N. *Books, Culture, and Character*. Boston: Houghton Mifflin Co., 1906.

Lasswell, Harold. *Propaganda Technique in the World War*. New York: Alfred A. Knopf, 1927.

_____. "The Structure and Function of Communication in Society." In *The Communication of Ideas*, edited by Lyman D. Bryson, pp. 37–51. New York: Harper and Brothers, 1948.

Laurence, E. "The Progress of Electricity." *Harper's New Monthly* 39 (September 1869): 548–60.

Lawson, W. P. "The Miracle of the Movie." *Harper's Weekly* 60 (2 January 1915): 7–9.

_____. *The Movies: Their Importance and Supervision*. New York: National Board of Censorship, 1915.

Lazarsfeld, Paul F. "An Episode in the History of Social Research: A Memoir." In *The Intellectual Migration: Europe and America, 1920–1960*, edited by Donald Fleming and Bernard Bailyn, pp. 270–337. Cambridge: Harvard University Press, 1969.

_____. "The Psychological Aspects of Market Research." *Harvard Business Review* 13 (October 1934): 54–71.

_____. *Qualitative Analysis: Historical and Critical Essays*. Boston: Allyn and Bacon, 1972.

_____. *Radio and the Printed Page*. New York: Duell, Sloan, and Pearce, 1940.

_____. "Radio Research and Applied Psychology." In Special Issues of *Journal of Applied Psychology*, edited by Paul F. Lazarsfeld, 23 (February 1939) and 24 (December 1940).

Lazarsfeld, Paul F.; Berelson, Bernard; and Gaudet, Hazel. *The People's Choice: How the Voter Makes Up His Mind in a Presidential Campaign*. New York: Duell, Sloan, and Pearce, 1944.

Lazarsfeld, Paul F., and Field, Harry. *The People Look at Radio*. Chapel Hill: University of North Carolina Press, 1946.

Lazarsfeld, Paul F., and Kornhauser, Arthur W. *The Techniques of Market Research from the Standpoint of a Psychologist*. New York: American Management Association, 1935.

Lazarsfeld, Paul F., and Stanton, Frank N., eds. *Communications Research, 1948–1949*. New York: Harper and Brothers, 1949.

_____. *Radio Research, 1941*. New York: Duell, Sloan, and Pearce, 1941.

_____. *Radio Research, 1941–1943*. New York: Duell, Sloan, and Pearce, 1944.

Leatherwood, Dowling. *Journalism On the Air*. Minneapolis: Burgess Publishing Co., 1939.

Leavis, F. R. *For Continuity*. Cambridge: Minority Press, 1933.

Lee, Alfred M. *The Daily Newspaper in America*. New York: Macmillan Co., 1947.

Lefferts, Marshall. "The Electric Telegraph: Its Influence and Geographical Distribution." *Bulletin of American Geographical and Statistical Society* 2 (January 1857): 242–64.

Lerner, Daniel, and Lasswell, Harold, eds. *The Policy Sciences*. Stanford: Stanford University Press, 1951.

Lerner, Daniel, and Nelson, Lyle M., eds. *Communication Research: A Half-Century Appraisal*. Honolulu: University Press of Hawaii, 1977.

Lescarboura, Austin C. "Radio For Everybody." *Scientific American* 126 (March 1922): 166.

Leupp, Constance D. "The Motion Picture as a Social Worker." *Survey* 24 (27 August 1910): 739–41.

Levien, Sonya. "New York's Motion Picture Law." *American City* 9 (October 1913): 319–21.

Lindley, Lester G. "The Constitution Faces Technology: The Relationship of the National Government to the Telegraph, 1866–1884." Ph.D. dissertation, Rice University, 1971.

Lindsay, Vachel. *The Art of the Moving Picture*. New York: Macmillan Co., 1915.

Lippmann, Walter. *Liberty and the News*. New York: Harcourt, Brace and Howe, 1920.

———. *The Phantom Public*. New York: Harcourt, Brace and Co., 1925.

———. *Public Opinion*. 1922. Reprint ed. Glencoe: Free Press, 1965.

Lodge, Oliver. *Modern Views of Electricity*. 3rd ed., rev. London: Macmillan and Co., 1907.

———. *Past Years: An Autobiography*. London: Hodder and Stoughton, 1931.

———. *The Work of Hertz and Some of His Successors*. London: Electrician Printing and Publishing Co., 1894.

Loew, Marcus. "The Motion Picture and Vaudeville." In *The Story of the Films*, edited by Joseph P. Kennedy, pp. 285–300. Chicago: A. W. Shaw, 1927.

"The Long Arm of the Radio is Reaching Everywhere." *Current Opinion* 72 (May 1922): 684–87.

Lott, George E., Jr. "The Press-Radio War of the 1930's." *Journal of Broadcasting* 14 (Summer 1970): 275–86.

Lounsbury, Myron D. " 'Flashes of Lightning': The Moving Picture in the Progressive Era." *Journal of Popular Culture* 3 (Spring 1970): 769–97.

Lowenthal, Leo. "Historical Perspectives of Popular Culture." In *Mass Culture: The Popular Arts in America*, edited by Bernard Rosenberg and David M. White, pp. 46–58. Glencoe: Free Press, 1957.

———. *Literature, Popular Culture, and Society*. Englewood Cliffs: Prentice-Hall, 1961.

Lumley, F. E. *The Propaganda Menace*. New York: Century Co., 1933.

Lumley, Frederick H. *Measurement in Radio*. Columbus: Ohio State University, 1934.

Lumsdaine, Arthur. "On Mass Communication Experiments and the Like." In *Communication Research: A Half-Century Appraisal*, edited by Daniel Lerner and Lyle M. Nelson, pp. 37–69. Honolulu: University Press of Hawaii, 1977.

Lynd, Robert S. *Knowledge for What?: The Place of Social Science in American Culture*. Princeton: Princeton University Press, 1939.

Lynd, Robert S., and Lynd, Helen M. *Middletown: A Study in Modern American Culture*. New York: Harcourt, Brace, and Co., 1929.

Lyons, Eugene. *David Sarnoff*. New York: Harper and Row, 1966.

Mabee, Carleton. *Samuel F. B. Morse: The American Leonardo*. New York: Alfred A. Knopf, 1944.

McClenachan, C. T. *Detailed Report of the Proceedings Had in Commemoration of the Successful Laying of the Atlantic Telegraph Cable*. New York: E. Jones and Co., 1859.

MacGowan, Kenneth. *Behind the Screen: The History and Techniques of the Motion Picture*. New York: Delacorte Press, 1965.

Mackintosh, W. A. "Innis on Canadian Economic Development." *Journal of Political Economy* 61 (June 1953): 185–94.

MacLaurin, W. Rupert. *Invention and Innovation in the Radio Industry*. New York: Macmillan Co., 1949.

MacLeish, Archibald, *The Fall of the City*. New York: Farrar and Rinehart, 1937.

McLuhan, Marshall. "Effects of the Improvement of Communications Media." *Journal of Economic History* 20 (December 1960): 566–75.
————. "G. K. Chesterton: A Practical Mystic." *Dalhousie Review* 15 (1936): 455–64.
————. *The Gutenberg Galaxy*. Toronto: University of Toronto Press, 1962.
————. "Innis and Communication." *Explorations*, no. 3 (August 1954): 96–104.
————. "Interview." *Playboy* 16 (March 1969): 54.
————. "The Later Innis." *Queen's Quarterly* 60 (Autumn 1953): 385–94.
————. *The Mechanical Bride: Folklore of Industrial Man*. 1951. Reprint. Boston: Beacon Press, 1967.
————. *Understanding Media: The Extensions of Man*. New York: New American Library, 1965.
————. "Notes on the Media as Art Forms." *Explorations*, no. 1 (December 1953): 6–13.
McLuhan, Marshall, and Carpenter, Edmund, eds. *Explorations in Communication*. Boston: Beacon Press, 1960.
McLuhan, Marshall, and Fiore, Quentin. *The Medium is the Massage*. New York: Bantam Books, 1967.
McMeans, Orange E. "The Great Audience Invisible." *Scribner's Magazine* 73 (March 1923): 410–16.
McNamara, Eugene, ed. *The Interior Landscape: The Literary Criticism of Marshall McLuhan, 1943–1962*. New York: McGraw-Hill Book Co., 1969.
McQuail, Denis. *Towards a Sociology of Mass Communication*. London: Collier-Macmillan, 1969.
Mancini, Ernesto. "Telegraphy Without Wires." *The Chautauquan* 26 (February 1898): 511–15.
Mann, Donald. "Telegraphing of Election Returns, Presidential Messages, and Other Documents." *American Telegraph Magazine* 1 (November 1852): 74–78.
Marconi, Guglielmo. "Origin and Development of Wireless and Telegraphy." *North American Review* 168 (May 1899): 625–29.
————. "The Practicability of Wireless Telegraphy." *Fortnightly Review* 77 (June 1902): 931–41.
————. "Recent Advances in Wireless Telegraphy." *Annual Report of the Smithsonian Institution* (1906): 131–45.
————. "Syntonic Wireless Telegraphy." *Journal of the Society of the Arts* 49 (17 May 1901): 506–17.
Marek, Kurt W. *Archaeology of the Cinema*. London: Thames and Hudson, 1965.
Matthews, Brander. "Are the Movies a Menace to the Drama?" *North American Review* 205 (March 1917): 447–54.
Matthews, Fred H. *Quest For An American Sociology: Robert E. Park and the Chicago School*. Montreal: McGill-Queens University Press, 1977.
Maver, William. "Progress in Wireless Telegraphy." *Annual Report of the Smithsonian Institution* (1904): 275–80.
————. "Wireless Telegraphy: Its Past and Present Status and Its Prospects." *Annual Report of the Smithsonian Institution* (1902): 261–74.
Maxim, Hudson. "Radio—The Fulcrum." *Nation* 119 (23 July 1924): 91.
Mead, George H. "Cooley's Contribution to American Social Thought." *American Journal of Sociology* 35 (March 1930): 693–706.
Merritt, Russell. "Nickelodeon Theaters 1905–14: Building an Audience for the Movies." In *The American Film Industry*, edited by Tino Balio, pp. 59–79. Madison: University of Wisconsin Press, 1976.
Merton, Robert K. *Social Theory and Social Structure*. Glencoe: Free Press, 1957.
Metz, Robert. *CBS: Reflections in a Bloodshot Eye*. New York: Playboy Press, 1975.
Miller, Jonathan. *Marshall McLuhan*. New York: Viking Press, 1971.
Miller, Perry. *The Life of the Mind in America*. New York: Harcourt, Brace and World, 1965.

Mills, C. Wright. *The Power Elite*. New York: Oxford University Press, 1956.
_____. *The Sociological Imagination*. New York: Oxford University Press, 1959.
"The Modern Motion Picture Theater." *Motion Picture News* 8 (6 December 1913).
Moffett, Cleveland. "Marconi's Wireless Telegraph." *McClure's* 13 (June 1899): 99–
    112.
Morley, John. "On Popular Culture: An Address." *Eclectic Magazine* 88 (February
    1877): 129–40.
Morris, Charles F. "A Beautiful Picture Theater." *The Nickelodeon* 1 (March 1909):
    65–67.
Morse, Edward L., ed. *Samuel F. B. Morse: Letters and Journals*. 2 vols. Boston:
    Houghton Mifflin Co., 1914.
Morton, Robert A. "The Amateur Wireless Operator." *Outlook* 94 (15 January 1910):
    131–35.
_____. "Regulation of Radiotelegraphy." *Scientific American* 73 (Supplement, 23
    March 1912): 180–81.
Mott, Frank L. *American Journalism*. New York: Macmillan Co., 1941.
"'Movie' Manners and Morals." *Outlook* 113 (26 July 1916): 694–95.
"The Moving Pictures and the National Character." *Review of Reviews* 42 (September
    1910): 315–20.
"Moving Pictures in Indianapolis." *Survey* 24 (23 July 1910): 614.
Muensterberg, Hugo. *The Photoplay: A Psychological Study*. New York: D. Appleton
    and Co., 1916.
Musson, Bennet, and Grau, Robert. "Fortunes in Films: Moving Pictures in the
    Making." *McClure's* 40 (December 1912): 193–202.
National Broadcasting Company. Advisory Council Reports. 1927–35.
Neill, Robin. *A New Theory of Value: The Canadian Economics of H. A. Innis*.
    Toronto: University of Toronto Press, 1972.
Noble, David F. *America By Design: Science, Technology, and the Rise of Corporate
    Capitalism*. New York: Alfred A. Knopf, 1977.
North, Francis R. *A Recreation Survey of the City of Providence*. Providence: Provi-
    dence Playground Association, 1912.
North, Joseph H. *The Early Development of the Motion Picture, 1887–1900*. New
    York: Arno Press, 1973.
North, Simon N. D. *History and Present Condition of the Newspaper and Periodical
    Press of the United States*. Washington, D.C.: Census Office, 1884.
Oboler, Arch. *Fourteen Radio Plays*. New York: Random House, 1940.
O'Brien, Howard V. "It's Great to be a Radio Maniac." *Collier's Weekly* 74 (13
    September 1924): 15–16.
The Ownership of Wireless Equipment. New York: Marconi Wireless Telegraph Co.,
    1914.
Page, Leslie J., Jr. "The Nature of the Broadcast Receiver and Its Market in the
    United States from 1922 to 1927." *Journal of Broadcasting* 4 (Spring 1960):
    174–82.
Pallen, Conde B. "Newspaperism." *Lippincott's Monthly* 38 (November 1886): 470–77.
Park, Robert E. "American Newspaper Literature." *American Journal of Sociology* 32
    (March 1927): 806–13.
_____. "The City: Suggestions for the Investigation of Human Behavior in the Urban
    Environment." *American Journal of Sociology* 20 (March 1916): 577–612.
_____. *The Collected Papers of Robert Park*. 3 vols. Vol. 1, *Race and Culture*. Vol. 2,
    Human Communities. Vol. 3, *Society*. Glencoe: Free Press, 1950–55.
_____. "Community Organization and the Romantic Temper." *Social Forces* 3 (May
    1925): 675–77.
_____. *The Crowd and the Public*. Originally *Masse und Publikum*, 1904. Translated
    from German by Charlotte Elsner. Edited and with an introduction by Henry
    Elsner, Jr. Chicago: University of Chicago Press, 1972.

————. "Foreign Language Press and Social Progress." *Proceedings of the National Conference of Social Work* (1920): 493–500.

————. "Human Ecology." *American Journal of Sociology* 42 (July 1936): 1–15.

————. "Immigrant Community and Immigrant Press." *American Review* 3 (March–April, 1925): 143–52.

————. *The Immigrant Press and Its Control*. New York: Harper and Brothers, 1922.

————. "Morale and the News." *American Journal of Sociology* 47 (November 1941): 360–77.

————. "Natural History of the Newspaper." *American Journal of Sociology* 29 (November 1923): 80–98.

————. "News and the Power of the Press." *American Journal of Sociology* 47 (July 1941): 1–11.

————. "News As a Form of Knowledge." *American Journal of Sociology* 45 (March 1940): 669–86.

————. "Physics and Society." *Canadian Journal of Economics and Political Science* 6 (May 1940): 135–52.

————. "Reflections on Communication and Culture." *American Journal of Sociology* 44 (September 1938): 187–205.

————. "The Urban Community as a Spatial and a Moral Order." *Publications of the American Sociological Society* 20 (1925): 1–14.

————. "The Yellow Press." *Sociology and Social Research* 12 (September–October 1927): 1–12.

Park, Robert E., and Burgess, E. W. *Introduction to the Science of Sociology*. Chicago: University of Chicago Press, 1921.

Park, Robert E.; Burgess, E. W.; and McKenzie, R. D. *The City*. Chicago: University of Chicago Press, 1925.

Parsons, Frank. *The Telegraph Monopoly*. Philadelphia: C. F. Taylor, 1899.

Parsons, Talcott, and White, Winston. "The Mass Media and the Structure of American Society." *Journal of Social Issues* 16, no. 3 (1960): 67–77.

Patten, Simon N. *Product and Climax*. New York: B. W. Huebsch, 1909.

Patterson, Joseph M. "The Nickelodeon." *Saturday Evening Post* 180 (23 November 1907): 10.

Peel, J. D. Y., ed. *Herbert Spencer on Social Evolution: Selected Writings*. Chicago: University of Chicago Press, 1972.

Pennsylvania State Board of Censorship. *Rules and Standards*. Harrisburg: J. L. L. Kuhn, 1918.

Perry, Lawrence. "Commercial Wireless Telegraphy." *The World's Work* 5 (March 1905): 3194–201.

Perry, Ralph Barton, ed. *The Thought and Character of William James*. 2 vols. Boston: Little, Brown and Co., 1935.

Phelan, J. J. *Motion Pictures as a Phase of Commercialized Amusements in Toledo, Ohio*. Toledo: Little Book Press, 1919.

Pickett, Calder M. "Six New York Newspapers and their Response to Technology in the Nineteenth Century." Ph.D. dissertation, University of Minnesota, 1959.

————. "Technology and the N.Y. Press in the 19th Century." *Journalism Quarterly* 37 (Summer 1960): 398–407.

Pierce, Lucy F. "The Nickelodeon." *The World Today* 15 (October 1908): 1052–57.

Powdermaker, Hortense. *Hollywood: The Dream Factory*. Boston: Little, Brown, and Co., 1950.

Pratt, George. "'No Magic, No Mystery, No Sleight of Hand.'" *Image* 8 (December 1959): 192–211.

Pray, Isaac C. *Memoirs of James G. Bennett and His Times*. New York: Stringer and Townsend, 1855.

Preece, W. H. "Aetheric Telegraphy." *Journal of the Society of the Arts* 47 (5 May 1899): 519–25.

_____. "Wireless Telephony." *The Independent* 52 (4 October 1900): 2368–69.
Presbrey, Frank. *The History and Development of Advertising*. New York: Doubleday and Co., 1929.
Prescott, George. *History, Theory and Practice of the Electric Telegraph*. Boston: Ticknor and Fields, 1860.
"The Problem of Radio Reallocation." *Congressional Digest* 7 (October 1928): 255–86.
Purssell, John W. "In Defense of the Amateur Wireless Operator." *Scientific American* 106 (8 June 1912): 515.
Quandt, Jean B. *From the Small Town to the Great Community: The Social Thought of Progressive Intellectuals*. New Brunswick: Rutgers University Press, 1970.
Ramsaye, Terry. *A Million and One Nights: A History of the Motion Picture*. New York: Simon and Schuster, 1926.
_____. "The Motion Picture." *Annals of the American Academy of Political and Social Science* 128 (November 1926): 1–19.
Ransom, John Crowe. "Reconstructed But Unregenerate." In *I'll Take My Stand*, pp. 1–27. New York: Harper and Brothers, 1930.
Reeves, Earl. "The New Business of Broadcasting." *Review of Reviews* 72 (November 1925): 529–32.
Reid, James D. *The Telegraph in America*. New York: Derby Brothers, 1879.
Report of the National Board of Censorship of Motion Pictures. New York: National Board of Censorship, 1913.
"Research in Mass Communication." Microfilm. Madison: State Historical Society of Wisconsin, Mass Communication Research Center, 1940.
Rice, Melville C. "The Penny Arcade as a Side Show." *The Nickelodeon* 1 (January 1909): 23.
Richards, John A. *A Talk on Telegraphic Topics*. Chicago: n.p., 1882.
Riegel, O. W. *Mobilizing for Chaos: The Story of the New Propaganda*. New Haven: Yale University Press, 1934.
Riley, John W., and Riley, Matilda W. "Mass Communication and the Social System." In *Sociology Today*, edited by Robert K. Merton, Leonard Broom, and Laurence Cottrell, pp. 537–78. New York: Basic Books, 1959.
Rorty, James. "The Impending Radio War." *Harper's* 163 (November 1931): 714–26.
_____. *Our Master's Voice: Advertising*. New York: John Day Co., 1934.
Rosenberg, Bernard, and White, David M., eds. *Mass Culture: The Popular Arts in America*. Glencoe: Free Press, 1957.
Rosenberg, L. H. "A New Era in Wireless." *Scientific American* 124 (4 June 1921): 449.
Rosewater, Victor. *History of Cooperative Newsgathering in the United States*. New York: D. Appleton and Co., 1930.
Rothafel, Samuel L., and Yates, Raymond F. *Broadcasting: Its New Day*. New York: Century Co., 1925.
Royal Commission on Broadcasting Report. 2 vols. Ottawa: E. Cloutier, 1957.
Royal Commission on National Development in the Arts, Letters, and Sciences. 2 vols. Vol. 1, *Report, Royal Commission on National Development in the Arts, Letters, and Sciences, 1949–51*. Vol. 2, *Royal Commission Studies: A Selection of Essays*. Ottawa: E. Cloutier, 1951.
Sarno, Edward F. "The National Radio Conferences." *Journal of Broadcasting* 13 (Spring 1969): 189–202.
Savage, Willinda. "John Dewey and 'Thought News' at the University of Michigan." *Michigan Quarterly Review* 56 (Spring 1950): 204–9.
Schubert, Paul. *The Electric Word: The Rise of Radio*. New York: Macmillan Co., 1928.
Schudson, Michael. *Discovering the News: A Social History of American Newspapers*. New York: Basic Books, 1978.

Schwarzlose, Richard. "Harbor News Association: The Formal Origins of the AP."
Journalism Quarterly 45 (Summer 1968): 253–60.
Seckler, David. *Thorstein Veblen and the Institutionalists: A Study in the Social
Philosophy of Economics*. Boulder: Colorado Associated University Press, 1975.
Shaffner, Kenneth F. *Nineteenth Century Aether Theories*. New York: Pergamon
Press, 1972.
Shaffner, Taliaferro P. *The Telegraph Manual*. New York: Pudney and Russell, 1859.
Shanks, W. F. S. "How We Get Our News." *Harper's Magazine* 34 (May 1867): 511–22.
Shenstone, W. A. "Some Recent Theories of the Ether." *Living Age* 246 (9 September
1905): 724–34.
Shils, Edward A. "Daydreams and Nightmares: Reflections on the Criticism of Mass
Culture." *Sewanee Review* 65 (Autumn 1957): 587–608.
————. "The Study of the Primary Group." In *The Policy Sciences*, edited by Daniel
Lerner and Harold Lasswell, pp. 44–69. Stanford: Stanford University Press,
1951.
Siddall, Dudley. "Who Owns Our Radio Broadcasting Stations?" *Radio Broadcast* 4
(August 1925): 726–30.
Sklar, Robert. *Movie-Made America*. New York: Random House, 1975.
Slaughter, N. H. "Wireless Telephony." *Annual Report of the Smithsonian Institution*
(1919): 177–92.
Slide, Anthony. *Early American Cinema*. New York: A. S. Barnes, 1970.
Slosson, Edwin E. "Voices in the Air." *New York Independent* 108 (22 April 1922):
385–86.
Smith, Robert R. "The Origin of Radio Network News Commentary." *Journal of
Broadcasting* 9 (Spring 1965): 113–22.
Smith, William H. "The Press as a News Gatherer." *Century Magazine* 42 (August
1891): 524–36.
Smythe, Dallas W. "Some Observations on Communications Theory." *Audio-Visual
Communication Review* 2 (Winter 1954): 24–37.
Snyder, Carl. "Wireless Telegraphy and Signor Marconi's Triumph." *Review of Re-
views* 25 (February 1902): 173–76.
————. "The World's New Marvels: The Wireless Telephone." *Collier's Weekly* 52 (25
October 1913): 22–23.
Spalding, John W. "1928: Radio Becomes a Mass Advertising Medium." *Journal of
Broadcasting* 8 (Winter 1963–64): 31–44.
Stackhouse, W. L. "Telegraphic Communication in Michigan." *Michigan History
Magazine* 24 (Winter 1940): 75–90.
The Standards of the National Board of Censorship. New York: National Board of
Censorship, 1914?.
Starr, Michael E. "Prime Time Jesus." *Cultural Correspondence*, no. 4 (Spring 1977):
20–26.
Stearn, Gerald E., ed. *McLuhan: Hot and Cool*. New York: Dial Press, 1967.
Stedman, Raymond W. *The Serials: Suspense and Drama by Installment*. Norman:
University of Oklahoma Press, 1971.
Stelzle, Charles. "How One Thousand Workingmen Spent Their Spare Time." *Outlook*
106 (4 April 1914): 762–66.
Stevens, A. A. "The Way to Larger Culture." *Harper's Monthly* 107 (June 1903):
47–49.
Stillman, W. J. "Journalism and Literature." *Atlantic Monthly* 68 (November 1891):
687–95.
Strother, French. "The Unfolding Marvels of Wireless." *World's Work* 43 (April 1922):
647–61.
Summers, Harrison B. *Radio Censorship*. New York: H. W. Wilson, 1939.
————. *A Thirty-Year History of Programs on National Radio Networks in the United*

States, 1926–1956. Columbus: Ohio State University, 1958.

Sumner, Charles A. *The Postal Telegraph*. San Francisco: Bacon and Co., 1879.

Symonds, John Addington. "Culture: Its Meanings and Uses." *New Review* 7 (July 1892): 105–15.

Talbot, Frederick A. *Moving Pictures: How They Are Made and Worked*. Philadelphia: J. B. Lippincott Co., 1912.

Taylor, Deems. "Radio: A Brief for the Defense." *Harper's* 166 (April 1933): 554–63.

Tevis, Charles W. "Censoring the Five Cent Drama." *The World Today* 19 (October 1910): 1132–39.

Theall, Donald F. *The Medium is the Rear View Mirror: Understanding McLuhan*. Montreal: McGill-Queens University Press, 1971.

Thompson, Robert L. *Wiring a Continent: The History of the Telegraph Industry in the United States, 1832–1866*. Princeton: Princeton University Press, 1947.

Thompson, Silvanus P. "Telegraphy Across Space." *Journal of the Society of the Arts* 46 (April 1898): 453–60.

———. "Telegraphy Without Wires." *Saturday Review* 83 (26 June 1897): 708–9.

Thoreau, Henry D. *Walden*. Riverside Editions. Boston: Houghton Mifflin Co., 1957.

Toll, Robert C. *Blacking Up: The Minstrel Show in Nineteenth-Century America*. New York: Oxford University Press, 1974.

"Trade Notes." *Moving Picture World* 1 (30 March 1907): 57–58.

Trowbridge, John. "The First Steps in Wireless Telegraphy." *The Chautauquan* 29 (July 1899): 375–78.

———. "Telegraphing Through the Air Without Wires." *The Chautauquan* 15 (April 1892): 54–57.

———. "Wireless Telegraphy." *Popular Science Monthly* 56 (November 1899): 59–73.

Turnbull, Laurence. *Electro-Magnetic Telegraph, with an Historical Account of its Rise, Progress and Present Condition*. Philadelphia: A. Hart, 1853.

Tyler, Tracy F., ed. *Radio as a Cultural Agency*. Washington, D.C.: National Committee on Education by Radio, 1934.

Tylor, Edward B. *Primitive Culture: Researches into the Development of Mythology, Philosophy, Religion, Art, and Custom*. 2 vols. New York: Henry Holt and Co., 1877.

Usher, Ellis B. "The Telegraph in Wisconsin." *Proceedings of the State Historical Society of Wisconsin of 1913* (1914): 91–109.

Vail, Alfred. *The American Electro Magnetic Telegraph*. Philadelphia: Lea and Blanchard, 1845.

Vail, Theodore N. *The A T & T Co. and Its Relations with and Obligations toward Wireless Communication*. New York: n.p., 1915.

Vardac, Nicholas A. *Stage to Screen: Theatrical Method from Garrick to Griffith*. Cambridge: Harvard University Press, 1949.

"Vaudeville in Picture Theaters." *The Nickelodeon* 1 (March 1909): 85–86.

"Vaudeville or Not?" *The Nickelodeon* 1 (November 1909): 134.

Veblen, Thorstein. *The Instinct of Workmanship and the State of the Industrial Arts*. New York: Macmillan Co., 1914.

———. *The Place of Science in Modern Civilization and Other Essays*. New York: Macmillan Co., 1919.

Vice Commission of Chicago. *The Social Evil in Chicago*. Chicago: Gunthrop Warner, 1911.

Vorse, Mary Heaton. "Some Picture Show Audiences." *Outlook* 97 (24 June 1911): 442–47.

Wade, Herbert T. "Wireless Telephony by the De Forest System." *Review of Reviews* 35 (June 1907): 681–85.

Wagenknecht, Edward. *Movies in the Age of Innocence*. Norman: University of Oklahoma Press, 1962.

Warner, Charles D. "What is Your Culture to Me?" *Scribner's Monthly* 4 (August 1872): 470–78.

Watkins, Melville H. "A Staple Theory of Economic Growth." *Canadian Journal of Economics and Political Science* 19 (May 1963): 141–58.

Wayland, H. L. "Results of the Increased Facility and Celerity of Inter-Communication." *New Englander* 16 (November 1858): 790–806.

Whalen, Grover A. "Radio Control." *Nation* 119 (23 July 1924): 90–91.

Whicher, Stephen E.; Spiller, R. E.; and Williams, W. E., eds. *The Early Lectures of Ralph Waldo Emerson*. Vol. 2, *1836–1838*. Cambridge: Harvard University Press, Belknap Press, 1964.

White, Llewellyn. *The American Radio: A Report on the Broadcasting Industry in the United States from the Commission on Freedom of the Press*. Chicago: University of Chicago Press, 1947.

White, W. C. "Radiotelephony." *Scientific American* 80 (Supplement, 4 September 1915): 146–47.

Whitman, Walt. "Democracy." *Galaxy* 4 (December 1867): 919–33.

———. *Democratic Vistas*. London and New York: Walter Scott, 1888.

"Who Will Ultimately Do the Broadcasting?" *Radio Broadcast* 2 (April 1923): 524–25.

Wilkins, Burleigh Taylor. "James, Dewey, and Hegelian Idealism." *Journal of the History of Ideas* 17 (June 1956): 332–46.

Willey, Malcolm, and Rice, Stuart. "The Agencies of Communication." In *Recent Social Trends in the United States*, prepared by the President's Research Committee on Social Trends, pp. 167–217. New York: McGraw-Hill Book Co., 1933.

Williams, Raymond. "Culture and Civilization." In *Encyclopedia of Philosophy*, 1967 ed., s.v., pp. 270–76.

———. *Culture and Society, 1780–1850*. New York: Harper and Row, 1958.

———. *Keywords: A Vocabulary of Culture and Society*. New York: Oxford University Press, 1976.

———. *Television: Technology and Cultural Form*. New York: Schocken Books, 1975.

Wilson, Ben Hur. "Telegraph Pioneering." *The Palimpsest* 6 (November 1925): 373–93.

Wilson, William Bender. *From the Hudson to the Ohio*. Philadelphia: Kensington Press, 1902.

"Wireless Amateurs to the Rescue." *Literary Digest* 52 (1 January 1916): 13–14.

"The Wireless Telephone Tests." *Wireless Age* 3 (November 1915): 111–16.

Wolfenstein, Martha, and Leites, Nathan. *Movies: A Psychological Study*. Glencoe: Free Press, 1950.

Wright, Charles R. "Functional Analysis and Mass Communication." *Public Opinion Quarterly* 24 (Winter 1960): 605–20.

Yates, Raymond F. "The Long Arm of Radio." *Current History* 15 (March 1922): 980–85.

———. "What Will Happen to Broadcasting?" *Outlook* 136 (19 April 1924): 604–6.

Index